# REA's Test Prep Books Are The Best!
## (a sample of the hundreds of letters REA receives each year)

" I studied this guide exclusively and passed the [CLEP Introductory Sociology] test with 12 points to spare. "
*Student, Dallas, TX*

" This [REA] book was much better than reading a college textbook. Get it, it's worth it! By the way, I passed [the CLEP test] with flying colors!!! "
*Student, Poughkeepsie, NY*

" Your book was such a better value and was so much more complete than anything your competition has produced — and I have them all! "
*Teacher, Virginia Beach, VA*

" Compared to the other books that my fellow students had, your book was the most useful in helping me get a great score. "
*Student, North Hollywood, CA*

" Your book was responsible for my success on the exam, which helped me get into the college of my choice... I will look for REA the next time I need help. "
*Student, Chesterfield, MO*

" Just a short note to say thanks for the great support your book gave me in helping me pass the test... I'm on my way to a B.S. degree because of you! "
*Student, Orlando, FL*

*(more on next page)*

*(continued from front page)*

" I just wanted to thank you for helping me get a great score
on the AP U.S. History exam... Thank you for making great test preps! "
*Student, Los Angeles, CA*

" Your *Fundamentals of Engineering Exam* book was the absolute best
preparation I could have had for the exam, and it is one of the major
reasons I did so well and passed the FE on my first try. "
*Student, Sweetwater, TN*

" I used your book to prepare for the test and found that the advice and the
sample tests were highly relevant... Without using any other material, I earned
very high scores and will be going to the graduate school of my choice. "
*Student, New Orleans, LA*

" What I found in your book was a wealth of information sufficient to shore up
my basic skills in math and verbal... The section on analytical ability was
excellent. The practice tests were challenging and the answer explanations most
helpful. It certainly is the *Best Test Prep for the GRE!* "
*Student, Pullman, WA*

" I really appreciate the help from your excellent book. Please keep up
the great work. "
*Student, Albuquerque, NM*

" I am writing to thank you for your test preparation... your book helped me
immeasurably and I have nothing but praise for your *GRE* preparation."
*Student, Benton Harbor, MI*

## THE BEST TEST PREPARATION FOR THE

# CLEP

## Introductory Business Law

 **With REA's TEST*ware*® on CD-ROM**

**Lisa M. Fairfax**

Professor of Law and Director, Business Law Program
University of Maryland School of Law
Baltimore, Maryland

 **Research & Education Association**
*Visit our website at:*
**www.rea.com**

**Research & Education Association**
61 Ethel Road West
Piscataway, New Jersey 08854
E-mail: info@rea.com

The Best Test Preparation for the
**CLEP INTRODUCTORY BUSINESS LAW EXAM**
With TEST*ware*® on CD-ROM

Printed in the United States of America

Library of Congress Control Number 2007933106

ISBN-13: 978-0-7386-0316-2
ISBN-10: 0-7386-0316-3

Windows® is a registered trademark of Microsoft Corporation.

REA® and TEST*ware*® are registered trademarks of Research & Education Association, Inc.

## About the Author

Lisa M. Fairfax is Professor of Law and Director of the Business Law Program at the University of Maryland School of Law. An honors graduate of Harvard Law School and Harvard College, she is an award-winning teacher of courses encompassing contracts, business associations, securities regulation, and unincorporated business entities.

Professor Fairfax is a recognized scholar in the areas of corporate governance, fiduciary obligations, securities fraud, and securitization. One of her articles was selected as one of the best corporate and securities articles of 2002 and reprinted in the Corporate Practice Commentator. A subsequent article on the same subject was selected in 2003 and reprinted in the Securities Law Review.

At the University of Maryland School Law, she was selected Teacher of the Year by students in 2003 and Professor of the Year by the Black Law Students Association in 2002 and 2006.

Professor Fairfax is a member of the Committee on Corporate Laws of the Business Section of the American Bar Association and the Executive Committee of the Securities Regulation Section of the Association of American Law Schools.

Before joining academia, she practiced corporate law with Ropes & Gray in Boston, Mass., and Washington, D.C. Her practice included public offerings, private placements, mergers and acquisitions, and venture capital transactions.

## Author Dedication

I would like to dedicate this book to Roger for always being there and giving me the support I need; to Fatima, Regina, and Nadia, for all of your encouragement during this and other projects. I also would like to extend my special thanks to LaMonica, for our amazing and enduring friendship; my mother, Elizabeth, for every sacrifice made on my behalf—every one of them is appreciated; and my mother-in-law, Charlene, for making me a part of the family from the very beginning, and, of course, for the gift of your son.

## About Research & Education Association

Founded in 1959, Research & Education Association (REA) is dedicated to publishing the finest and most effective educational materials—including software, study guides, and test preps—for students in middle school, high school, college, graduate school, and beyond.

REA's test preparation series includes books and software for all academic levels in almost all disciplines. REA publishes test preps for students who have not yet entered high school, as well as high school students preparing to enter college. Students from countries around the world seeking to attend college in the United States will find the assistance they need in REA's publications. For college students seeking advanced degrees, REA publishes test preps for many major graduate school admission examinations in a wide variety of disciplines, including engineering, law, and medicine. Students at every level, in every field, with every ambition can find what they are looking for among REA's publications.

REA's series presents tests that accurately depict the official exams in both degree of difficulty and types of questions. REA's practice tests are always based upon the most recently administered exams, and include every type of question that can be expected on the actual exams.

REA's publications and educational materials are highly regarded and continually receive an unprecedented amount of praise from professionals, instructors, librarians, parents, and students. Our authors are as diverse as the subject matter represented in the books we publish. They are well known in their respective disciplines and serve on the faculties of prestigious colleges and universities throughout the United States and Canada.

We invite you to visit us at *www.rea.com* to find out how "REA is making the world smarter."

## Acknowledgments

In addition to our author, we would like to thank Larry B. Kling, Vice President, Editorial, for his overall direction; Pam Weston, Vice President, Publishing, for setting the quality standards for production integrity and managing the publication to completion; John Cording, Vice President, Technology, for coordinating the design, development, and testing of REA's TEST*ware*® software; Diane Goldschmidt, Senior Editor, for editorial contributions and project management; Alice Leonard, Senior Editor, Michael Reynolds, Senior Editor, and Molly Solanki, Associate Editor, for editorial contributions; Heena Patel and Amy Jamison, Technology Project Managers, for their design contributions and software testing efforts; Christine Saul, Senior Graphic Designer, for designing our cover; and Jeff LoBalbo, Senior Graphic Designer, for coordinating pre-press electronic file mapping. We also gratefully acknowledge the team at Aquent Publishing Services for page composition, copyediting, and proofreading this edition.

# CONTENTS

# CLEP INTRODUCTORY BUSINESS LAW
## Independent Study Schedule

The following study schedule allows for thorough preparation for the CLEP Introductory Business Law exam. Although it is designed for four weeks, it can be reduced to a two-week course by collapsing each two-week period into one. Be sure to set aside enough time—at least two hours each day—to study. But no matter which study schedule works best for you, the more time you spend studying, the more prepared and relaxed you will feel on the day of the exam.

| Week | Activity |
|---|---|
| 1 | Read and study Chapter 1 of this book, which will introduce you to the CLEP Introductory Business Law exam. Then take Practice Test 1 on CD-ROM to determine your strengths and weaknesses. Assess your results by using our raw score conversion table. You can then determine the areas in which you need to strengthen your skills. |
| 2 & 3 | Carefully read and study the Introductory Business Law review included in Chapters 2 through 8 of this book. |
| 4 | Take Practice Test 2 on CD-ROM and carefully review the explanations for all incorrect answers. If there are any types of questions or particular subjects that seem difficult to you, review those subjects by again studying the appropriate sections of the CLEP Introductory Business Law review chapters. |

<u>Note:</u> If you care to, and time allows, retake Practice Tests 1 and 2 printed in this book. This will help strengthen the areas in which your performance may still be lagging and build your overall confidence.

# CHAPTER 1

## Passing the CLEP Introductory Business Law Exam

# Chapter 1

# PASSING THE CLEP INTRODUCTORY BUSINESS LAW EXAM

## ABOUT THIS BOOK AND TESTware®

This book provides you with complete preparation for the CLEP Introductory Business Law exam. Inside you will find a targeted review of the subject matter, as well as tips and strategies for test taking. We also give you two practice tests, all based on the official CLEP Introductory Business Law exam. Our practice tests contain every type of question that you can expect to encounter on the actual exam. Following each practice test you will find an answer key with detailed explanations designed to help you more completely understand the test material.

The practice exams in this book and software package are included in two formats: in printed format in this book, and in TESTware® format on the enclosed CD. **We strongly recommend that you begin your preparation with the TESTware® practice exams**. The software provides the added benefits of instant scoring and enforced time conditions.

## ABOUT THE EXAM

### Who takes CLEP exams and what are they used for?

CLEP (College-Level Examination Program) examinations are typically taken by people who have acquired knowledge outside the classroom and wish to bypass certain college courses and earn college credit. The CLEP is designed to reward students for learning—no matter where or how that knowledge was acquired. The CLEP is the most widely accepted credit-by-examination program in the country, with more than 2,900 colleges and universities granting credit for satisfactory scores on CLEP exams.

Although most CLEP examinees are adults returning to college, many graduating high school seniors, enrolled college students, military personnel, and international students also take the exams to earn college credit or to demonstrate their ability to perform at the college level. There are no prerequisites, such as age or educational status, for taking CLEP examinations. However, because policies on granting credits vary among colleges, you should contact the particular institution from which you wish to receive CLEP credit.

There are two categories of CLEP examinations:

1. **CLEP General Examinations**, which are five separate tests that cover material usually taken as requirements during the first two years of college. CLEP General Examinations are available for English Composition (with or without essay), Humanities, Mathematics, Natural Sciences, and Social Sciences and History.

2. **CLEP Subject Examinations** include material usually covered in an undergraduate course with a similar title. For a complete list of the subject examinations offered, visit the College Board website.

## Who administers the exam?

The CLEP tests are developed by the College Board, administered by Educational Testing Service (ETS), and involve the assistance of educators throughout the United States. The test development process is designed and implemented to ensure that the content and difficulty level of the test are appropriate.

## When and where is the exam given?

The CLEP Introductory Business Law exam is administered each month throughout the year at more than 1,300 test centers in the United States and can be arranged for candidates abroad on request. To find the test center nearest you and to register for the exam, you should obtain a copy of the free booklets *CLEP Colleges* and *CLEP Information for Candidates and Registration Form*. They are available at most colleges where CLEP credit is granted, or by contacting:

CLEP Services
P.O. Box 6600
Princeton, NJ 08541-6600
Phone: (800) 257-9558 (8 a.m. to 6 p.m. ET)
Fax: (609) 771-7088
Website: *www.collegeboard.com/clep*

## CLEP Options for Military Personnel and Veterans

CLEP exams are available free of charge to eligible military personnel and eligible civilian employees. All the CLEP exams are available at test centers on college campuses and military bases. In addition, the College Board has developed a paper-based version of 14 high-volume/high-pass-rate CLEP tests for DANTES Test Centers. Contact the Educational Services Officer or Navy College Education Specialist for more information. Visit the College Board website for details about CLEP opportunities for military personnel.

Eligible U.S. veterans can claim reimbursement for CLEP exams and administration fees pursuant to provisions of the Veterans Benefits Improvement Act of 2004. For details on eligibility and submitting a claim for reimbursement, visit the U.S. Department of Veterans Affairs website at *www.gibill.va.gov/pamphlets/testing.htm*.

## SSD Accommodations for Students with Disabilities

Many students qualify for extra time to take the CLEP Introductory Business Law exam, but you must make these arrangements in advance. For information, contact:

College Board Services for Students with Disabilities
P.O. Box 6226
Princeton, NJ 08541-6226
Phone: (609) 771-7137 (Monday through Friday, 8 a.m. to 6 p.m. ET)
TTY: (609) 882-4118
Fax: (609) 771-7944
E-mail: *ssd@info.collegeboard.org*

Our TEST*ware*® can be adapted to accommodate your time extension. This allows you to practice under the same extended-time accommodations that you will receive on the actual test day. To customize your TEST*ware*® to suit the most common extensions, visit our website at *www.rea.com/ssd*.

## HOW TO USE THIS BOOK

### What do I study first?

Read over the course review and the suggestions for test-taking, take the first practice test to determine your area(s) of weakness, and then go back and focus your study on those specific problems. Studying the reviews thoroughly will reinforce the basic skills you will need to do well on the exam. Make sure to take the practice tests to become familiar with the format and procedures involved with taking the actual exam.

To best utilize your study time, follow our Independent Study Schedule, which you'll find in the front of this book. The schedule is based on a four-week program, but can be condensed to two weeks if necessary by collapsing each two-week period into one.

## When should I start studying?

It is never too early to start studying for the CLEP Introductory Business Law exam. The earlier you begin, the more time you will have to sharpen your skills. Do not procrastinate! Cramming is not an effective way to study, since it does not allow you the time needed to learn the test material. The sooner you learn the format of the exam, the more time you will have to familiarize yourself with it.

## FORMAT AND CONTENT OF THE EXAM

CLEP Introductory Business Law covers the material one would find in an introductory college-level class in the subject. The exam emphasizes understanding the functions of contracts in American business law. Questions on the exam also cover the history of American law, legal systems and procedures, agency and employment, sales, as well as other topics.

The exam consists of 100 multiple-choice questions, each with five possible answer choices, to be answered in 90 minutes.

The approximate breakdown of topics is as follows:

5–10%   History and Sources of American Law/Constitutional Law
5–10%   American Legal Systems and Procedures
25–35%  Contracts
25–30%  Legal Environment
10–15%  Torts
5–10%   Miscellaneous

## ABOUT OUR COURSE REVIEW

The review in this book provides you with a complete background of all the important facts, concepts and principles relevant to the exam. It will help reinforce the facts you have already learned while better shaping your understanding of the discipline as a whole. By using the review in conjunction with the practice tests, you should be well prepared to take the CLEP Introductory Business Law.

## SCORING YOUR PRACTICE TESTS

### How do I score my practice tests?

The CLEP Introductory Business Law is scored on a scale of 20 to 80. To score your practice tests, count up the number of correct answers. This is your total raw score. Convert your raw score to a scaled score using the conversion table on the following page. (Note: The conversion table provides only an estimate of your scaled score. Scaled scores can and do vary over time, and in no case should a sample test be taken as a precise predictor of test performance. Nonetheless, our scoring table allows you to judge your level of performance within a reasonable scoring range.)

### When will I receive my score report?

The test administrator will print out a full Candidate Score Report for you immediately upon your completion of the exam (except for CLEP English Composition with Essay). Your scores are reported only to you, unless you ask to have them sent elsewhere. If you want your scores reported to a college or other institution, you must say so when you take the examination. Since your scores are kept on file for 20 years, you can also request transcripts from Educational Testing Service at a later date.

## STUDYING FOR THE CLEP

It is very important for you to choose the time and place for studying that works best for you. Some students may set aside a certain number of hours every morning, while others may choose to study at night before going to sleep. Other students may study during the day, while waiting on a line, or even while eating lunch. Only you can determine when and where your study time will be most effective. But be consistent and use your time wisely. Work out a study routine and stick to it!

When you take the practice tests, try to make your testing conditions as much like the actual test as possible. Turn your television and radio off, and sit down at a quiet table free from distraction. Make sure to time yourself.

# PRACTICE-TEST RAW SCORE CONVERSION TABLE *

| Raw Score | Scaled Score | Course Grade | Raw Score | Scaled Score | Course Grade |
|---|---|---|---|---|---|
| 100 | 80 | A | 48 | 49 | C |
| 99 | 80 | A | 47 | 49 | C |
| 98 | 80 | A | 46 | 48 | C |
| 97 | 79 | A | 45 | 48 | C |
| 96 | 79 | A | 44 | 47 | C |
| 95 | 78 | A | 43 | 47 | C |
| 94 | 78 | A | 42 | 47 | C |
| 93 | 77 | A | 41 | 47 | C |
| 92 | 77 | A | 40 | 46 | D |
| 91 | 76 | A | 39 | 46 | D |
| 90 | 75 | A | 38 | 45 | D |
| 89 | 74 | A | 37 | 45 | D |
| 88 | 73 | A | 36 | 44 | D |
| 87 | 73 | A | 35 | 44 | D |
| 86 | 72 | A | 34 | 43 | D |
| 85 | 72 | A | 33 | 43 | D |
| 84 | 71 | A | 32 | 42 | D |
| 83 | 70 | A | 31 | 41 | D |
| 82 | 70 | A | 30 | 40 | F |
| 81 | 69 | A | 29 | 39 | F |
| 80 | 69 | A | 28 | 38 | F |
| 79 | 68 | A | 27 | 37 | F |
| 78 | 67 | A | 26 | 36 | F |
| 77 | 66 | A | 25 | 35 | F |
| 76 | 66 | A | 24 | 34 | F |
| 75 | 65 | A | 23 | 34 | F |
| 74 | 64 | A | 22 | 33 | F |
| 73 | 63 | A | 21 | 33 | F |
| 72 | 63 | A | 20 | 32 | F |
| 71 | 62 | A | 19 | 32 | F |
| 70 | 61 | A | 18 | 31 | F |
| 69 | 61 | A | 17 | 31 | F |
| 68 | 60 | A | 16 | 30 | F |
| 67 | 59 | A | 15 | 29 | F |
| 66 | 59 | A | 14 | 28 | F |
| 65 | 58 | B | 13 | 28 | F |
| 64 | 57 | B | 12 | 27 | F |
| 63 | 57 | B | 11 | 27 | F |
| 62 | 56 | B | 10 | 26 | F |
| 61 | 56 | B | 9 | 25 | F |
| 60 | 55 | B | 8 | 24 | F |
| 59 | 55 | B | 7 | 23 | F |
| 58 | 54 | B | 6 | 22 | F |
| 57 | 54 | B | 5 | 21 | F |
| 56 | 53 | B | 4 | 20 | F |
| 55 | 53 | B | 3 | 20 | F |
| 54 | 52 | B | 2 | 20 | F |
| 53 | 52 | B | 1 | 20 | F |
| 52 | 51 | B | 0 | 20 | F |
| 51 | 51 | B | | | |
| 50 | 50 | C | | | |
| 49 | 50 | C | | | |

* This table is provided for scoring REA practice tests only. The American Council on Education recommends that colleges use a single across-the-board credit-granting score of 50 for all 34 CLEP computer-based exams. Nonetheless, on account of the different skills being measured and the unique content requirements of each test, the actual number of correct answers needed to reach 50 will vary. A 50 is calibrated to equate with performance that would warrant the grade C in the corresponding introductory college course.

Start off by setting a timer for the time that is allotted for each section, and be sure to reset the timer for the appropriate amount of time when you start a new section.

As you complete each practice test, score your test and thoroughly review the explanations to the questions you answered incorrectly; however, do not review too much at one time. Concentrate on one problem area at a time by reviewing the question and explanation, and by studying our review until you are confident that you completely understand the material.

## TEST-TAKING TIPS

Although you may not be familiar with computer-based standardized tests such as the CLEP Introductory Business Law exam, there are many ways to acquaint yourself with this type of examination and to help allevi- ate your test-taking anxieties. Listed below are ways to help you become accustomed to the CLEP, some of which may be applied to other standard- ized tests as well.

**Read all of the possible answers**. Just because you think you have found the correct response, do not automatically assume that it is the best answer. Read through each choice to be sure that you are not making a mis- take by jumping to conclusions.

**Use the process of elimination**. Go through each answer to a question and eliminate as many of the answer choices as possible. By eliminating just two answer choices, you give yourself a better chance of getting the item correct, since there will only be three choices left from which to make your guess. Remember, your score is based only on the number of questions you answer correctly.

**Work quickly and steadily**. You will have only 90 minutes to work on 100 questions, so work quickly and steadily to avoid focusing on any one question too long. Taking the practice tests in this book will help you learn to budget your time.

**Acquaint yourself with the computer screen**. Familiarize yourself with the CLEP computer screen beforehand by logging on to the College Board website. Waiting until test day to see what it looks like in the pretest tutorial risks injecting needless anxiety into your testing experience. Also, familiarizing yourself with the directions and format of the exam will save you valuable time on the day of the actual test.

**Be sure that your answer registers before you go to the next item**. Look at the screen to see that your mouse-click causes the pointer to darken the proper oval. This takes less effort than darkening an oval on paper, but don't lull yourself into taking less care!

## THE DAY OF THE EXAM

On the day of the test, you should wake up early (hopefully after a decent night's rest) and have a good breakfast. Make sure to dress comfortably, so that you are not distracted by being too hot or too cold while taking the test. Also plan to arrive at the test center early. This will allow you to collect your thoughts and relax before the test, and will also spare you the anxiety that comes with being late. As an added incentive to make sure you arrive early, keep in mind that no one will be allowed into the test session after the test has begun.

Before you leave for the test center, make sure that you have your admission form and another form of identification, which must contain a recent photograph, your name, and signature (i.e., driver's license, student identification card, or current alien registration card). You will not be admitted to the test center if you do not have proper identification.

If you would like, you may wear a watch to the test center. However, you may not wear one that makes noise, because it may disturb the other test-takers. No dictionaries, textbooks, notebooks, briefcases, or packages will be permitted and drinking, smoking, and eating are prohibited.

*Good luck on the CLEP Introductory Business Law exam!*

# CHAPTER 2
## History and Sources of American Law

# Chapter 2

# HISTORY AND SOURCES OF AMERICAN LAW

## 2.1 ORIGINS OF THE LEGAL SYSTEM

### Common Law

Broadly speaking, **law** represents a set of rules or principles established by government or some other controlling body that members of society must follow and obey. This definition of law includes rules and principles established by cases and statutes. A **legal system** refers to a system of established laws. Both laws and legal systems are designed to promote fairness, consistency, and order within society.

While the exact origins of laws are unknown, efforts to create a legal system to regulate society began as early as 1792 B.C.E. during the time of Babylon. Ultimately those efforts took the form of the development of a **civil law** or **code law** system, pursuant to which a single comprehensive code was developed and laws were established by reference to such code. Most of the countries in the world follow some form of civil law system. These modern civil law systems have their roots in codes established during the Roman Empire.

The civil law system is distinct from a **common law** or **case law** system. Common law is essentially judge-made law whereby judges make decisions on a case-by-case basis, and those decisions generate a body of rules and principles. Thus, while judges in a common law system decide cases by referring to their own decisions or the decisions of other courts, judges in a civil law system refer to a set code when making their judicial determinations. The common law system originated in England and the English system serves as the foundation for common law systems used today. In the late 1700s, Sir William Blackstone published what is considered to be the most comprehensive historical treatment of English common law, entitled *Commentaries on the Law of England*. Many modern common law systems refer to Blackstone's work.

Civil law and common law represent the two dominant legal systems used by Western society. The American legal system is a common law system, and thus incorporates many principles from English common law. In addition to England and the United States, most countries colonized by England such as Australia, Canada, and New Zealand follow the common law system. Countries with civil law systems include France, Spain, Germany, and Latin American countries.

### *Stare Decisis* and Precedent

In order to ensure that decisions are consistent with one another, judges in a common law system are bound to follow decisions of previous cases involving similar fact patterns. Such previous decisions are referred to as **precedent**. The notion that judges must make decisions consistent with precedent is called *stare decisis*. The principle of *stare decisis* is designed to promote certainty and consistency among courts and case law. *Stare decisis* encourages judges to follow the decisions of courts with equal authority, and even the decisions of courts with lesser authority. Moreover, judges are obliged to follow the decisions of courts with higher authority. Then too, *stare decisis* also means that judges must follow their own decisions or the decisions of their own court. While judges have the discretion to overturn their own court's prior decisions, *stare decisis* means that they do so rarely and very reluctantly. Instead, courts overturn prior decisions only when the previous decision clearly violates principles of justice and fairness.

## 2.2 SOURCES OF LAW

There are many different sources of American law including the federal constitution, state constitutions as well as various federal, state, and local statutes.

### The U.S. Constitution

The U.S. or federal Constitution represents the governing and supreme law of the United States. The Constitution establishes **three branches** of government: Article I creates the legislative branch, Article II creates the executive branch, and Article III creates the judicial branch.

The legislative branch, known as **Congress** or the federal legislature, is divided into two houses, the **Senate** and the **House of Representatives**. Congress is responsible for making the laws. Members of the legislature are deemed to act as representatives of the people.

The executive branch constitutes the president, the vice president, and other executive officers. The president has broad powers, but is primarily responsible for enforcing the laws.

The judicial branch is comprised of the court system. Article III establishes the **Supreme Court** and Article I authorizes Congress to establish federal courts "inferior" to the Supreme Court. The Supreme Court consists of nine justices who are appointed by the president with the advice and consent of the Senate. The judiciary interprets the law. In addition, the judiciary can review the decisions of federal and state legislatures to ensure that they do not violate the Constitution. This process, known as **judicial review**, was set forth in the 1803 decision of *Marbury vs. Madison,* 5 U.S. 137 (1803). Judicial review gives courts the ability to declare a federal or state law unconstitutional, and thereby invalidate it.

The Constitution establishes a system of **checks and balances**, whereby each branch of government has specific power and authority, and can check or balance out the power exercised by other branches.

## The Bill of Rights and Other Constitutional Amendments

At present, there are twenty-seven amendments to the Constitution. The first ten amendments to the Constitution are referred to as the **Bill of Rights**. These amendments are aimed at protecting citizens from government intrusion, and thus prevent the government from making laws that interfere in certain rights deemed fundamental. The Bill of Rights prohibits government from intruding on such rights as the freedom of speech, the freedom of religion, and the right to be free from cruel and unusual punishment. The Bill of Rights also grants citizens important rights such as the right to jury trial and counsel in special cases. Although the Bill of Rights originally only applied to the federal government, most provisions have been interpreted to extend to the states as well. The remaining constitutional amendments cover a range of topics including abolishing slavery, granting women the right to vote, and limiting the president to two terms in office.

## Federal Statutes

The Constitution grants Congress the power to make legislation. Thus, Article I of the Constitution empowers Congress to make laws concerning taxes, foreign and interstate commerce, and the nation's defense. Based on this power, Congress has passed a variety of different federal statutes. The Constitution also enables Congress to make all laws **"necessary and proper"** for carrying out its responsibilities. Congress has passed many laws pursuant to this "necessary and proper" clause. Moreover, Congress has passed many statutes based on its power to regulate interstate commerce under Section 8, Article I of the Constitution. Courts have construed that power as the ability to pass legislation regarding any conduct that affects interstate commerce. For example, Congress was able to enact federal statutes prohibiting discrimination under the interstate commerce clause because discrimination restricts people's freedom to travel and gain employment across state lines.

## States' Constitutions and Statutes

The American system is one of **federalism**, which means that the states and the federal government share the power of governing. Thus, every state has three branches of government as well as a state constitution, and every state has considerable autonomy to govern the affairs of its citizens. Indeed, the tenth amendment to the Constitution provides that powers not conferred on the federal government are reserved for the states. Hence, states have all powers not specifically delegated to the federal government.

However, Article VI of the Constitution provides that the U.S. Constitution, laws made in pursuit of the Constitution, and all U.S. treaties shall be the "supreme law of the land." This **"supremacy clause"** has been interpreted to mean that state constitutions and statutes cannot violate the federal constitution or federal law.

## Local Laws

Local governments, such as city councils or county boards, also may pass laws. Such laws are referred to as **ordinances**, and are aimed at addressing purely local matters, such as parking or minor traffic violations.

## Uniform Laws

In an effort to harmonize the laws of various states, there are many **uniform laws.** Such laws are established by a group of experts seeking to create uniform legislation on a given topic. Each state is then given the opportunity to adopt the law in whole or in part. One of the most prominent uniform laws is the **Uniform Commercial Code** ("UCC"), which provides for legislation concerning various aspects of commercial law. The UCC has been adopted by all states except Louisiana. Other uniform laws include the Model Business Corporations Act and the Uniform Partnership Act of 1914, which was superceded by the Uniform Partnership Act of 1984. Because states can and often do alter a uniform law once it is adopted, such laws vary from state to state. However, uniform laws create basic consistency among state law on various topics.

## 2.3 CONSTITUTIONAL LAW

The Constitution, particularly through its various amendments, regulates a variety of different behaviors. For example, the Constitution prohibits the government, as well as private actors with significant public responsibilities, from engaging in practices that would violate the Constitution. The discussion below pinpoints some of the most prominent of these prohibitions.

### First Amendment

The First Amendment provides that "Congress shall make no law respecting an establishment of religion, or prohibiting the free exercise thereof; or abridging the freedom of speech, or of the press; or the right of the people peaceably to assemble, and to petition the government for a redress of grievances." This Amendment has not been interpreted as an absolute prohibition. Instead, courts will analyze government activity in order to determine if it constitutes an inappropriate intrusion on these protected rights.

With respect to religion, the First Amendment has been interpreted as prohibiting the government from establishing an official religion or otherwise entangling itself in the affairs of religious institutions. Moreover, this amendment prevents the government from establishing any law that interferes with a person's ability to exercise her religion unless the government can demonstrate a compelling interest for establishing the law.

The government's ability to interfere with a person's freedom of speech depends on the nature of the speech being regulated. Indeed, Congress may prohibit speech that has a **"clear and present"** danger of inciting violence or generating other "substantive evils" or significant negative consequences. The classic example of such speech is yelling "fire" in a crowded theater. Congress also has a broad ability to regulate **commercial speech**, defined as speech regarding commercial or economic activities. The Supreme Court has held that the First Amendment imposes no restrictions on the government's ability to regulate commercial speech that concerns an illegal activity or that is misleading. However, regulations related to other forms of commercial speech will be deemed unconstitutional unless they directly advance a substantial governmental interest and are tailored to serve that interest. Government regulations based on **content**, however, are subject to **strict scrutiny**, which means they will be sustained only if they are narrowly tailored to serve a compelling government interest. **Content-neutral** restrictions, otherwise referred to as **time, place, and manner** restrictions, are subject to **intermediate scrutiny**. Thus, such restrictions need only be narrowly tailored to meet an important government objective.

## Due Process

Both the Fifth Amendment and the Fourteenth Amendment contain a **"due process"** clause requiring that no person shall be "deprived of life, liberty, or property without due process." The Fourteenth Amendment applies to the states, while the Fifth Amendment applies to the federal government. The Supreme Court has found that both amendments protect the same interests. The Court has defined due process as the right to receive notice of any actions that would deprive a person of life, liberty, or property as well as the right to have an opportunity to present a case in a fair procedure before a neutral decision-maker. Hence, these amendments also govern the procedures in a criminal trial because such trials may restrict a person of her life or liberty.

## Takings

The Fifth Amendment also restricts governmental **takings**. This means that the government cannot take the property of an individual for public use without just compensation. Thus, the government must compensate individuals not only when it appropriates their property for public use (such as governmental taking of property in order to build a freeway or subway station), but also when the government significantly damages or impairs the value of a person's property.

## Equal Protection

The Fourteenth Amendment contains an equal protection clause providing that no state shall deny any person "the equal protection of the laws." Although this clause applies only to states, the Court has interpreted the Fifth Amendment as preventing the federal government from denying all persons equal protection.

As interpreted, both the Fifth and Fourteenth Amendments apply to governmental laws that are **discriminatory**, i.e., that differentiate between people. In order for a law or regulation to be deemed discriminatory it must (a) be facially discriminatory because on its face it distinguishes between groups of people, (b) be applied in a discriminatory manner, which means applied differently to different groups, or (c) have a discriminatory purpose.

For purposes of determining whether a law violates equal protection, the Court divides people into three classes, and then applies different standards of review based on which class the regulation impacts. Thus, if regulation involves a **suspect** classification, then the court will apply strict scrutiny to the government's regulation. A suspect classification means a classification based on race, religion, national origin or alienage, or otherwise involving a fundamental right. Similar to First Amendment cases, this means that the government must demonstrate that the regulation is narrowly tailored to serve a compelling government interest. Regulations that must satisfy strict scrutiny are almost always found to be unconstitutional.

If a government regulation involves a **quasi-suspect classification**, which includes gender and legitimacy, then courts apply **intermediate scrutiny**. Thus, the regulation will be valid so long as it is substantially tailored to meet an important government interest. This less exacting standard means that such regulations have a greater chance of surviving challenges based on their constitutionality.

All other classifications are subject to a **rational basis test**, pursuant to which government regulation will be upheld so long as it is rationally related to a legitimate government interest.

# CHAPTER 3
## American Legal Systems and Procedures

# Chapter 3

# AMERICAN LEGAL SYSTEMS AND PROCEDURES

## 3.1 CRIMINAL LAW AND CIVIL LAW

The American legal system focuses on both **criminal law** and **civil law**. Criminal law constitutes law that addresses crimes and punishment of crimes, and thus regulates the behavior of individuals to ensure that such behavior is consistent with society's conception of socially and morally appropriate behavior. As a result, criminal laws represent crimes against society and hence the state. In contrast, civil law, such as torts and contracts, represents law that regulates the relationships between parties. Courts help settle disputes regarding alleged violations of criminal or civil law.

## 3.2 THE COURT SYSTEM

The following discussion of the American court system will focus primarily on civil law and lawsuits, and then will provide a comparison of how those suits differ in the criminal law context. Both the federal and state court system have three levels of courts: a trial court, an appeals or appellate court, and a supreme court. State courts have a structure similar to the federal court system, though the specific names of each court differ. Hence, the discussion below will use the federal court system as an example of both court's structure.

The federal trial court is referred to as the U.S. or **federal district court**. There are ninety-four district courts throughout the United States and its territories, such as Puerto Rico and Guam, and at least one federal district court in every state. If a party appeals the district court's decision, she can bring a case in the appeals or appellate court, known as the **federal circuit court of appeals** or the **federal court of appeals**. The party is allowed this first appeal as a matter of right. There are twelve federal appeals courts that hear cases from several different district courts within a specific geographic area. For example, cases decided by federal district courts in Maryland, North Carolina, South Carolina, Virginia, and West Virginia can all be appealed to the U.S. Court of Appeals for the Fourth Circuit. However, the D.C. Circuit hears only cases on appeal from the federal district court in Washington, D.C.

If a party wishes to appeal the decision of the federal circuit court, then she may seek to bring a case to the U.S. Supreme Court. Unlike the federal appeals court, the Supreme Court has the discretion to determine if it will review decisions on appeal. When seeking to appeal a case to the Supreme Court, a party must petition the Court for a **writ of certiorari**. If four of the nine justices agree to hear a case, the writ of certiorari will be granted. However, in the vast majority of cases, the Supreme Court declines to hear a case, and thus the writ of certiorari is denied. This is because the Court only grants petitions for compelling reasons. If the Supreme Court agrees to hear a case and renders a decision, its decision is final as it is the highest court in the land.

There are also specialized federal courts that hear issues focused on a particular subject, such as federal tax courts and federal bankruptcy courts. States also have specialized courts including family court, probate court, and small claims court.

## 3.3 COURT FUNCTIONS AND PROCEDURES

### Court Functions

A trial court is a court of **original jurisdiction**, which means it is the first court to consider an action. As its name suggests, the trial court constitutes the court in which the actual trial occurs, i.e., where parties present their evidence to a judge or jury.

An appeals or appellate court only has **appellate jurisdiction**, which means the power to review decisions of the lower court. For example, federal circuit courts have the power to review decisions of the federal district court. Appellate jurisdiction is limited to reviewing, affirming, revising, or modifying decisions of the lower court, and thus appeals courts do not conduct trials. In general, appellate courts give deference to lower court decisions and only **reverse** or set aside the lower court's decision if it reflects a **clear abuse of discretion**. However, on issues involving interpretation of law, appellate courts do not defer to the lower court, and hence reverse such decisions when they reflect an improper or unconstitutional application of the law. If the appellate court decides to reverse or set aside a decision, it also may **remand** it. This means that the appellate court will send the case back to the lower court for a new trial so that the lower court can take other actions consistent with the appellate court's finding.

A supreme court also has appellate jurisdiction, but such jurisdiction is limited to reviewing the decision of the appellate court. Like the appeals court, a supreme court can remand a case back to the appellate court and instruct it to take actions consistent with its findings. Distinct from state supreme courts, the U.S. Supreme Court has the power to review decisions from federal circuit courts, as well as state supreme courts. In addition, the Constitution grants the Supreme Court original jurisdiction to hear certain cases including cases (a) between two or more states, (b) between the federal government and a state, (c) involving officials of foreign countries, or (d) by a state against citizens of another state or country. In reviewing decisions, supreme courts give deference to decisions of fact and only overturn such decisions if they are clearly erroneous. However, a supreme court's review of decisions involving interpretations of legal rules is **de novo**, which means it is entirely new and does not defer to the lower court's judgment.

## Commencing the Lawsuit

Most court cases follow a similar procedure, both at the federal level or the state level. However, the **Federal Rules of Civil Procedures** (the "Federal Rules") govern the procedures for filing a civil suit in federal court. States have adopted their own rules of procedures, but such rules generally parallel the federal rules.

As an initial matter, any party bringing suit must have **standing**, which is the legal right to bring the suit. Standing refers to the notion that the person who brings suit must have or imminently have a legally recognized injury, sometimes referred to as an **injury-in-fact**. In a civil lawsuit, the person who brings the suit is called the **plaintiff**, while the person who is being sued is called the **defendant**. The documents parties file in connection with their lawsuit are called **pleadings**.

Upon bringing the action, the plaintiff files a **complaint** with the trial court setting forth the basis of her lawsuit. The court must then issue to the defendant a copy of the complaint and a **summons**, which represents notice that a lawsuit has been filed against the defendant. The defendant must respond to the complaint. The defendant's response is called an **answer** to the complaint. In the answer, the defendant must admit or deny the allegations within the complaint. The defendant also may raise **affirmative defenses** (defenses that would prevent the plaintiff from holding the defendant liable) or **counterclaims** (claims that the defendant has against the plaintiff). In addition, the defendant can file a **motion**, which represents a request for the court to take some action. The defendant may file a **demurrer**, which essentially represents a motion to dismiss the case because the plaintiff's complaint does not establish a legal basis for any remedy against the defendant. Rule 12(b) of the Federal Rules also allows a defendant to make a motion to dismiss based on (a) lack of subject matter jurisdiction, (b) lack of person jurisdiction, (c) lack of venue, (d) the failure to join necessary parties, (d) lack of process, and (e) lack of service of process. Each of these motions, other than the motion for lack of subject matter jurisdiction, referred to as a **Rule 12b(6) motion**, must be made at the first available opportunity or they will be deemed waived. Other pre-trial motions include a **motion to strike** (take out certain matters) or a **motion for a more definitive statement** when the pleadings are vague or ambiguous.

At any time, either party can file a **motion for summary judgment**. A judge will grant such a motion upon a finding that (a) there is no genuine issue of material fact, and as a result, (b) one party is entitled to prevail in the case as a matter of law.

If the plaintiff's case is not dismissed, the parties will proceed toward trial. Before the trial actually occurs, the parties have a right to **discovery**, which is the ability to gain information concerning the other party and her witnesses. The judge also may conduct conferences before the trial begins and guide parties in settlement discussions.

## The Civil Jury Trial

As discussed above, the first court in which the plaintiff brings her suit is the trial court. In the trial court, each party presents her evidence to either a judge or a jury. Most civil cases are tried before a jury. The jury that hears evidence at trial also is called a **petit jury**. There are twelve members of a petit jury in federal court. In a jury trial, the judge rules on the evidence, and generally guides the jury on questions of law and proper rules of procedure. The petit jury delivers a **verdict**, deciding whether the defendant should be held liable for the complained action. At trial, the plaintiff has the **burden of proof** (the obligation to establish her claims first). At the end of the plaintiff's presentation of her case, the defendant can file a **motion for dismissal** or a **motion for a directed verdict**, which constitutes a motion claiming that the plaintiff has not established enough evidence to prove her case.

If such motions are not granted, then the defendant must present evidence to defend the plaintiff's claims. After the defendant has had the opportunity to present her case, the petit jury retires to a separate room to decide the outcome of the case. Such a process is called **deliberation**.

In a civil case, the jury must decide that the plaintiff proved her case by a **preponderance of the evidence**, meaning that the evidence favoring the plaintiff's allegations is stronger than the evidence presented against her position. Generally, the jury verdict must be unanimous. If the jury fails to reach consensus, it is referred to as a **hung jury**, and the parties must have a new trial with a different jury.

Once the jury renders its verdict, the losing party can make several post-trial motions, including a motion for a new trial, or a motion for a **judgment notwithstanding the verdict** (known as **judgment n.o.v.**). A judgment n.o.v. requires the court to find that the evidence does not support the jury's verdict. If the court makes such a finding, it will overturn the jury's verdict.

## The Appeals Process

The losing party at trial has the right to appeal the decision to an appeals court. The party seeking to appeal the decision is known as the **appellant**, while the other party is referred to as the **appellee** or **respondent**. As discussed in section 3.3, Court Functions earlier in this chapter, there are no trials at the appeals court level. Instead, the appeals court reviews the trial record and, in some circumstances, allows each party to present arguments to the court, known as **oral arguments**. The court then delivers its opinion.

If the appellant loses her appeal, she can seek another appeal to the Supreme Court. However, such an appeal is discretionary and generally only granted in cases with broad legal or policy implications. The Supreme Court only grants a petition for review when there is a compelling reason, such as when federal courts are divided over an important federal law or an important question not settled by the Supreme Court. Mere errors in prior proceedings are not viewed as compelling reasons to grant a petition.

If the appellant's appeal is denied or the time for bringing an appeal otherwise expires, the judgment becomes final, and cannot be challenged in another proceeding. Such finality is known as **res judicata**, and it prevents the parties from re-litigating the same action.

## The Criminal Trial

Because criminal matters constitute crimes against the state, there is no plaintiff. Instead, a representative of the state or federal government, known as the **prosecution**, brings a case against the defendant. Before going to trial, the prosecution must present an **indictment** (the written charges against the defendant) to a **grand jury**, which is a group of between sixteen and twenty-three jurors who decide whether there is sufficient evidence to charge the defendant with a crime. The Fifth Amendment of the Constitution requires that all criminal cases be presented to a grand jury. In order to assist its decision making, the grand jury has broad powers to subpoena witnesses and documents. If the grand jury decides that there is adequate evidence to charge the defendant with the crimes presented by the prosecution, it will return the prosecution's indictment. The criminal trial then will proceed in much the same manner as a civil trial, with the prosecution bearing the burden of proof.

The Constitution also guarantees additional rights in a criminal trial such as the right to a speedy trial, the right to a trial by jury for serious offenses, as well as the right to counsel. Additionally, in order for a criminal defendant to be found guilty, the petit jury must find that the prosecution established the defendant's guilt **beyond a reasonable doubt**.

If the defendant is found guilty, she can challenge her conviction by making appeals. Once the defendant has had the opportunity to appeal her case or the time has expired to make appeals, the defendant may be eligible to apply for a **writ of habeas corpus**. Such a writ represents the defendant's request for a new proceeding to determine if she is being unlawfully deprived of her liberty. Habeas corpus is limited to people in custody. This typically means people serving prison sentences who allege that they are being unlawfully detained. Habeas corpus also can be used only after other remedies have been exhausted. Defendants in federal court must bring such a writ in federal court, while defendants in state court may bring such an action in either state or federal court.

## 3.4 JURISDICTION

In order for a court to hear a case, it must have both **subject matter jurisdiction** and **personal jurisdiction**.

## Subject Matter Jurisdiction

Subject matter jurisdiction constitutes the power to decide the type of case at issue. Federal courts do not have broad subject matter jurisdiction because they can only hear particular types of cases. Thus, such courts are known as courts of **limited jurisdiction**. Federal courts' subject matter jurisdiction results from either **diversity jurisdiction** or **federal question jurisdiction**. Federal question jurisdiction refers to the courts' power to hear cases arising under the Constitution, federal laws, or U.S. treatises. Federal question jurisdiction is exclusive, and hence cases involving such questions may be brought in federal court only. Diversity jurisdiction refers to the courts' ability to hear cases where the parties are "diverse," which means that the opposing parties are citizens from different states or one of the parties is a citizen of a foreign country, *and* the amount in controversy exceeds $75,000. Federal courts' diversity jurisdiction is not exclusive, which means state courts also may hear such cases.

State courts have broad subject matter jurisdiction to hear any case not reserved exclusively for the federal courts, and thus are courts of **general jurisdiction**.

Subject matter jurisdiction cannot be waived and either party can raise lack of subject matter jurisdiction at any time.

## Personal Jurisdiction

**Personal jurisdiction** constitutes power over the particular parties in a case. When a plaintiff brings his case in a given court, the plaintiff is granting such court personal jurisdiction over him. Thus, personal jurisdiction poses a concern only for a defendant. Personal jurisdiction over the defendant can be established in one of the following ways:

(a) The Supreme Court in *Pennoyer v. Neff*, 95 U.S. 714 (1877), held that a defendant's *physical presence* in a state is sufficient to allow courts within the state to exercise personal jurisdiction over her.

(b) A person can be subject to personal jurisdiction in her state of *permanent residence*, known as **domicile**; a corporation's domicile is the state in which it is incorporated.

(c) A person can *consent* to personal jurisdiction by voluntarily appearing in court or otherwise agreeing to a court's exercise of jurisdiction.

(d) Under *International Shoe v. Washington*, 326 U.S. 310 (1945), if a defendant has sufficient *minimum contacts* or relationships with a state, then a court within that state can exercise personal jurisdiction over the defendant even if he has never entered the state. Consistent with *International Shoe*, many states have passed **long-arm statutes** that allow them to exercise personal jurisdiction over defendants having sufficient minimum contacts within their state. Hence, such personal jurisdiction is also known as **long-arm jurisdiction**.

Personal jurisdiction may be waived. As a result, if a defendant fails to challenge personal jurisdiction at the first available opportunity, it will be viewed as waived.

## Venue

Even when a court has both subject matter jurisdiction and personal jurisdiction, the plaintiff's lawsuit must be brought in a court that has proper **venue**. There are generally several state or federal courts that have subject matter jurisdiction and personal jurisdiction over the parties. Venue represents a geographic limitation on such courts' jurisdiction by limiting the courts in which a plaintiff may bring her suit to courts in the geographic area in which she resides or where the events occurred.

# CHAPTER 4
## Contracts

# Chapter 4

# CONTRACTS

## 4.1 MEANINGS OF TERMS

### Contract

The **Restatement (Second) of Contracts** ("Restatement") is a set of statements reflecting generally agreed upon pronouncements of common law contract rules. Section 1 of the Restatement defines a **contract** as "a promise or a set of promises for the breach of which the law gives a remedy, or the performance of which the law in some way recognizes a duty." Thus, at its core, contract law is concerned with enforcing promises between parties, but only those promises that the law recognizes as enforceable. In this respect, a contract is a transaction where one or both parties make a legally enforceable promise. Contract law provides the principles for determining whether a promise is enforceable.

### Express Contract

An **express contract** is a promise stated in words, either oral or written.

### Goods

As will be discussed in Chapter 8, Article 2 of the UCC governs all transactions for the sale of goods. The UCC defines **goods** as all things that are movable at the time of the contract.

### Implied Contract

An **implied contract** is a promise that is inferred from a person's conduct or the circumstances of the transaction.

### Promise

A **promise** is an undertaking or commitment to act or refrain from acting in a specified way in the future. When an exchange is entirely instantaneous, there is no contract because neither party makes a promise to the other. Thus, if A purchases a clock from B for $100 and at the point of sale A gives B $100 and B gives A the clock, this is an instantaneous exchange. In such an exchange, each party has fully performed her obligation and no promises have been made. The exchange therefore is not a contract, but is referred to as an **executed exchange**. In contrast, if A promises to purchase a clock from B in two weeks for $100, there is no immediate exchange. Rather a contract has been formed because A has promised to perform some future event—purchase the clock.

## Promisor, Promisee, and Beneficiary

The person who makes a promise is the **promisor**, while the person to whom the promise is made is the **promisee**. When the promise or commitment will benefit someone other than the promisee—that someone is referred to as a **beneficiary**. For example, if A promises to buy a clock from B in two weeks, A is the promisor and B is the promisee. If A promises to buy the clock from B to give to C, then C is the beneficiary of the exchange.

## Quasi-Contract

A **quasi-contract** arises in the absence of a promise and thus is not a contract at all. Instead, a quasi-contract is a transaction that creates a basis for recovery to prevent **unjust enrichment**, which means a situation where one person unfairly benefits from a transaction. Quasi-contracts arise when one party confers a benefit on another party, and courts permit the party who confers the benefit to bring suit against the other party in order to recover the value of the benefit. An action to avoid unjust enrichment is referred to as **restitution**. Quasi-contracts are sometimes referred to as contracts that are **implied-in-law**. Both terms capture the idea that no contract has been formed, but rather that courts will view a transaction as creating a basis for recovery in order to prevent injustice. For example, A, who is a doctor, is seated next to B at a restaurant. When B begins choking, A administers emergency treatment. In this case, there is no contract because A and B have not exchanged promises. Thus, A can seek to recover from B in an action for unjust enrichment, based on the notion that B has unjustly benefited from the medical services performed by A and should be required to pay A. The transaction between A and B would be referred to as a quasi-contract.

# 4.2 FORMATION OF CONTRACTS

## Mutual Assent

In order for a contract to be formed, there must be **mutual assent** on the part of the parties who are seeking to enter into the contract. This means that each party to the contract must manifest or reveal her intent to be bound to a given exchange. Some courts refer to this manifestation of intent as a **"meeting of the minds"** to capture the notion that there must be mutual agreement about the exchange to be performed. Because it reflects the intention of both parties, courts will enforce the resulting exchange by providing some remedy when one of the parties fails to honor that exchange. In this regard, mutual assent is not only a necessary component of any contract, but also represents the rationale for enforcing the contract.

## Nature of Assent

The concept behind mutual assent is that no party will be bound to a contract in which he did not intend to enter. However, often courts must determine each party's intention when there is disagreement. When making that determination, courts use an **objective standard**. An objective standard means that courts determine intent by analyzing how a reasonable person would construe the words and conduct of the parties, generally without considering words or actions an individual may have intended, but did not communicate (**subjective intent**). Thus, in an exchange between A and B, if A reasonably construes B's words and actions as assent to the contract, then B will be bound to the contract, even if he secretly did not intend to be. In this regard, the contract is formed even if one party did not intend to be bound, negating a true "meeting of the minds." Courts have adopted this objective formulation of assessing mutual assent because it is deemed to be more fair and more dependable. Indeed, if courts focused on a subjective standard, people would be able to give the impression of assenting to a contract, while later disaffirming the contract, based on the notion that the impression did not reflect their actual subjective intent. Instead of a meeting of the minds, it is more accurate to say that mutual assent is demonstrated when a reasonable person can construe both parties' actions as revealing an intent to be bound to the exchange.

When interpreting the parties' conduct, courts will look at the communication between the parties in light of all the facts and circumstances.

## Elements of Mutual Assent

There are two factors that must be shown in order to demonstrate mutual assent. Those two factors are an **offer** on the part of one party and an **acceptance** on the part of the other. Thus, mutual assent occurs when one party reveals an intent to make an offer and the other party reveals an intent to accept that offer on particular terms.

## Offer

**Section 24** of the Restatement defines an offer as a "manifestation of willingness to enter into a bargain, so made as to justify another person in understanding that his assent to that bargain is invited and will conclude it." The person making the offer is called the **offeror** and the person to whom the offer is made is called the **offeree**. An offer must be communicated to the offeree. It also must be directed at a particular person or group. This means that a communication may not be construed as an offer if the intended beneficiaries cannot be determined. Indeed, an offer is only intended for the person to whom it is communicated, and only the intended offeree can accept the offer. The offer not only must invite acceptance, but also must give the impression that once that acceptance is granted, a contract will be created without any further action being necessary.

A critical issue in analyzing whether a given communication is an offer is determining whether or not the communication intends to invite acceptance or if it is a preliminary negotiation requiring some further action. A preliminary negotiation is often referred to as a solicitation or **invitation to make an offer**. For example, when someone sends a mass mailing to a variety of people in a manner where it is clear that the person sending the mailing does not intend to be bound to all of the people who were sent the mailing, the mailing is most likely an invitation to make an offer. Similarly, advertisements are not construed as offers because it is unlikely that the advertiser seeks to be bound to the public at large. Instead, advertisements generally constitute invitations to make offers to the advertiser. However, some advertisements may invite acceptance by their terms, such as advertisements that indicate that the first person to respond will receive a specific item. Such an advertisement may be construed as an offer.

## Termination of Offer

Once a party manifests her intent to accept an offer, there is mutual assent and a contract can be formed. However, an offer may be terminated prior to acceptance.

## Termination by Lapse of Time

If the offeror indicates that an offer must be accepted within a stated time, then the offer will terminate once that time has passed. Even if the offer does not indicate a specific time when acceptance is due, the offer will nevertheless terminate once a reasonable period of time has passed without an acceptance.

## Termination by Death or Mental Incapacity

If an offeror dies prior to the time that an offer is accepted, then the offer is terminated. This is true even if the offeree has no knowledge of the offeror's death. Similarly, if an offeror is deemed to be mentally incompetent after an offer is made, then the offer is terminated, if acceptance has not occurred before the offeror is judged to be incompetent.

Once acceptance occurs, an offeror's death or mental incompetence does not negate the contract. In other words, an offeror's death or mental incompetence must occur after the offer is made, but prior to acceptance, in order to impact the formation of the contract. As a result, if an offeror dies after a contract has been accepted, the contract has been formed and the contract will become the obligation of the deceased offeror's estate.

## Termination by Revocation

As a general rule, an offeror may terminate the offer any time prior to the offeree's acceptance. Such termination by the offeror is referred to as **revocation**.

An offer may be revoked either directly or indirectly. Directly, the offeror can indicate by words that she no longer wishes to be bound by the offer. This indication serves to revoke the offer.

Indirectly, an offer may be revoked when the offeror takes actions that are inconsistent with the intent to be bound, and the offeree has knowledge of those actions. For example, if A offers to sell B a house, the offer would be revoked if B discovered, through a reliable source, that the house had been sold before B accepted the offer. However, if B does not discover that the house has been sold, then the offer is not revoked, because B has no knowledge of A's inconsistent actions. Thus, revocation by indirect means is risky. Indeed, even though A apparently already has sold the house, A's failure to sell the house to B upon B's acceptance would constitute a breach of contract because A never revoked the offer to B.

Offers may not be revoked prior to termination in three circumstances:

(a) if the offeree has paid to keep the offer open for some period of time (see **option contract** discussed below),

(b) if the offeror has agreed to keep the offer open for some period of time, and the offeree has relied on that promise to her detriment, or

(c) if the offeree already has begun performance under the contract (see **unilateral contract** discussed below).

With regard to this last exception, where acceptance and performance of the contract are the same thing and the offeree already has begun performance (and thus partial acceptance), then the offeror must give the offeree time to complete that performance and acceptance. For example, if A offers to pay B $100 to clean her house, A cannot revoke the offer once B has begun to clean, but must allow B to finish cleaning.

## Termination by Rejection

An offer also can be terminated by the offeree's rejection. An offer is rejected when the offeree's words or conduct indicate that the offeree does not intend to accept the offer. In this regard, a rejection is analyzed under an objective and not a subjective standard. Because rejection terminates the offer, once an offeree has rejected an offer, she cannot attempt to later accept it.

## Termination by Counteroffer

A **counteroffer** is both a rejection of the original offer and a new offer, and thus serves to terminate the original offer. A counteroffer occurs when the offeree responds to the offer by proposing a different bargain. In this way, the counteroffer transforms the original offeree into the offeror. All the rules of offer and termination will apply to this new offer. Also, because the counteroffer is a rejection, the offeree cannot accept the original offer if the counteroffer is not accepted.

Like a rejection, the counteroffer must reveal the offeree's intention to reject the new offer and propose a different arrangement. In assessing the offeree's response, one must distinguish between actions that represent a counteroffer and those that represent a request for information or a suggestion for changes. Such actions do not clearly indicate an intent to reject the original offer, and thus should not be construed as a counteroffer.

## Acceptance

An offer is accepted when the offeree reveals her agreement to comply with the terms of the offer. Only the person who was invited to accept the offer may accept it. This is because an offer is viewed as personal to the intended offeree.

Under common law, an offer was not viewed as accepted unless the acceptance corresponded exactly with the terms of the offer. This rule, known as the **"mirror image" rule**, meant that any response by the offeree that changed the terms of the agreement—however slightly—would be treated as a rejection. The modern approach treats responses as acceptances, so long as the changes to the original offer are minor. However, if the response to the offer represents a material change in the terms of the offer, then it will be treated as a rejection and a counteroffer.

## Mailbox Rule

An acceptance is effective as soon as it is dispatched. This is known as the **"mailbox" rule**. Based on the rule, under common law, an acceptance is effective when it is mailed. Today, the rule has been expanded to encompass other forms of communication such as emails and faxes. With regard to those forms of communications, acceptance is effective when the offeree sends it.

All other communications are effective upon receipt. Thus, both an offer and a revocation are only effective when they are received. Similarly, a counteroffer and a rejection are only effective when they are received.

These rules have an important impact on contract formation. For example, if A receives an offer from B on January 1 and mails an acceptance on January 3, that acceptance will be effective on January 3 and hence will create a contract on that date. This is true even if B mailed a revocation on January 2. Since the revocation probably would not be received until after the acceptance was sent, it would be too late to terminate the offer.

However, the mailbox rule will not apply if the offeree seeks to accept an offer after she has rejected the offer or made a counteroffer. For example, if the offeree originally mailed a rejection to the offer, but later changed her mind and mailed an acceptance, the mailbox rule would not apply to any of the communications. Instead, whichever communication the offeror received first is the one that would be effective.

## Unilateral and Bilateral Contracts

Courts make a distinction between a **unilateral contract** and a **bilateral contract**. When at the time a contract is formed, one party already has performed her obligation so that there is only one performance obligation remaining, the contract is called a unilateral contract. In other words, a unilateral contract arises when the act of acceptance is also the act of performance. Thus, a unilateral contract is created if A promises to pay B $100 to mow her lawn because B's acceptance occurs once he mows the lawn. Then too, this contract is a unilateral one because once B has mowed the lawn and his acceptance is complete, the only outstanding obligation is A's promise to pay B.

A bilateral contract refers to a contract where two promises are outstanding at the time of contract formation. In a bilateral contract, two promises are exchanged, while in a unilateral contract, a promise is exchanged for a performance. Thus, if A promises to pay B $100 to mow her lawn and B promises to mow the lawn, the contract is created once B manifests his agreement to mow the lawn. However, once the contract is created, both A and B still have to perform obligations under the contract.

As discussed above, when a contract is unilateral, an offer cannot be revoked once performance has begun. In fact, once performance has begun, the offeror no longer has the power to revoke, regardless of how minimal the performance is. However, merely preparing to perform is not enough to prevent the offeror from revoking the offer.

## Option Contract

When the offeree pays for the offeror's promise to keep the offer open for a period of time, the offer will become irrevocable during that period of time. Moreover, the ability to accept the offer will not be terminated by rejection or counteroffer by the offeree. Nor will it be terminated by death or the mental incompetence of the offeror. Instead, the offer must remain open during the period of the option contract and can be accepted any time during that period.

## Offer and Acceptance Under the UCC

See **Section 8.1** of Chapter 8.

## 4.3 CONSIDERATION

### In General

In order for a contract to be legally enforceable, it must be supported by **consideration** or some substitute for consideration (see **promissory estoppel**). Thus, in addition to an offer and acceptance (mutual assent), a person seeking to enforce a contract also must establish the existence of consideration.

### Elements of Consideration

In order to constitute consideration, two factors must be present, (a) there must be a **bargained-for exchange**, and (b) the promisee must incur some **legal detriment**.

### Bargained-For Exchange

Under this element, the parties to the contract must bargain for or agree to some exchange. In order to constitute a "bargain," the promise or performance must induce the action of the other party. In this regard, consideration requires either an exchange of promises or an exchange of a promise for a performance. *Performance* may consist of an act, forbearance, or the creation, modification, or destruction of a legal relationship.

If one party is intending to confer a **gift** on the other party, then there is no bargained-for exchange, because the person receiving the gift is not making a return promise or otherwise performing some act or forbearance. Thus, if A promises to give B a gold watch, there is no consideration for A's promise to B because B has not made a return promise or performance. Moreover, if the promisee does engage in some performance, the performance must *induce* the exchange, and not merely serve as a condition for receiving the gift. For example, suppose A tells B, "if you give me my shopping bag, I will give you the gold watch that is in it." In this situation, it is probably not the case that A decided to give B the watch merely because B passed her the shopping bag. Hence, the fact that B gives A her shopping bag is not considered a bargained-for performance, because it does not actually induce A to give B the watch. Instead, the watch is best viewed as a gift.

If a performance has already occurred or a promise has already been made, then it generally cannot serve as the basis for consideration because it cannot be considered to have induced a bargain. This is known as the doctrine of **"past consideration,"** and such consideration is generally insufficient. Suppose A mows B's lawn. The next day, B promises to pay A for her services. B's promise to pay could not have induced A to mow B's lawn because A mowed the lawn before the promise was given. Hence, there is no bargained-for exchange and no consideration for A's promise. However, there are exceptions to this doctrine if (a) the prior performance would have been enforceable, but has been barred because of some technical rule, or (b) the prior performance occurred at the promisor's request.

## Legal Detriment

A promisee suffers a legal detriment if he (a) does something or promises to do something that he is not legally required to do, or (b) refrains or promises to refrain from doing something that he legally has the right to do. Based on this formulation, the promise to refrain from an illegal act will not constitute a legal detriment, because the promisee does not have the legal right to engage in such conduct. However, a promise to refrain from swearing does represent a legal detriment, because people have a legal right to swear. Similarly, a promise to refrain from bringing a lawsuit or asserting a claim represents a legal detriment if the suit or claim has merit.

In addition, the promise to perform a **pre-existing duty** (a duty that a person already is obligated to perform) will not constitute a legal detriment. Suppose A contracts with B to sing at A's party for $1,000, and after the contract B demands an additional $500 to sing at A's party. If A agrees to the additional amount, there is no consideration for it because B already was obligated to sing for A. In other words, B suffered no legal detriment in exchange for the receipt of the additional $500.

However, courts have recognized a variety of exceptions to the pre-existing duty rule. First, a legal detriment will be found if performance differs from the one required by the pre-existing duty, even if only slightly so. Hence, in the singing example above, a legal detriment will be found if, for example, B agrees to sing an extra song or arrive early to A's party. Second, a legal detriment will be found if the pre-existing duty is owed to a third party. Thus, if C agreed to pay B the extra $500 to sing at A's party, this new promise from C to A will constitute a legal detriment despite the fact that B already had a pre-existing duty to sing for A. Third, the pre-existing duty will not prevent a finding of a legal detriment if performance of the duty would have been excused because of impracticality (see **Discharge of Contracts** discussed in Section 4.12). Fourth, an agreement under the UCC may be modified without consideration so long as the modification is in good faith (see Section 8.2 of Chapter 8). This basically means that under the UCC, the pre-existing duty rule does not apply.

A legal detriment does not require that the promisor benefit. A legal detriment can exist in the absence of an identifiable benefit to the promisor.

## Illusory and Alternative Promises

An agreement where one of the parties does not actually promise to do anything lacks consideration because one of the promises is an **illusory promise**. For example, if B agrees to sing at A's party "if she feels like it," B's promise is illusory. Similarly, if an agreement allows a promisee to choose alternative performances, each of the performances must impose a legal detriment or the agreement lacks consideration. Thus, if A tells B, "I will pay you $1000 and you can sing at my party, if you feel like it, or sing at my grandmother's party." In that case, B's promise to sing at A's grandmother's party would be a legal detriment, but because the promise to sing at A's party represents an illusory promise, the entire agreement lacks consideration.

A requirement contract, which means a contract to buy all that a person requires, is enforceable. This is because although it appears illusory, there is a legal detriment. Indeed, one party is agreeing to sell all of her goods or services and the other party is agreeing to purchase them. Under the UCC, requirement contracts cannot be unreasonably disproportionate to the estimated amount of goods or to the customary amount of goods created, if there is no estimate.

## Adequacy of Consideration

Courts generally do not evaluate the adequacy of the consideration. However, if something can be construed as **token consideration** because it lacks any value, then courts will find it legally insufficient. Similarly, if the parties to a contract state that consideration has been given, but it was not, then the statement will be viewed as **sham consideration** and be legally insufficient.

## Substitutes for Consideration

Some contracts will be enforced even when they lack consideration. The primary doctrine used to substitute for consideration is **promissory estoppel** or **detrimental reliance**. Under that doctrine, a promise will be enforced without consideration if:

(a) the promisor should reasonably expect her promise to induce action or forbearance by the promisee,

(b) the promise does in fact induce justifiable action or forbearance, and

(c) injustice can be avoided only by enforcement.

Promissory estoppel is an equitable remedy designed to allow the enforcement of promises that a promisee reasonably and forseeably relies upon.

In addition to promissory estoppel, a promise to pay a claim or debt that has been barred by law, or discharged in bankruptcy, is enforceable despite the lack of consideration.

## 4.4 CAPACITY

### Legal Capacity

**Legal capacity** or **capacity** refers to the legal ability to form a contract. Proof of a lack of capacity makes a contract voidable, enabling the person who lacks capacity to void the contract.

### Contracts with Minors

People who are below the age of majority are referred to as "**infants**" or "**minors**." The age of majority varies by state, but in most states it is eighteen. However, in some states, married persons are treated as adults regardless of their age. The determination of a person's age is an objective fact. Thus it does not matter if a person looks older than he is or is close to reaching the age of majority.

Minors are generally deemed to lack the capacity to enter into contracts. As a result, contracts with minors are voidable, but only by the minor, not the adult. A contract is voidable by a minor during the time that he is a minor and for a reasonable time after he reaches the age of majority. Moreover, a minor may agree to **affirm** a contract once he reaches the age of majority, either by expressly indicating an intention to be bound by the contract, or by failing to reject or **disaffirm** the contract within a reasonable time after reaching majority.

As a general matter, once a minor disaffirms a contract, neither the minor nor the other party will be obligated to perform any of the obligations under the contract. In addition, the adult in the contract must return anything of value given by the minor. The minor generally must return any goods or benefits that he still retains, but is not liable for property that has been consumed or destroyed.

However, there are exceptions to the rule regarding contracts with minors. First, a minor will be bound to pay the reasonable value of any contract for **necessities**. Necessities represent goods or services that a minor reasonably needs for her livelihood. The other party's ability to hold a minor responsible for his contracts for necessity constitutes an action in restitution, and thus is based on a theory of unjust enrichment. It is also based on a public policy concern for ensuring that people are willing to provide necessities to minors. Second, while an adult generally must take precautions to make sure that she does not contract with a minor, some jurisdictions will enforce a contract against a minor who intentionally misrepresented his age, causing the other party to reasonably rely on the misrepresentation. In these circumstances, such jurisdictions will require the minor to fully perform his obligations under the contract. Apart from these circumstances, certain statutes covering particular matters (such as insurance contracts or student loan contracts) provide that a minor cannot avoid performance based on lack of capacity.

## Mental Incapacity

An adult is presumed to have capacity. However, if an adult can establish that she has a mental condition that is disabling, then she can disaffirm her contract based on **mental incapacity**. In order to avoid a contract based on mental incapacity, the allegedly incompetent person must prove that, at the time she entered into the contract, she was unable to understand the nature and consequences of her actions.

A contract with a person who is mentally incompetent is voidable by the mentally incompetent person or her representative. If a mentally incompetent person seeks to avoid contract liability, the parties must be restored to their original positions. Thus, unlike a minor, a mental incompetent must return the value of any property or services she has received, even if they have been consumed or destroyed. In other words, the other party will be allowed to recover in restitution any unjust enrichment. However, if the other party to the contract knew or had reason to know of a person's mental incompentency and the contract was not on fair terms, then a mentally incompetent person may be allowed to avoid the contract without making restitution.

## Contracts with Intoxicated Persons

A contract entered into by a person who is intoxicated (based on alcohol or drug abuse) is also voidable by the intoxicated person. However, in order to avoid a contract based on intoxication, a person must prove that she was severely intoxicated such that (a) she did not understand the nature and significance of her actions, and (b) the other party had reason to know of the intoxication. Given the potential for abuse, courts are reluctant to allow avoidance based on intoxication.

## Joint Obligations

An offer can be made to, and be accepted by, more than one person. When this occurs, the offeror has undertaken a joint obligation to all of the offerees who accept. Thus, the offeror will be obligated to provide performance to each offeree, and will be liable to each offeree, if she fails to render such performance when due or if the performance is defective.

# 4.5 CONTRACTS FOR THE BENEFIT OF THIRD PARTIES

## Third Party Beneficiaries

Contracts may be formed that are intended to benefit some third party, creating a **third party beneficiary** contract. The general rule is that a contract confers rights and imposes duties only on the actual parties to the contract. However, under certain circumstances, a third party may have the right to enforce a contract. In these circumstances, the party who is to render performance to a third party is referred to as the **promisor**, while the party whose right to performance is being conferred on a beneficiary is referred to as the **promisee**. For example, if X enters into a contract with Y pursuant to which X agrees to pay Y to build a house for Z, Y is the promisor because she will render performance to Z, while X is the promisee because her right to performance from Y is being rendered to Z. Z in this case is the third party beneficiary.

## Intended Beneficiary and Incidental Beneficiary

Not all third party beneficiaries have enforceable rights. Instead, a distinction is made between an **intended beneficiary** and an **incidental beneficiary**. A person is an **intended beneficiary** if:

(a) recognition of a right to performance is appropriate to effectuate the intention of the parties, and

(b) *either* (i) the performance of the promise will satisfy the promisee's obligation to pay money to the beneficiary (see **creditor beneficiary** discussed below), or (ii) the promisee intends to confer a benefit on the beneficiary (see **donee beneficiary** discussed below).

The first aspect of an intended beneficiary's status depends on whether the parties intended to grant a third party an independent right of enforcement. In assessing this factor, courts will examine several issues including whether or not the third party was designated in the contract, whether performance was made directly to the third party, and whether the third party had any rights within the contract.

The second aspect of an intended beneficiary's status depends upon the relationship between the beneficiary and the promisee. If a promisee is conferring a benefit on a third party in order to satisfy a prior obligation, the beneficiary is referred to as a **creditor beneficiary**. If the promisee merely intends to confer a gift, the third party is referred to as a **donee beneficiary**. Hence, in the above-mentioned house example, if the house is being built for Z in order to satisfy a payment that X owes to Z, then Z is a creditor beneficiary. If X owes no debt to Z, then Z is a donee beneficiary.

A person who is not an intended beneficiary is an **incidental beneficiary** and has no rights to enforce a contract.

## Vesting of Beneficiary's Rights

Once the beneficiary's rights vest, the promisee and promisor cannot modify or terminate the contract without the beneficiary's consent. After vesting, if the contract is modified or terminated without the beneficiary's consent, the change is not binding on the beneficiary. Instead, the beneficiary can enforce the performance identified under the original agreement.

A beneficiary's rights vest when she (a) manifests her assent to the contract, (b) brings suit to enforce the contract, or (c) materially changes her position in justifiable reliance on the contract. Once a beneficiary's rights have vested, the contracting parties are obligated to perform the contract on behalf of the beneficiary.

## Beneficiary's Rights

Once a beneficiary's rights have vested, she has an enforceable claim against the promisor and may sue the promisor directly to enforce the contract. However, if the beneficiary is unable to recover fully from the promisor, the beneficiary's ability to bring an action against the promisee depends on her status. If the beneficiary is a donee beneficiary, then she does not have an enforceable claim against the promisee because the promisee's act was gratuitous. If the beneficiary is a creditor beneficiary, then she may bring suit against the promisee because the promisee's actions were designed to satisfy a preexisting obligation owed to the beneficiary. In other words, the contract between the promisor and the promisee does not terminate the obligation the promisee owes to a third party who is a creditor beneficiary. Thus, the creditor beneficiary has the right to receive satisfaction of that obligation from the promisee even if the promisor fails to meet her obligations.

## Promisor's Rights

Because the beneficiary's rights arise from the contract between the promisor and the promisee, the promisor can raise any defense against the beneficiary that she would have been able to raise against the promisee. However, the beneficiary cannot be held liable for improper actions by the promisee. This means that the promisor's ability to raise a defense represents a right to **offset** (or deduct amounts from damages) any claims she has against the amount she owes to the beneficiary, but the promisor cannot force the beneficiary to pay her for claims associated with the promisee. Then too, the promisor cannot raise a defense against the beneficiary that arose out of the transaction between the beneficiary and the promisee. For example, assume that X contracts with Y so that Y can build a house for Z. X has entered into the contract because he owes Z money, but X and Z disagree regarding the precise amount owed. In a suit between Y and Z, Y could not raise as a defense whether X actually owed Z the money at issue because such a defense is based on a separate contract, and is a claim personal to X.

## Promisee's Rights

Notwithstanding the fact that she has conferred the contract's benefits on a third party, the promisee is a party to the contract and hence has the right to enforce the promisor's promise. However, whether or not the promisee can bring an action against the promisor depends upon the status of the beneficiary. If the promisor fails to perform her obligations owed to a creditor beneficiary, the promisee either can compel the promisor to render specific performance under the contract or seek damages for nonperformance. Moreover, if the promisor fails to perform and the creditor beneficiary brings suit against the promisee, the promisee may sue the promisor to recover any damages she sustained as a result of any suit by the creditor beneficiary.

The general rule is that the promisee cannot bring an action against the promisor when the contract involves a donee beneficiary because such a beneficiary cannot bring suit against the promisee. However, some courts allow the promisee to bring an action requiring the promisor to specifically perform her obligation even for a donee beneficiary under the contract.

## Intended Beneficiaries of Government Contracts

Many government contracts are made with the intention of benefiting particular groups of people. Because granting the members of these groups a right to sue the government would be impractical, the presumption is that members of the public are incidental beneficiaries to government contracts and thus have no enforceable rights under the contract. However, this presumption can be rebutted if (a) the government contract or a statute clearly confers a private right of enforcement, or (b) the government has a specific legal obligation to provide some service to the members of the public identified in the contract.

# 4.6 ASSIGNMENT AND DELEGATION

## Assignment of Rights

An **assignment** involves a transaction pursuant to which one party transfers her rights under a contract to another. The Restatement defines an assignment as the "manifestation of an intention to transfer a right to a third person." The transfer must represent a complete relinquishment of such right so that it is immediately enforceable. Hence, if a power to control or revoke the right is retained, then an assignment has not occurred. A party may assign a right that is conditional; such a right cannot be enforced until the condition has been satisfied. By contrast, the transfer of a right expected to arise at some future time is not a valid assignment because the transfer cannot be immediately enforceable.

## Identification of Parties and Effect of Assignment

Like third party beneficiary contracts, the parties to an assignment are referred to by specific titles to identify their role and obligations in the transaction. The person who assigns her rights is initially called the **obligee**, but upon assignment becomes the **assignor**. The person to whom the right is assigned is called an **assignee**. The other party to the contract is the **obligor**, signaling her obligation to the assignee. Thus, if X and Y have a contract that Y later assigns to Z, X is the obligor, Y is the assignor (previously the obligee) and Z is the assignee.

Once an assignment has been made, the assignee is entitled to performance from the obligor, while the assignor is no longer entitled to such performance. Although the obligor does not have to consent to the assignment in order for it to be valid, the obligor must receive *notice* of the assignment. If the obligor completes performance on behalf of the assignor before receiving notice of the assignment, he has no further responsibility to the assignee. However, once the obligor has notice of the assignment, he must hold performance for the benefit of the assignee. Moreover, if he performs for the assignor after such notice, he will be liable to the assignee.

## Restrictions on Assignment

If a contract states that assignments are prohibited, the statement is construed only as a prohibition against **delegation** (see **delegation** discussed below) and thus does not prohibit assignments. Instead, an assignment will be valid unless the contract specifically states that assignments are void. However, if an assignment is made with respect to an agreement stating that assignments are prohibited, the assignment will be treated as a breach of contract and will allow the obligor to bring an action against the assignor.

An assignment will be void if it conflicts with a statute or public policy, or if it materially adversely impacts the rights of the obligor. With respect to this latter factor, an assignment would be invalid if it would (a) materially change the obligor's duty, (b) increase the burden or risk imposed by the contract, (c) impair the obligor's prospects of getting a return performance, or (d) substantially reduce the contract's value to the obligor.

## Assignee, Assignor, and Obligor's Rights

Similar to a beneficiary, an assignee has an enforceable right against the obligor because she is considered the **real party in interest**. Yet like a promisor in a third party beneficiary contract, an obligor can raise any defense against the assignee that she would have been able to raise against the assignor. Then too, the obligor's ability to raise such defenses represents a right to *offset* the assignee's claim, and thus the assignee cannot be held directly liable to the assignor for improper actions by the assignee.

The obligor also can raise any defenses against the assignee that she would have been able to raise against the assignor that relate to *other* transactions so long as the defenses arose before the obligor had notice of the assignment. For example, suppose A contracts with B to mow B's lawn for $50. A later assigns the right of payment to C and notifies B. B (who is now the obligor) may raise any defenses arising out of the contract such as a claim that A mowed the lawn improperly. In addition, suppose A had a separate contract with B to wash B's car, and A broke B's window while washing the car. In the lawn contract, B can raise this defense against C so long as the window was broken before B received notice of A's transfer to C. Raising such a defense means that B can offset any claims owed by A, but if the claims exceed the amount of the assignment (i.e., the damage to the window was more than $50), the assignee will not be responsible for paying the excess.

If the obligor's defense against the assignee is successful, the assignee can bring an action against the assignor because, by assigning the contract, the assignor implicitly warrants that the right being assigned is not subject to any defenses. In addition, if the assignment is **irrevocable** (see **irrevocable** discussed below), then the assignee may bring suit against the assignor if she wrongfully revokes the assignment by, for example, transferring it to a third party or accepting performance from the obligor.

## Revocability

**Revocability** relates to situations when an assignment can be taken away from the assignee. An assignment that is supported by consideration is **irrevocable**. An assignment that is not supported by consideration is **revocable**, and such an assignment is referred to as a **gratuitous assignment**. However, a gratuitous assignment will become irrevocable under certain circumstances including when (a) the obligor has performed her obligations to the assignee, (b) the assignor delivers the assignment in writing to the assignee, or (c) the assignor reasonably expects that the assignee will change her position in reliance on the assignment, and such a change occurs to the assignee's detriment (i.e., when there has been detrimental reliance). In addition, if an assignor seeks to assign a right that is embodied in a **tangible object**, the assignment will become irrevocable once the object is transferred. For example, the right to attend a play is embodied in a ticket, which is a tangible object. If that right is assigned along with the ticket it becomes irrevocable.

If an assignment is irrevocable, then the assignor does not have the right to terminate it or transfer the same right to a third party, and any attempt to do so would result in a breach by the assignor. An assignment that is revocable may be terminated by (a) the assignor's death or bankruptcy, (b) a subsequent assignment of the same right to another party, (c) notice of revocation from the assignor to either the assignee or the obligor, or (d) the assignor's acceptance of performance from the obligor.

## Delegation of Duties

When a person transfers a duty, it is called a **delegation**. Thus, the key difference between a delegation and an assignment is that delegation transfers a duty while assignment transfers a right. Like an assignment, parties to a delegation are given specific titles. A person who delegates her duty under an agreement is initially called the **obligor** and after the delegation becomes the **delegator**. The person who assumes the duty is referred to as the **delegate**, while the other party to whom performance is owed is called the **obligee**. X and Y have a contract that Y delegates to Z. Y is the delegator, Z is the delegate and X is the obligee.

## Effect of Delegation

When a contract is delegated, the obligee must accept performance from the delegate. However, unless the obligee agrees to release her from liability, the delegator remains liable under the contract until the delegate has performed. Once a delegate performs under the contract, the delegator's contractual duty has been met.

Neither the delegator nor the obligee can compel the delegate to perform *unless* the delegate promises she will perform and her promise is supported by consideration. If that occurs, the other parties to the contract can compel performance or bring suit against the delegate for nonperformance.

## Exceptions to Delegation

Some duties cannot be delegated. Duties that involve some personal service or skill or that would materially change the obligor's expectancy under the contract may not be delegated. Hence, duties to perform services such as painting someone's portrait or performing surgery are generally too personal to be delegated. Moreover, a contract provision prohibiting assignment will be construed to prohibit a delegation. However, any duty, even personal ones, can be delegated if the obligee consents to the delegation.

## 4.7 STATUTE OF FRAUDS

### Oral Contracts

As a general rule, oral contracts are valid and enforceable. However, certain agreements will not be enforceable unless they are in writing and signed by the party sought to be bound. The **Statute of Frauds** is a general rule referring to circumstances in which agreements must be in writing, and by extension when oral agreements will be unenforceable. The Statute's writing requirement stems from the notion that oral promises may be unreliable. However, if a contract does not fall within the Statute of Frauds, then it does not have to be in writing in order to be enforceable.

## Contracts that Fall Within the Statute of Frauds

There are six basic agreements that are covered by the Statute of Frauds:

1. A promise by an executor or administrator to pay the estate's debts.

2. A promise to pay the debt of another, referred to as a **surety** promise. Such a promise must not represent the primary promise, but rather must serve as a guarantee for another promise. For example, if Y says to a builder, "if you build X a pool house, I will pay for it," the transaction is not a surety because Y's promise is the primary one. As a result, this promise does not fall within the Statute of Frauds and does not have to be in writing. However, if Y says to the builder, "if you build X a pool house and he does not pay you, I will," then the transaction is a surety because Y is promising to guarantee X's primary payment. As a result, the promise falls within the Statute of Frauds and must be in writing.

3. A promise made in consideration of marriage.

4. A promise for the sale of land or creating an interest in land. This includes promises involving leases for more than one year, easements for more than one year, and mortgages or other security interests in land.

5. A promise that by its terms cannot be performed within one year. This covers promises that take more than a year to perform as well as promises that will not be completed within a year from the date on which the contract was entered. This also covers agreements that by their terms are not capable of being performed during the promisor's lifetime. However, as long as an agreement is capable of being performed within a year, it does not fall within the Statute of Frauds, even if actual performance occurs after a one-year period.

6. Contracts for the sale of goods for the price of $500 or more.

Both the UCC and state statutes also contain classes of contracts that are subject to the writing requirement.

## Writing Requirement

The Statute of Frauds requires that contracts that fall within its scope must be in writing and signed by the person to be bound. In order for the writing to be sufficient, it must (a) reasonably identify the subject matter of the contract, (b) contain enough information to indicate that a contract has been formed, and (c) state with reasonable certainty the essential terms of the contract. As a general matter, this means that the writing must identify the parties as well as the terms and conditions of the exchange. In addition, the party to be charged or her agent must sign the writing.

When a contract falls within the Statute of Frauds but fails to meet the writing requirement, it is unenforceable by the party seeking to rely on the Statute. Hence, any party to a contract can rely upon the Statute of Frauds to avoid enforcement of a contract.

## Exceptions

There are exceptions to the writing requirement embodied in the Statute of Frauds. Such exceptions are treated as taking the contract **"out of the Statute of Frauds."**

(a) If a party admits in a pleading, testimony or otherwise in court, that a contract was made, the contract is enforceable against the party to the extent of the **admission**.

(b) Performance also may take a contract out of the Statute of Frauds. What constitutes performance differs depending on the type of contract at issue. With regard to the sale of goods, if payment has been made and accepted or goods have been delivered and accepted, then the contract is enforceable to the extent of such payment or delivery. For example, suppose X enters into an oral contract with Z pursuant to which X will sell Z 1,000 hats for $1 each. If X delivers 700 hats and Z accepts delivery, the contract is enforceable to the extent of the 700 hats. Z will be obligated to pay X $700 for the hats, but will not have any obligation for the remaining 300 hats. Similarly, if Z pays X $400, X will be obligated to deliver 400 hats to Z. With regard to a sale of land, a contract will be taken out of the Statute of Frauds when there has been some partial performance. States define such performance differently, but it generally includes a change of possession, valuable improvements and some form of payment. With regard to contracts that cannot be performed within a year, full performance is necessary to take such contracts out of the Statute of Frauds.

(c) Courts also will use the doctrine of **promissory estoppel** to take a contract out of the Statute of Frauds. As an initial matter, if a party falsely claims to have written and signed an agreement or promises to do so, then the party cannot avoid enforcement of the contract based on the Statute of Frauds. In addition, courts rely upon the more traditional doctrine of promissory estoppel to take contracts out of the Statute of Frauds. The elements of promissory estoppel are that (a) a promise is made where there is a reasonable expectation of some action or forbearance, (b) the promise induces justifiable reliance, and (c) enforcement is necessary to prevent injustice. In the context of the Statute of Frauds, this doctrine is applied when one party justifiably relies on the oral promise of another party, and as a result suffers some detriment.

# 4.8 SCOPES AND MEANINGS OF CONTRACTS

## Certainty of Terms

In order for a contract to be enforceable, the terms of the contract must be **definite and certain**. Courts impose this requirement for a number of reasons. If the contract terms are not definite and certain, then the court cannot determine each party's duties and whether there has been a breach of those duties. Moreover, when the terms are not definite and certain, a court may find that no mutual assent has occurred because the lack of definiteness and certainty suggests that no mutual agreement could have been made. Older case law required that in order to be definite and certain a contract had to contain all of the **essential terms**. Those essential terms included the names of parties, the price, the subject matter, and the time for performance.

Certainty and definiteness are important for both offers and acceptance. In regard to an offer, the Restatement states that an offer cannot occur if the terms are not reasonably certain. Similarly, the Restatement states that an intention to manifest acceptance may not be found where one or more terms are left open. However, when both parties reveal an intent to be bound, the UCC provides that courts should seek to construe the contract so that it can be enforced by defining terms based on (a) the course of performance of the contract between the parties, (b) the parties' prior course of dealing, or (c) the manner in which the term is used in the trade, known as trade usage.

## Rules of Interpretation and Construction

When seeking to determine the meaning of a contract, courts refer to a variety of different principles designed to interpret the agreement. The overarching purpose of rules of **interpretation** is to determine the parties' intent. In so doing, courts will refer to the following factors, listed in order of importance:

1. **Express words and conduct of the party**, which means that courts will assess the actual words the parties used in creating the contract, and will review such words in context of the entire agreement;

2. **Course of performance**, which involves analyzing the meaning of a contract by reference to the manner in which the parties conducted themselves in the course of performing the contract at issue;

3. **Course of dealing**, which means assessing a contract by relying on the manner in which the parties have conducted themselves during prior transactions with each other; and

4. **Trade usage**, which refers to examining the manner in which words are used customarily or in the market applicable to the parties.

While the above rules are designed to assist the court in assessing what the parties' intend the contract to mean, courts also will use a variety of **rules of construction** when trying to determine how the contract should be construed. Some of the most prevalent rules include:

(a) preferring an interpretation that makes the contract valid and enforceable,

(b) interpreting the contract as a whole; thus specific clauses should not defeat the general purpose of a contract,

(c) giving specific provisions more weight than general ones,

(d) preferring negotiated or hand-written terms over standard terms, and

(e) construing any contract ambiguities against the drafter.

## Implied Terms

In addition to rules of construction and interpretation, courts will imply certain terms in order to clarify a contract's meaning. These implied terms are also known as gap fillers. Thus, courts impose an **implied obligation of good faith** in every contract. Also, when a contract does not indicate a level of performance, courts will imply an **obligation to use reasonable efforts**. In some cases, this implied obligation will serve as consideration for a contract that appears illusory because one party appears to have no performance obligations. For example, suppose X promises to sell pizzas made by Y, and in exchange X agrees to split any profits he makes with Y. This promise appears illusory because X does not appear to have any obligation to sell pizzas; his only promise appears to be to split profits he makes, if any. However, if courts imply an obligation to use reasonable efforts, then X's promise includes an obligation to use reasonable efforts to make some profit by selling pizza. In that case, the implied obligation serves to fill a gap in the contract terms and to create consideration for X's promise, thereby making the promise an enforceable contract.

## The Parol Evidence Rule

The **Parol Evidence Rule** is a rule regarding the kinds of evidence admissible when a party seeks to offer evidence designed to explain an agreement that is in writing. The rule is basically designed to exclude written or oral evidence of commitments made prior to the actual written agreement because such evidence tends to be unreliable. Such written or oral evidence is referred to as **parol evidence**.

In determining the admissibility of parol evidence, a court must first determine if the written contract is **integrated**. If a written contract represents a full, final, and complete record of the parties' agreement, then the contract is integrated. Such integration is referred to as **complete** or **total integration**. If the contract is completely integrated, parol evidence is inadmissible. However, if the written contract does not constitute a complete integration, parol evidence is admissible so long as it is consistent with the written agreement.

In determining whether a contract is integrated, courts generally examine the **"four corners"** of the written contract, which means that courts will examine only the document itself. However, some courts extend their analysis beyond the four corners of the agreement and assess other evidence to determine if the contract is integrated.

There are exceptions to the Parol Evidence Rule that enable the admissibility of parol evidence even if it is inconsistent with the written agreement, or the document is otherwise completely integrated. Thus, parol evidence can be admitted to demonstrate that there is a basis for avoidance of the contract. In addition, such evidence can be admitted to demonstrate the existence of a collateral or additional agreement, or to establish that the agreement at issue was subject to a **condition** (see **condition** discussed below).

## Conditions

Many contracts are subject to one or more conditions. A **condition** is an event that is not certain to occur. A contract is subject to a condition when the parties agree that performance is contingent on the occurrence of that uncertain event. If the condition is not met or excused, then neither party has a duty to comply with her performance obligations. The absolute duty to perform a contract does not arise until the condition has been met or excused.

There are three forms of conditions.

(a) A **condition precedent** is a condition that must occur before a duty to perform arises.

(b) A **condition concurrent** is a condition that occurs at the same time as performance.

(c) A **condition subsequent** is a condition that cuts off a pre-existing duty.

In order for the obligation of performance to arise, a condition must either be performed or excused. When a condition is excused, a party has an immediate obligation to perform. An excuse can occur in a variety of different ways.

(a) An excuse can occur by **hindrance** when a party prevents a condition from occurring or fails to cooperate in order to ensure the occurrence of a condition.

(b) One party's **material breach** (see **material breach** discussed in Section 4.9 below) of the contract will excuse a condition such that the breaching party's obligation will be deemed absolute, enabling the breach to be treated as a total breach.

(c) One party's **anticipatory repudiation** (see **anticipatory repudiation** discussed in Section 4.9 below) of the contract will excuse a condition such that the repudiating party's duty to perform becomes absolute, and thus the repudiation can be treated as a total breach.

(d) One party's **substantial performance** (see **substantial performance** discussed in Section 4.9 below) of a condition will excuse the lack of complete performance of the condition.

(e) If the party for whom the condition was designed to benefit agrees to a **waiver** of the condition by indicating by words or conduct that she will not insist on the condition, then the condition may be deemed excused. However, if the waiver is not supported by consideration, it is only effective if the condition is immaterial. When a condition is material, a waiver can become effective without consideration *only* if the non-waiving party detrimentally relies on the waiver. In that case, the condition is excused by **estoppel**.

# 4.9 BREACH OF CONTRACT AND REMEDIES

## Breach

When a promisor is under an absolute duty to perform (because all conditions have been met or excused), the promisor's failure to perform in accordance with the terms of the contract represents a **breach**. However, while any failure to perform represents a breach, the promisee's remedy depends upon the nature of the breach.

## Partial or Trivial Breach

A breach is considered **partial** or **trivial** if the promisor substantially performs under the contract. Thus, **substantial performance** is sometimes referred to as the opposite of a **material breach**. While a trivial defect in performance generally will be treated as substantial performance, a different rule applies when the performance relates to a sale of goods. In that case, a promisee can reject most goods that do not conform to the contract (see **Section 8.2** of Chapter 8). Then too, if a breach is minor, but intentional, some courts will consider it material and thus nontrivial.

When a breach is trivial, a promisee can bring suit to recover damages related to the breach, but is not entitled to suspend her performance. Thus, suppose A contracts with B to pay B $5,000 to sing at A's party which is planned from 8 p.m. to 2 a.m. Under the contact, B also agrees to arrive at the party at 7:30 p.m. in order to set up and rehearse. If B arrives at 7:40 p.m. he has committed a breach because he has failed to render performance in accordance with the contract terms. However, because arriving ten minutes late should not impair the value of the contract, the breach would be considered trivial. As a result, while A could bring suit against B for damages associated with B's late arrival, A could not refuse to satisfy her obligation of paying B $5,000.

## Material Breach

A breach is considered **material** when it is so central to the contract that it significantly impairs the contract's value to the promisee. If a breach is material, there has not been substantial performance. In addition to her ability to bring suit to recover damages, a material breach allows the promisee to suspend her performance and wait for the promisor to cure the breach. However, she cannot terminate the contract. Because a material breach does not terminate the contract, the promisee cannot seek alternative arrangements for the contract. In the above singing example, a material breach would occur if B does not arrive until 10 p.m. because B's ability to perform from 8 p.m. to 2 a.m. is a central part of the contract. However, if the breach is only material, then A could not hire another singer to replace B because such an action would be construed as a termination of the contract.

## Total Breach

Courts look at a variety of factors to determine if a breach is **total**. Such factors include whether (a) there is a likelihood of cure, (b) further delay will prevent the promisee from making alternative arrangements, or (c) prompt performance is a critical element of the contract. All total breaches are material breaches.

A total breach discharges the promisee's obligation, allowing her to withhold performance, terminate the contract and bring suit to recover damages related to the full value of the contract. If a breach is total, a promisee is allowed to seek alternative arrangements for the fulfillment of her contract. In the above singing example, if B has not arrived at the party by midnight, B's breach is likely both material and total because it would be difficult for B to cure the breach and it is unlikely that she will be able to find another singer for her party if she does not act quickly once B fails to arrive as scheduled. Unlike a material breach, once a breach is total, A is allowed to seek alternative arrangements such as hiring another singer.

## Anticipatory Repudiation

A breach only can occur if a party fails to perform when performance is due. This means that a breach cannot occur before performance is due. Thus, if a party promises delivery of a good at 5 p.m., a breach cannot occur until 5 p.m. However, if a party unlawfully indicates that she will not perform when performance is due, then she has committed an **anticipatory repudiation** of the contract. An anticipatory repudiation occurs when the party makes clear either by her words or conduct that she does not intend to perform or that she will only perform under circumstances that go beyond the contract terms.

When there is an anticipatory repudiation, and the indicated inaction would be serious enough to qualify as a material or total breach, the non-repudiating party can halt performance and treat the other party's repudiation as a total breach, unless there has been a **retraction**. A party can retract her repudiation by indicating a willingness to perform under the contract. A retraction is not valid if the non-repudiating party has (a) materially changed her position in reliance on the repudiation, or (b) indicated her willingness to treat the repudiation as a total breach.

## Demand for Assurances

Often a party will experience uncertainty regarding another party's intention to perform under the contract. In such a circumstance, the uncertain party may **demand assurance**, which involves a written request for reasonable assurances regarding a party's intention to perform. A party may demand assurance when he has reasonable grounds for insecurity regarding another party's performance. If the demand for assurance is reasonable, the party requesting it may suspend his performance until such assurance is received. Moreover, the requesting party may treat the failure to receive adequate assurance within a reasonable time period as an anticipatory repudiation, and hence a total breach.

## Remedies for Breach

When a breach occurs, the non-breaching party can bring an action for a remedy. There are a variety of different remedies, but their primary purpose is to compensate for economic loss.

## Expectation Damages

In most cases, a party will be awarded **expectation damages**. These are damages designed to approximate the amount necessary to compensate the party *if the breach had not occurred* and the contract had been fully performed. Some refer to these damages as restoring the **benefit of the bargain**. Expectation damages must be reasonable, foreseeable, and certain.

Expectation damages are comprised of **direct damages** plus **consequential damages**, and then are reduced by any costs or loss avoided. Direct damages constitute the difference between the value of the performance a party should have received and the value of the performance the party actually received. Consequential damages represent losses that result from other transactions that are dependent upon the breached contract. Consequential damages must be reasonable, foreseeable, and certain. Such damages include loss profits on collateral contracts or other special damages that are known and communicated.

A party's damage award will be reduced by any costs he avoided as a result of the breach. A party's damage award also will be reduced by any loss he did or could have avoided. This is known as a **duty to mitigate**. Thus, if a party continues performance after the breach or fails to make reasonable substitute arrangements after a breach, he will have violated his duty to mitigate and his damages will be reduced by the amount he could have received if he had halted performance or otherwise made alternative arrangements.

A party's expectation damages are calculated as follows:

**Direct Damages + Consequential Damages – Costs Avoided – Loss Avoided (Mitigation)**

When there has been substantial performance, the general measure of expectation damages will be the cost of replacement or completion. However, when substantial performance is done in good faith and the cost of replacement or completion would result in **economic waste** (i.e., a situation in which replacement or completion costs are significantly disproportionate to the actual harm caused by the breach), the measure of damages will be the **diminution in value**. Diminution in value refers to the difference between the value of the property as substantially complete and the value of the property upon full performance.

## Reliance Damages

If a party's expectation damages are too speculative, she will be awarded **reliance damages**. Reliance damages represent the amount of money a party has spent in justifiable reliance on a contract. Such damages are designed to refund any expenses incurred in connection with contract performance. Reliance damages must be reasonable and foreseeable and are subject to the duty to mitigate. In addition, if the breaching party can prove with reasonable certainty that the contract would have produced a loss for the non-breaching party, reliance damages will be reduced by the amount of that loss.

## Restitution

**Restitution** reflects the amount of benefit one party conferred on the other, i.e. the amount of damages reflecting unjust enrichment. Restitution is not limited to the contract price and unlike reliance damages, does not get reduced by the amount of money a party would have lost on a contract. This is because restitution is designed to prevent unjust enrichment, and hence is not awarded with reference to the contract terms. **Rescission** and **restitution** refer to the parties' ability to terminate the contract and then seek damages for unjust enrichment. Rescission and restitution damages are designed to put the parties in the position they would have been in if no contract had been formed. When a contract is voidable, the general remedy is rescission and restitution.

## Specific Performance and Injunctions

**Specific performance** reflects an order from the court to perform the contract pursuant to its terms. As a general rule, courts do not like to award specific performance. However, specific performance will be awarded when (a) the damage remedy is inadequate and (b) the equitable need for such performance outweighs the burden of supervision and harm to the defendant. A damage remedy will be deemed inadequate if it is too difficult to prove or if it will not fully compensate the non-breaching party. This may occur, for example, when the subject matter of a contract is unique. Courts will not order specific performance for contracts involving personal services, however, because of the difficulty with supervision as well as concerns regarding involuntary servitude.

In some cases when specific performance may not be appropriate, courts may nevertheless issue an **injunction**. An injunction represents an order prohibiting a party from engaging in certain conduct. A court will issue an injunction if (a) the damage remedy is inadequate and (b) the injunction is necessary to prevent irreparable harm to the non-breaching party. In the context of a breached contract, a court is likely to issue an injunction to prevent the breaching party from performing for a third party actions that she was obligated to perform for the non-breaching party. For example, in a contract where B breached her obligation to sing at A's party, a court is likely to award A an injunction that would prevent B from singing at C's party.

## Liquidated Damages

Under some contracts, the parties will stipulate the amount of damages to be awarded upon a breach. Courts will award such amount only if (a) damages were difficult to determine or estimate at the time the contract was formed, and (b) the stipulated amount represents a reasonable forecast of the amount necessary to compensate a non-breaching party for her loss. If these two prongs are met, the stipulated amount will be upheld and enforceable as a valid **liquidated damages** clause. If a court finds the damages to be unreasonable, then the stipulated amount will be construed as a **penalty**, and hence will be unenforceable.

## Non-recoverable Damages

As a general matter, punitive damages, non-economic damages (such as damages for emotional distress), and attorneys' fees are not recoverable.

## 4.10 BAR TO REMEDIES FOR BREACH OF CONTRACT (DEFENSES TO ENFORCEMENT)

Contracting parties may bring various defenses to a contract, the impact of which is to make the contract unenforceable. Both lack of capacity and the Statute of Frauds constitute defenses to the enforcement of a contract. The discussion below sets forth other defenses.

### Duress

**Duress** represents (a) an **improper threat** (b) that leaves the victim no reasonable alternative but to comply with an agreement. If a party is induced to enter into a contract under duress, the contract is voidable by the victim of duress. A classic example of duress is when a party is forced to sign a contract because the other party puts a gun to her head. In that case, the victim clearly has been threatened in a manner that leaves her with no reasonable alternative but to execute the contract.

Courts used to require that in order to qualify as duress, an improper threat had to be a threat of death or bodily harm. However, modern courts interpret improper threat more broadly to include conduct that is either unlawful or wrongful. Hence, an improper threat may include a threat to do something that would have adverse personal or economic consequences such as a threat to disclose embarrassing personal details or interfere in a person's business dealings. Courts also have found that a party's threat not to perform under a valid contract constitutes an improper threat for purposes of duress.

When assessing whether a party has a reasonable alternative, courts examine if there exists no practical means for a party to avoid the impact of the threat. This includes circumstances where it would be risky or unduly burdensome for a party to refuse to comply with a threat.

A contract *modified* under duress also is voidable to the extent of the modification. Duress with respect to modification requires an additional element. Thus, in addition to proving that the modification resulted from an improper threat that left the victim with no reasonable alternative but to comply, the victim must demonstrate that he protested the modification.

### Undue Influence

Undue influence represents those situations where one party takes unfair advantage of another to persuade her to enter into a contract. **Undue influence** involves two factors (a) a relationship of dominance pursuant to which one party has strong influence over another because (i) there exists a fiduciary or other relationship of trust, or (ii) a party is in a weakened state, and (b) the dominant party unfairly persuades the other party to enter into a relationship.

## Mistake

A contract entered into based on a **mistake** is voidable. A mistake represents an error about a fact in existence at the time the contract was made. There are two forms of mistakes, a **mutual mistake** and a **unilateral mistake**. A party can avoid enforcement based on a mutual mistake when (a) both parties are mistaken, (b) the mistake concerns a basic assumption on which the contract was made that has a material impact on performance, and (c) the party seeking to avoid performance has not assumed the risk of the mistake.

With regard to the second element, the party seeking avoidance must demonstrate that the fact relates to a core feature of the contract. Thus, suppose two parties entered into a transaction related to the sale of a dog, and both parties believed the dog had a black tail. If the dog's tail was actually dark brown, such a mistake does not appear to go to the basic assumption of the contract. In comparison, if both parties believed their transaction involved the sale of a dog and instead the animal sold was a cat, that mistake goes to a basic assumption of the contract because it relates to the essence of the bargain.

The third element of mistake involves a balancing test pursuant to which the court must determine if it is reasonable for the party seeking avoidance to bear the risk of the mistake. In determining whether a party should bear the risk of a mistake, a court will assess whether the agreement shifts the risk to a particular party as well as whether commercial standards or custom impose the risk on a particular party.

A party can avoid a contract based on **unilateral mistake** by demonstrating that (a) one party made a mistake, (b) the mistake concerns a basic assumption on which the contract was made that has a material impact on performance, (c) the party seeking to avoid performance has not assumed the risk of the mistake, and (d) equities favor avoidance. If there is a unilateral mistake, only one person is mistaken, and thus, it is more difficult to avoid enforcement. As a result, the party seeking avoidance must demonstrate not only that she will suffer severe hardship if the contract is enforced, but also that the other party will not suffer any harm if the contract is not enforced.

## Misrepresentation and Fraud

A **misrepresentation** is an assertion that is not in accord with the facts. However, even an expression of an opinion can form the basis of a misrepresentation if the opinion suggests that the speaker (a) has knowledge of facts upon which the opinion is based, or (b) has no knowledge of facts that would refute the opinion.

In order for a misrepresentation to form the basis to avoid a contract, it must be shown that (a) a misrepresentation was made, (b) it was **material**, and (c) the party seeking avoidance reasonably relied on it. A misrepresentation is material if it is likely to induce a reasonable person to agree to the contract or if the person making the misrepresentation knew or should have known that it was likely to induce a specific party to agree to the contract. A court will determine if reliance is reasonable by examining the facts and circumstances surrounding the given transaction.

Misrepresentation is distinct from **fraud**. In fact, fraud is a form of misrepresentation that is made with intent. Thus, a misrepresentation will constitute fraud if, in addition to materiality and justifiable reliance, it was made intentionally to induce reliance and if it was made with scienter. **Scienter** refers to a misrepresentation made with knowledge of its inaccuracy.

## Unconscionability

Some contracts are so egregious that they will be invalidated even if the other defenses are not applicable to them. Such contracts will be deemed unconscionable. A contract will be voidable based on **unconscionability** when a court believes that a contract is so one-sided and unfair that it would be unconscionable to enforce it. Some courts refer to such contracts as ones that "shock the conscious." Courts tend to divide unconscionability into substantive and procedural unconscionability. **Substantive unconscionability** exists when the terms of the agreement are grossly unfair or unduly favorable to one side, particularly when the terms are incomprehensible to a party or the average person. **Procedural unconscionability** focuses on the relationship between the contracting parties, and exists when one party lacks choice regarding whether to enter into a contract, or when there are otherwise gross inequities in the bargaining positions between the two parties. Hence when a contract is presented on a "take it or leave it" basis, known as a contract of **adhesion**, it is likely that a court will find procedural unconscionability because of the inability to bargain over the contract's terms.

In order for a contract to be voidable for unconscionability, a court must find both substantive and procedural unconscionability. However, courts will balance the two elements so that, for example, if a significant amount of substantive unconscionability exists, procedural unconscionability need not be as strong.

## Statute of Limitations

A contract will be unenforceable after the statute of limitations (the period in which a person may bring her claim) has expired. The statute of limitations for contracts varies by state, but is usually six years. The statute of limitations under the UCC is four years. Once the statute of limitations has expired, the contract action is barred by operation of law. However, a promisor's agreement to perform her obligation after the expiration of the statute of limitations will be sufficient to create a new contract, and the consideration under the old contract will be sufficient consideration for the new contract. In this regard, the past consideration rule does not apply to such promises.

## 4.11 DISCHARGE OF CONTRACTS

If a party is under an immediate duty to perform, the contract must be discharged either by performance or by some excuse for performance.

### Changed Circumstances

In some circumstances, a party will be excused from performing under a contract because of a change in circumstances. Changed circumstances entail three doctrines: **impossibility**, **impracticability** (or impracticality), and **frustration of purpose**. Discharge by impossibility occurs when (a) an event occurs after the contract is executed, (b) the nonoccurrence of which was a basic assumption of the contract, (c) the event makes contract performance *impossible*, and (d) the party seeking discharge did not assume the risk of the nonoccurrence. Courts assess most of these elements in the same manner that they are examined in the context of mistake. However, when analyzing whether an event represents a basic assumption of the contract, it must be proven that the event was **unforeseen**—an event that the parties did not contemplate when executing the contract. In order to satisfy the requirement of impossibility, performance must be literally impossible (i.e., incapable of being performed), and hence impossibility generally only can be established upon the death or physical impairment of a person necessary for performance. However, if a supervening statute makes a contract illegal, then such **supervening illegality** will make performance impossible.

Similar to impossibility, discharge by **impracticability** occurs when (a) an event occurs after the contract is executed, (b) the nonoccurrence of which was a basic assumption of the contract, (c) the event makes contract performance *impractical*, and (d) the party seeking discharge did not assume the risk of the nonoccurrence. A performance is impractical if it is unduly burdensome pursuant to which performance cannot occur without some significant loss or hardship.

Discharge by **frustration of purpose** occurs when (a) an event occurs after the contract is executed, (b) the nonoccurrence of which was a basic assumption of the contract, (c) the event *frustrates the material purpose* of the contract, and (d) the party seeking discharge did not assume the risk of the nonoccurrence. Frustration of purpose occurs when the exchange loses most of its value as a result of the event, such that the purpose of the contract is destroyed.

## Discharge by Rescission

Rescission will discharge a contract. Rescission can be mutual or unilateral. **Mutual rescission** occurs when both parties agree to rescind the contract. In order to be valid, the contract must be **executory** with respect to both parties, which means that both parties must still have some remaining performance obligation. In this circumstance, the rescission is valid because it is supported by consideration. In other words, both parties will suffer the legal detriment of refraining from receiving performance. **Unilateral rescission** occurs when only one party desires to rescind the contract. Courts will allow unilateral rescission if the party seeking to rescind has legal grounds to avoid enforcement of the contract such as by demonstrating undue influence, fraud, or duress.

## Discharge by Novation

A novation occurs when a new party assumes the obligations and benefits of a contract, discharging the prior contract. **Novation** requires (a) a previous valid contract, (b) agreement by all of the parties to the new contract, (c) an intention to immediately terminate duties under the previous contract, and (d) a new contract that is valid and enforceable. Unlike an assignment or delegation, novation extinguishes the rights and liabilities of the parties to the previous contract.

## Discharge by Accord and Satisfaction

An **accord** represents an agreement pursuant to which the original promisee agrees to accept different performance from the original promisor, in exchange for a release of the original agreement. An accord does not discharge the original obligation until there has been satisfaction. **Satisfaction** refers to actual performance of the accord agreement. Both accord and satisfaction are necessary to discharge a contract.

# 4.12 ILLEGAL CONTRACTS AND PUBLIC POLICY CONCERNS

An **illegal** contract is a contract that violates the law or a statute. Illegality renders the contract void and generally unenforceable. This means that neither party will be entitled to a contract remedy. Thus, if some performance has occurred under the contract, the general rule is that a court will not provide for restitution, but will leave the parties as it finds them so as not to partake in an illegal act. Courts tend to apply this rule when both parties are equally guilty or when the party seeking restitution is more at fault than the other party. The rule is applied based on a principle known as **"in pari delicto."** However, when the party seeking restitution is less culpable, courts may use their discretion to fashion an appropriate remedy.

Some contracts are not illegal, but rather violate a particular public policy. Public policy refers to a policy that is clearly identified in some statute or legislation. If a contract does not involve a public policy that is clearly articulated in a statute or piece of legislation, most courts are reluctant to hold that the contract violates public policy. This is because courts do not want to establish policy in the absence of some clear direction from the legislature. A contract that violates public policy is not necessarily unenforceable. Instead, courts must balance policy concerns with equitable concerns. This involves consideration of the seriousness of the misconduct, the nature of the public policy, and the relative guilt of the parties. In this regard, courts will use their discretion to determine if restitution should be awarded.

# CHAPTER 5
## The Legal Environment

# Chapter 5

# THE LEGAL ENVIRONMENT

## 5.1 ETHICS

### Theories of Ethics

**Ethics** refers to moral principles of right and wrong. There are several theories of ethics. For example, **deontological** theories are based on the notion that ethical behavior is guided by duties or obligations. Proponents of this theory maintain that we have clear obligations that must shape our actions regardless of their consequences. John Locke referred to these obligations as **natural rights**, and maintained that such rights demand that we not harm anyone's life, health, or liberty. Moreover, Locke viewed these rights as (a) **natural**, meaning that they were not created by any government or other body, (b) **universal**, meaning that they applied to everyone, and (c) **inalienable**, meaning that they could not be transferred. Locke's concept of natural rights is memorialized in the **Declaration of Independence**, which states that man is endowed with certain inalienable rights including life, liberty, and the pursuit of happiness. Another influential proponent of a deontological theory of ethics was Immanuel Kant. Kant argued that our ethical duties should be guided by one principle, which he called the **categorical imperative**. This imperative mandates particular actions, regardless of their consequences or our personal preferences. One core principle of the categorical imperative is that we treat people "as ends and not means to an end."

In contrast to deontological theories, **consequentialism** views ethical behavior in terms of its consequences. Hence, those theories maintain that an action should be judged by its impact, rather than its motives. Thus, an action is morally right if its consequences are morally appropriate. In other words, "the ends justify the means." One principle consequentialism theory is **utilitarianism**. Utilitarianism maintains that an action is justified as long as it does the greatest good for the greatest number of people. Both Jeremy Bentham and John Stuart Mill advocate some version of utilitarianism.

## Legal Ethics

Laws tend to embody ethical concepts, and hence seek to regulate various behaviors so that they conform to society's understanding of morally appropriate behavior. **Legal ethics** refers to the rules of ethics that govern the practice of law and the conduct of lawyers. Each state has established ethical rules for lawyers practicing within the state. Most states base their rules on the American Bar Association's **Model Rules of Professional Conduct** ("Model Rules").

## Malpractice

**Malpractice** constitutes conduct that is improper or unethical. Malpractice is essentially a tort action of negligence against lawyers for failing to satisfy their professional duty of care owed to their clients. Thus, in order to establish a malpractice claim, the typical elements of negligence must be satisfied including duty, breach, causation and damages. In this context, ethical rules impose a duty on lawyers not only to act in the best interests of their clients, but also not to act in ways that would be adverse to their clients' interests. Hence, such laws automatically impose a duty of care on lawyers. A breach of that duty is established by demonstrating that the lawyer's behavior fell short of the professional standards of care. In this respect, demonstrating that the lawyer breached one of the ethical rules proscribed in the Model Rules may prove negligence, and thus malpractice.

## Attorney/Client Privilege

The **attorney/client privilege** protects communications between an attorney and her client so that neither party can be compelled to disclose such communications in court. In order to raise the privilege, it must be proven that (a) there is an attorney/client relationship, and (b) the communication was confidential because it was not disclosed in the presence of others, and was not intended to be disclosed to others. The privilege belongs to the client. This means that the client can waive the privilege, thereby compelling an attorney to disclose confidential communications. It also means that the attorney is prohibited from disclosing such communications unless the client consents to the disclosure.

## Conflicts of Interests

Because lawyers represent many different clients, there exists the possibility that such representation may impact the interests of one or more clients in a negative manner. Thus, the Model Rules establish procedures regarding how lawyers should address conflicts of interests.

First, the Model Rules limit a lawyer's ability to represent clients when there is a **concurrent conflict of interests**. A concurrent conflict of interests arises when (a) the representation of one client will be directly adverse to another client or (b) there is a significant risk that the representation of a client will materially limit the lawyer's ability to provide effective representation to another client. The Model Rules provide that the lawyer cannot engage in representation when such a conflict exists unless she reasonably believes that she will be able to provide competent and diligent representation and the client consents in writing to the representation. However, if the representation involves the assertion of a claim by one client against another in the same litigation or proceeding, the representation is prohibited and the client cannot consent to it.

A lawyer's ethical obligations also extend to her former clients. Thus, a lawyer cannot represent a client in the same or a substantially related matter in which the client's interests are materially adverse to the interests of her former client unless the former client consents in writing to the representation. Then too, a lawyer may not use the information of a former client in a manner that is disadvantageous to the former client, or otherwise disclose that information unless required by law.

The Model Rules also limit the extent to which lawyers can engage in business dealings with their clients. Thus, the Model Rules provide that a lawyer cannot enter into a business transaction with a client or knowingly acquire an interest adverse to a client unless the client (a) consents in writing to the transaction, (b) is given an opportunity to seek independent legal advice about the transaction, and (c) both the terms and the process by which the transaction occurs are fair, reasonable, and fully disclosed in writing to the client.

With respect to all of these matters, a client's consent must be **informed consent**. This means consent after the lawyer has adequately informed the client about the conflict and not only has explained to her the material risks associated with the conflict, but also has made available to her reasonable alternatives to the proposed conflict.

## 5.2 SOCIAL RESPONSIBILITY OF CORPORATIONS

### Social Responsibility Defined

**Corporate social responsibility** refers to the idea that corporations should be concerned with the impact of their policies on the broad range of **stakeholders** or **constituents** that are affected by those policies. Such stakeholders or constituents include employees, customers, creditors, suppliers, and the local and broader community. Corporate social responsibility includes a corporate focus on protecting and preserving the environment as well as corporate charitable giving.

Some people view the corporation as owing a duty only to shareholders and their financial concerns. This conception of the corporation is referred to as **shareholder primacy**. The famous case of *Dodge v. Ford Motor Company*, 170 N.W. 668 (Mich. 1919), reflects this conception, stating that the corporation is organized primarily for the profit of its shareholders. In contrast to shareholder primacy, other people believe that while the corporation owes an obligation to its shareholders and their financial interests, corporations also have a social and ethical responsibility to operate in a manner that benefits other stakeholders. This has been referred to as the **social entity** or **stakeholder** theory of the corporation. Several scholars argue that if a corporation focuses on other constituents, that focus will benefit the corporation as a whole, including its shareholders.

While corporate law does not necessarily impose a legal obligation on the corporation to behave in a socially responsible manner, it does recognize the corporation's ability to do so in various ways.

## Ethical Behavior

Most corporate statutes allow corporations to consider ethical factors when carrying out their responsibilities. Corporations are also required to act in accordance with the law.

## Charitable Contributions

Every state corporation statute allows corporations to devote resources to charitable endeavors, including educational, humanitarian, scientific, and philanthropic matters as well as matters that promote the public welfare. Some states provide that corporations can make such donations even if they do not enhance corporate profit. In fact, courts will uphold corporate donations so long as they are reasonable.

## Other Constituents

A host of federal and state statutes require the corporation to pay heed to other constituents, including employment laws, environmental laws, and laws regulating consumer affairs. However, corporate law also recognizes the corporation's ability to address the concerns of other constituents when directors and officers carry out their duties. Indeed, more than thirty states have enacted statutes that allow corporate officers and directors to consider the interests of non-shareholders from employees and customers to the local and broader community. Such statutes, known as **other constituency statutes**, are aimed at recognizing corporations' right to behave in a socially responsible manner.

## 5.3 GOVERNMENT REGULATION AND ADMINISTRATIVE AGENCIES

In some situations, the government will create agencies, known as **administrative agencies**, to perform specific legislative functions and administer particular federal statutes. Such agencies are created by acts known as **enabling acts**, which establish the agency's goals and powers, and grant the agency its authority to make rules and regulations regarding a specified issue or issues. Rules adopted by the agency must comply with the Constitution and the agency's enabling act as well as other federal laws that govern administrative procedures.

The executive or legislative branch directly supervises some agencies. However, most agencies are independent, and hence are not supervised by the legislature or the executive branch. Agencies are required to hold public meetings. The **Federal Information Act** also requires agencies to provide citizens with information they request, unless the information falls within certain exempted categories such as information pertaining to national defense or trade secrets.

Some of the more prominent agencies include:

- the National Labor Relations Board, which administers federal labor laws,

- the Securities and Exchange Commission, which oversees the purchase and sale of securities,

- the Social Security Administration, which manages the nation's social security system,

- the Federal Communications Commission, which regulates radio, television, and other forms of interstate communications, and

- the Environmental Protection Agency, which regulates air and water pollution as well as addresses problems associated with certain toxic substances.

Claims regarding administrative agency rules are brought before the administrative agency in hearings conducted by their own judges, known as **administrative law judges**, or other bodies within the agency. The **Administrative Procedure Act** sets standards for federal agency rule making as well as standards for hearings conducted by such agencies. Those standards relax the traditional rules of evidence within an administrative proceeding. Administrative agencies generally allow their decisions to be appealed to one or two review boards within the agency. An administrative agency decision also may be appealed to courts. However, a court appeal is not allowed until all administrative remedies have been exhausted.

Courts also can review the rules and regulations of administrative agencies. When courts review an agency's rules and regulations, the Administrative Procedure Act provides that courts should not overturn agency actions unless they are found to be **arbitrary** or **capricious**, or not in accordance with the law.

## 5.4 ENVIRONMENTAL LAW

Several statutes, treaties, regulations, and policies exist that are aimed at protecting the environment and preserving environmental resources. The collection of these laws is referred to as **environmental law**.

### National Environmental Policy Act

The 1969 **National Environmental Policy Act** ("NEPA") was enacted along with various other federal environmental statutes to protect the environment from the actions of public and private actors. One of NEPA's primary purposes was to declare a national environmental policy and promote efforts to prevent or eliminate damage to the environment. NEPA also seeks to ensure that public and private actors better understand the ecological system and the environmental impact of their decisions. To further this goal, NEPA established a **Council on Environmental Quality** to be responsible for gathering information on the quality of the environment and for advising the president on the preparation of the **Environmental Quality Report**. This report includes an assessment of the environment and environmental policies, current and future environmental trends as well as potential remedies for deficiencies in the nation's environmental programs and policies.

## Environmental Protection Agency

In 1970, the **Environmental Protection Agency** ("EPA") was established to oversee pollution control efforts. The EPA is charged with working with federal, state, and local officials to protect the national environment and provide guidance regarding effective environmental policies. The EPA has broad authority to regulate environmental programs. Pursuant to that authority, the EPA researches issues associated with pollution and the environment, sets standards for environmental quality, monitors public and private actors to ensure their compliance with such standards, and even sanctions such actors for any noncompliance.

## Air Quality Regulations

**Air pollution**, which refers to chemicals and other harmful pollutants in the atmosphere, is believed to be responsible for many deaths and respiratory diseases as well as for eroding many natural resources. To address problems created by such pollution, Congress and the states have passed several statutes aimed at reducing air pollution. Most notably, beginning in 1963 Congress enacted a series of acts and amendments aimed at making the air quality safe and healthy, with the most recent amendment in 1990. Such acts are referred to as the **Clean Air Act**. The Clean Air Act authorizes the EPA to determine what constitutes appropriate levels of common air pollutants (such as ground-level ozone, carbon monoxide, and lead) and set standards for meeting those levels. Such standards, known as **National Ambient Air Quality Standards**, are designed to reduce the presence of pollutants in the air to levels that are consistent with promoting good health and preserving the environment. States must ensure that they are in compliance with such standards, and the EPA can sanction states for their failure to comply.

## Water Quality Regulations

States and Congress also have passed numerous statutes aimed at protecting the nation's water supply. The most prominent federal statute is the **Clean Water Act**, which regulates the discharge of pollutants into the water. The Clean Water Act authorizes the EPA to determine the permissible levels of contaminants in the water to ensure a safe water supply, and to set standards aimed at meeting those levels. Companies must obtain permits from the EPA that impose limits on the amount of pollutants they can discharge, and can be assessed penalties for violations of those permits. The EPA also requires such companies to monitor their activities in this area, and report on those monitoring efforts.

## Regulations Regarding Hazardous Waste

There are a variety of different statutes aimed at ensuring the proper disposal and handling of hazardous waste. The **Comprehensive Environmental Response, Compensation, and Liability Act** ("CERCLA") focuses on the clean up of abandoned or historical hazardous waste sites. CERCLA established a fund, known as the **Superfund**, with the goal of locating, investigating, and cleaning up such sites. In connection with this effort, the EPA identifies particularly egregious sites and places them on a **National Priorities List**. Sites on this list then become the EPA's priority in its clean-up efforts. Such sites also are the target of **remediation** efforts, which represent actions designed to permanently reduce the health and safety risk associated with the site. CERCLA makes both current and past owners and operators of hazardous waste sites liable for cleaning up such sites, while enabling states to sue private actors for the costs of remediation and removal of waste. Then too, people who own or occupy facilities that produce, use, or store hazardous waste must provide local and state officials with information on their handling of such waste.

The **Resource Conservation and Recovery Act** requires anyone who handles hazardous wastes to keep particular records of their activities, and comply with various rules and standards regarding their disposal of waste. Unlike CERCLA, this Act focuses on disposal rules for active waste sites.

Other environmental acts focus on monitoring particular activities that pose a threat to the nation's natural resources. For example, the **Toxic Substances Control Act** regulates chemical substances, while the **Federal Environmental Pesticide Control Act** regulates the handling of pesticides being exported from and imported into the United States.

## 5.5 SECURITIES AND ANTITRUST LAW

### Securities Regulation

Both federal and state laws regulate the offers and sales of securities. The primary federal statutes are the **Securities Act of 1933, as amended** ("Securities Act") and the **Securities Exchange Act of 1934, as amended** ("Exchange Act"). The Exchange Act created the **Securities and Exchange Commission** ("SEC") to oversee the regulation of these federal securities laws. States also have passed laws aimed at regulating securities transactions within their states. These laws are commonly referred to as **"blue sky"** laws.

The Securities Act defines securities broadly to include notes, stock, bonds, debentures, stock subscriptions, voting trust certificates, limited partnership interests, investment contracts, and fractional interests in oil, gas or other mineral rights. The definition is designed to cover traditional securities such as stock and bonds as well as unconventional transactions, where the underlying purpose is to provide investment income. Most of these unconventional transactions are analyzed by determining if they are **investment contracts**. Under the test articulated in *SEC v. Howey Co.*, 328 U.S. 293 (1946), an investment contract represents (a) an investment of money, (b) in a common enterprise, (c) when the purchaser is led to expect profits, (d) solely or primarily from the efforts of others. If a transaction satisfies each of these prongs it will be deemed an investment contract, and therefore a security. The determination focuses on whether a transaction was intended to serve as an investment vehicle or has some other purpose. Once an instrument or agreement is defined as a security, then it will be subject to the federal and state securities laws.

## Securities Act Registration

**Section 5** of the Securities Act provides that securities cannot be offered or sold unless they have been registered with the SEC. Registration involves filing a **registration statement** with the SEC, which contains information about the securities to be registered as well as the company that is issuing the security. Included within the registration statement is a **prospectus**, which is a document containing information that must be delivered to investors prior to their securities' purchase. The prospectus is designed to contain all of the material information an investor needs to evaluate the security, particularly any risk associated with purchasing the security. Other information within the registration statement must be filed with the SEC, but need not be delivered to investors.

The Securities Act imposes strict rules on companies that are in registration. In particular, the Act limits the type of information companies in registration may disclose to the public in order to reduce the potential for fraud, and ensure that all investors receive accurate and consistent information regarding a company and its securities. Once a company issues its securities pursuant to this registration process, it is referred to as a **public company**.

## Remedies for Violations of the Registration Process

The Securities Act imposes various remedies for violations of registration procedures and the registration process. **Section 12(a)(1)** of the Securities Act imposes civil liability on anyone who offers or sells a security in violation of Section 5. This means anyone who fails to register a security that should be registered or fails to comply with registration procedures. However, only a **statutory seller** is liable for such violation. A statutory seller is either (a) the person who directly sold securities to the purchaser, or (b) someone who solicited the purchaser for a financial gain or for the seller's interests. Statutory sellers are strictly liable for the violations of Section 12(a)(1), and thus there are no defenses to this action.

**Section 11** of the Securities Act imposes civil liability for material misrepresentations or omissions in the registration statement. In establishing liability, the plaintiff need only show the existence of a material misrepresentation or omission. The plaintiff does not need to show reliance or causation, and anyone who purchases in the registered offering can sue so long as he did not know about the truth at the time of his acquisition. Liability extends to the issuer, its directors, the chief executive officer, the chief financial officer, the underwriter, and any **expert** (which includes accountants and lawyers who render a professional opinion or certification in the registration statement). The issuer has strict liability. However, the issuer can avoid liability if he can show **negative causation**, which means demonstrating that the plaintiff's damages were caused by something other than the misrepresentation or omission (such as general market conditions).

Other defendants may raise a **due diligence defense**, depending on whether the defendant is an expert and whether the statement occurred in an **expertised portion** of the registration statement. Expertised portions are portions that are certified by an expert such as financial statements or legal opinions. The remaining portions of the registration are **nonexpertised**. An expert only has liability for the portions he certified. In that context, to establish a due diligence defense an expert must demonstrate that after reasonable investigation, he had no reasonable basis to believe that the registration statement contained material misstatements or omissions. People who are not experts must establish the same due diligence defense for nonexpertised portions of the registration statement. However, for expertised portions, non-experts do not need to perform an investigation. Rather, they must show that they had no reasonable grounds to believe that the expertised portion contained material misstatements or omissions.

The table below reflects the diligence defense for each defendant.

**Table 5-1. Due Diligence Defenses**

| Type of Defendant | Defense for Expertised Portion | Defense for Nonexpertised Portion |
|---|---|---|
| Issuer | No diligence defense | No diligence defense |
| Experts (accountants and lawyers) | After reasonable investigation, no reasonable basis to believe material misstatements or omissions present | No liability |
| Non-experts (directors, executive officers, and underwriters) | No reasonable basis to believe material misstatements or omissions present | After reasonable investigation, no reasonable basis to believe material misstatements or omissions present |

**Section 12(a)(2)** imposes civil liability for material misstatements or omissions in a prospectus or oral statements that relate to a prospectus. Liability extends to any statutory seller, and the plaintiff does not need to prove reliance or causation. However, the seller can avoid liability by showing (a) negative causation, (b) the plaintiff knew that the statements in the prospectus were not true at the time of her purchase, or (c) the seller did not know and could not have reasonably known that the statements were not true.

## Exempt Securities and Transactions

The Securities Act exempts certain securities from regulation. These are securities issued by the federal government, state governments, or any of their subdivisions; securities issued by a charitable organization; those issued by banks or savings and loan institutions; securities issued by a receiver or trustee in bankruptcy; securities issued with a maturity date of less than nine months; securities regulated by other federal laws; insurance or annuity contracts; securities issued for conversion or exchange to existing shareholders; and securities issued in transactions that occur significantly within one state. Each of these securities is automatically exempted from the requirements of the Securities Act.

The Securities Act also exempts certain transactions from registration. **Section 4** of the Securities Act exempts transactions by (a) any person other than an issuer or **underwriter** and (b) any transaction that does not involve a public offering. The definition of an underwriter is convoluted, but essentially relates to any person who is helping the corporation distribute its shares.

A transaction that does not involve a public offering is also referred to as a **private placement**. In *SEC v. Ralston Purina Co.*, 346 U.S. 119 (1953), the Supreme Court defined a private placement as a sale to persons who do not need the protection of the securities laws. Hence, whether a sale constitutes a private placement does not depend on the number of people involved in the sale, but rather turns on the relative sophistication of the investors.

Because of the complexity and uncertainty involved with determining whether a given transaction represented a private placement, the SEC enacted **Regulation D**, which provides specific categories of transactions that qualify as private placements. Regulation D does not negate the general rule that transactions qualifying as private placements will be exempt from the registration requirements. Rather it enables transactions that fit within specific rules to be automatically exempted. Regulation D relies on the concept of **accredited investor**. Accredited investors include institutional investors, people with over a million dollars in net worth, venture capital firms, trusts with assets over five million dollars, directors and executive officers of the issuing company, and other specified investors.

Regulation D sets out three categories of exempted transactions.

1. **Rule 504**, which allows an exemption for offers in which the aggregate price is less than $1 million. There are no restrictions on the number of people in the offering.

2. **Rule 505**, which allows an exemption for offers in which the aggregate offering price is less than $5 million and the number of purchasers is less than thirty-five, excluding accredited investors.

3. **Rule 506**, which does not have a dollar limitation, but allows exemptions only when there are less than thirty-five people (excluding accredited investors) in the offering and all of the people are sophisticated.

As these rules suggest, securities may be offered to an unlimited number of accredited investors without exemption so long as the other requirements are met. In addition to the above requirements, issuers must satisfy certain restrictions on the resale of the securities as well as restrictions on general advertising and solicitation. Issuers also must provide specified information to investors in certain circumstances.

The table below sets forth some of the key restrictions associated with the three rules under Regulation D.

### Table 5-2. Regulation D

| Transaction Type | Requirements | Key prohibitions |
|---|---|---|
| Rule 504 | Less than $1 million | • Not available for reporting or investment companies **unless state disclosure is required or an offering is made to accredited investors.**<br>• Resale restrictions<br>• No general advertising or solicitations |
| Rule 505 | • Less than $5 million<br>• No more than 35 nonaccredited investors<br>• Disclosure to non-accredited investors | • Resale restrictions<br>• Restrictions on general advertising or solicitations |
| Rule 506 | • No more than 35 nonaccredited investors<br>• Disclosure to nonaccredited investors<br>• Nonaccredited investors must be sophisticated | • Resale restrictions<br>• Restrictions on general advertising or solicitations |

The Securities Act also provides for other transaction exemptions. Thus, **Regulation A** provides an exemption for certain small offerings, while **Rule 147** allows exemptions for offerings that occur primarily within one state. **Regulation S** establishes an exemption for securities sold outside of the U.S., and **Section 701** of the Act exempts transactions involving offerings to employees.

## Resale of Securities

The Securities Act also restricts the resale of securities purchased in a private offering or securities sold on behalf of a **control person** (see control person discussed below). **Rule 144**, however, establishes certain rules for the proper resale, including the requirement that such securities must be held for at least one year, and sold through a broker in a transaction that involves a limited percentage of securities.

## Exchange Act Regulation

While the Securities Act essentially regulates the issuance of securities, the Exchange Act regulates all other aspects of securities transactions. In addition to regulating various practices such as fraud, the Exchange Act also regulates **stock exchanges**, the **over-the-counter market**, and individuals who assist investors with trading activities. Stock exchanges are organizations that provide a location for the purchase and sale of securities such as the New York Stock Exchange, while over-the-counter markets relate to securities transactions that occur by computer or phone such as NASDAQ.

The following companies are subject to the Exchange Act: (a) every company that issues shares to the public consistent with the Securities Act, (b) every company with securities registered on a national securities exchange, (c) every company with assets in excess of $5 million and at least 500 shareholders, and (d) every company that voluntarily registers. A company that is subject to the Exchange Act is referred to as a **reporting company**. This is because Exchange Act registration requires that a company file periodic reports containing financial and other material information including an annual report (known as a **10-K**), quarterly report (known as a **10-Q**), and current reports (known as an **8-K**).

The Exchange Act regulates the solicitation of shareholder votes or proxies by reporting companies, and requires that corporations issue information statements to investors whenever they solicit proxies, known as **proxy statements**. In addition, the Act regulates **tender offers** (offerings made to purchase all or a portion of the shares of a specific company) by imposing various reporting and other requirements on parties seeking to engage in a tender offer. The Act further prohibits **control persons** from acquiring **short swing profits**. Control persons are defined as directors, certain officers, and owners (either directly or indirectly) of more than ten percent of a corporation's shares. Short swing profits arise when a control person makes a profit from purchasing and selling her shares within a six-month period. The Exchange Act requires the control person to return any profit made from such a transaction.

One of the Exchange Act's most prominent prohibitions is its prohibition against securities fraud and **insider trading**. **Section 10(b)** and **Rule 10b-5** prohibit securities fraud. In order to be held liable for such fraud, the following elements must be proven:

(a) **Misstatement** or **omission**, which constitutes (a) an affirmative misrepresentation, (b) a failure to make statements necessary for other statements not to be misleading (half-truths), or (c) an omission when there is a duty to disclose;

(b) **Materiality**, which means a substantial likelihood that a reasonable investor would consider the statement or omission important in making a decision about a securities transaction;

(c) **In connection with** a securities transaction;

(d) **Scienter**, which means an intent to deceive or defraud;

(e) **Reliance**, which, based on the **Fraud on the Market Theory**, is presumed when stocks are traded in an active securities market;

(f) **Causation**; and

(g) **Damages**.

Courts also have interpreted the Exchange Act to prohibit insider trading. Insider trading represents trading on the basis of material information that is not available to the public. For purposes of insider trading, an insider includes any person in an employment relationship with the issuer. In addition, under the **misappropriation theory**, a person can be held liable for insider trading if she "misappropriates" information learned in the context of a fiduciary relationship or a relationship of special trust. Such relationships include relationships where (a) the parties have a history of sharing confidences, (b) the parties mutually agree to keep each other's confidences, and (c) the parties are spouses, siblings, or parents and children. Thus, suppose A and B are brother and sister and A discloses material non-public information to B. If B trades on that information, B can be held liable for insider trading even though she does not work for the company whose information was the subject of her trading activity.

## Antitrust Law

A **trust** refers to a group of corporations or businesses that combine together in order to enhance their economic strength and market power. Trusts are problematic because they tend to eliminate competition in the market, enabling one group to control a particular product and hence its price. Such control creates the possibility that the group will be able to charge unfair prices for its product or create a **monopoly**. A monopoly refers to a trust formed to dominate an industry. Antitrust laws are aimed at preventing trusts or monopolies that would lead to a company's ability to control the market in a way that would be economically disadvantageous for consumers. The Federal Trade Commission ("FTC") regulates trusts and monopolies.

In 1890, Congress passed the **Sherman Act** to prohibit agreements among corporations that would restrain trade or create monopolization in an industry. The Act constitutes the primary federal antitrust law and applies to all transactions impacting interstate commerce.

The Supreme Court has interpreted the Sherman Act as prohibiting only those agreements that unreasonably restrain trade. Hence, when examining if an agreement violates the Act, courts apply what is known as the **rule of reason**, which requires courts to assess whether or not a particular restraint on trade is reasonable. Generally restraints on trade will be upheld as reasonable if they have a legitimate business purpose and are economically efficient.

There are some actions that are deemed **per se** or automatic violations of the Sherman Act. These violations relate to **horizontal agreements**, which refer to those transactions between businesses in competition with one another. Such transactions are per se illegal because they tend to significantly reduce competition.

These transactions include:

- **Price fixing:** agreements between competitors to set particular prices for their products

- **Production quotas:** agreements to restrict the supply of products in order to drive up the prices of such products

- **Group boycotts:** agreements to refrain from doing business with a particular person or persons or entity in order to force such a person or entity to pay higher prices

- **Market division:** agreements among competitors to "divide the market" by splitting up geographic areas in order to eliminate competition in those areas

With regard to **vertical agreements**, which are agreements between buyers and sellers, price-related agreements are per se illegal. However, most other agreements require court scrutiny based on the rule of reason in order to be held illegal.

There are several vertical agreements that raise antitrust concerns.

- **Tie-in agreements:** agreements whereby a seller agrees to sell one product to a customer, but only on the condition that the customer purchases another product.

- **Exclusive distributor agreements:** agreements that grant an entity an exclusive right to manufacture a product within a given area. Some courts consider such agreements per se illegal, while others apply the rule of reason test to them. The **Clayton Act** (discussed below) prohibits such agreements with regard to commodities.

- **Exclusive dealing agreements:** agreements requiring a buyer to resell products to a specific manufacturer. The Clayton Act prohibits such arrangements if they tend to create a monopoly.

- Other business practices regulated under antitrust laws are those involving **price discrimination**. Price discrimination occurs when a seller charges different buyers different prices for the same product. The **Robinson-Patman Act** prohibits such discrimination if it has a negative impact on competition.

In addition to regulating particular business practices, antitrust laws also regulate business combinations. Specifically, the **Clayton Act** prohibits mergers and acquisitions that may reduce competition or create a monopoly. In addition, **Section 7A** of the Clayton Act, known as the **Hart-Scott-Rodino Act**, requires corporations to notify the FTC and the U.S. Justice Department whenever they engage in a merger. Mergers will be prohibited under the Act if the market related to the merger is substantially concentrated and if, after the merger, it would be difficult for new businesses to enter the market on a competitive basis.

## 5.6 EMPLOYMENT AND LABOR LAW

### Employment and Employment Law

**Employment law** refers to the collection of state and federal laws that govern the employment relationship, other than laws addressing collective bargaining and labor relations. These latter laws are referred to as labor law.

Unless an employee has a contract with her employer, she is deemed to be an **employee-at-will**, which means that either the employee or the employer can terminate the employment relationship at any time for any reason. There are public policy exceptions to this at-will doctrine. Thus, an employer cannot fire an employee based on reasons that would violate state or federal law, such as firings based on a person's race or sex (see **employment discrimination** discussed below). Courts also recognize **implied contracts** as an exception to the at-will doctrine. This means that if the employee can prove that the employer created an implied contract to fire the employee only for cause, such a contract will prevent the employer from firing an employee for any reason. Many implied contracts arise as a result of employee handbooks or personnel policies suggesting that employees only will be fired based on specified reasons.

### Minimum Wage and Child Labor

The federal and state governments have established a minimum wage requirement for employers. The **Fair Labor Standards Act** ("FLSA") establishes a federal minimum wage as well as policies for overtime pay for full-time and part-time workers employed by private entities and the government. The FLSA requires overtime pay of not less than one and a half times an employee's regular salary whenever the employee works more than forty hours during her workweek. The Act excludes certain employees from its coverage, such as professionals and executives. It also does not apply to certain small businesses.

The FLSA also seeks to protect children. Thus, the Act prevents employers from hiring children under fourteen or children over fourteen during school hours, and prohibits employers in hazardous industries from hiring children under eighteen.

### Family and Medical Leave

The **Family and Medical Leave Act** requires the government and certain private employers to give their employees leave for certain family and medical emergencies. Thus, employers must provide employees with up to twelve weeks of unpaid leave for (a) a serious health condition, (b) the birth of a child, adoption or placement with the employee of a child in foster care, or (c) the care of a spouse, child, or parent with a serious health condition. Moreover, employers must provide employees with the same or equivalent job when they return from leave. The Act applies to all government employers as well as private employers who employ at least fifty employees. Employees are covered if they have worked at least one year with an employer and for at least 1,250 hours during that year.

## Workers Compensation

**Workers compensation** laws are designed to ensure that employees who have work-related injuries receive compensation for those injuries without having to engage in litigation. Each state has a workers compensation statute. Such statutes set forth a specific level of benefits that employers must pay. Such statutes then require employers to pay such benefits whenever an employee has an injury that arises out of, or has occurred during, the course of her employment. Employers also must pay benefits to an employee's dependents if the employee is killed as a result of a work-related accident. The employer's obligation to pay the employee or her dependents arises regardless of who is at fault for the injury or accident. However, in exchange for such compensation, worker compensation statutes prevent employees from bringing lawsuits against their employers for such injuries.

## Unemployment Compensation

**Unemployment compensation** provides employees with compensation for a set period of time when they become unemployed through no fault of their own. The compensation system constitutes a combined federal and state insurance program, pursuant to which federal and state governments contribute money. In addition, employers contribute to the system based on taxes levied upon them.

Each state's compensation program must be approved by the U.S. Secretary of Labor and must comply with federal standards. However, state law determines a person's eligibility for unemployment compensation, including whether she is out of work due to her own fault. While eligibility rules differ from state to state, an employee must be actively seeking new employment in order to remain eligible for unemployment compensation.

State law also determines the amount of compensation that must be paid as well as the period of time during which employers must pay such compensation. However, federal law sets minimum compensation levels that states must follow. As a general matter, an employee's compensation payments will be based on a percentage of the compensation she received during her employment. Hence, an employee does not receive the same amount of compensation she received while she was working.

## Social Security

The **Social Security Act** was enacted to provide retirement and disability benefits to employees as well as benefits to survivors of employees. The Social Security Act created the **Social Security Administration** to oversee implementation of this benefit program.

Social security benefits are funded by taxes levied on both employers and employees pursuant to the **Federal Insurance Contributions Act**. Employers pay half of the benefits and employees pay the other half. In order to obtain the employee's portion, employers are required to withhold such amounts from the employee's salary. The taxes are then deposited into a fund used to pay out social security benefits.

## Protection for Retirement Benefit Plans

In general, there are two forms of retirement benefit or pension plans: **defined benefit plans** and **defined contribution plans**. Under defined benefit plans, employers make payments to retired employees based on the length of their employment and the wages they received. Defined contribution plans constitute plans in which employers make contributions to an employee's account and upon retirement, the employee receives benefits from that account.

Primarily federal law governs these plans. In 1974, Congress established the **Employee Retirement Income Security Act** ("ERISA") to regulate private pension plans. ERISA does not require such plans, but regulates employers engaged in interstate commerce that have a defined benefit plan. ERISA establishes various standards for the implementation of these plans. Thus, ERISA requires covered employers to provide employees with particular information regarding their benefit plans. It also requires employers to provide adequate funds for their plans, and to appoint an administrator for the plan who has a fiduciary responsibility to administer the plan in the best interests of the plan's employee beneficiaries. ERISA created the **Pension Benefit Guaranty Corporation** ("PBGC") to insure private benefit plans, and employers must pay premiums to the PBGC to support such insurance.

## Workplace Safety

Both federal and state laws regulate the workplace to ensure a healthy and injury-free work environment. The primary federal statute in this area is the **Occupational Safety and Health Act**. Because the Act was enacted under the interstate commerce clause, it applies to all employers who engage in interstate commerce. The Act authorizes the Secretary of Labor to create health and safety standards. To assist the Secretary, the Act also created the **Occupational Safety and Health Administration** ("OSHA"), a federal administrative agency that works with employers and employees to ensure compliance with workplace safety standards. OSHA can inspect and investigate workplaces, issue citations against employers, and impose civil and criminal penalties. In addition, the Act requires employers to maintain information on employee accidents, illnesses, and other matters that may impact the safety of the work environment. The Act also establishes the **National Institute for Occupational Safety and Health** to research health and safety issues and recommend regulations.

## Collective Bargaining

**Collective bargaining** refers to negotiations between employers and groups of employees to create a collective agreement regarding employment compensation and other benefits. Historically, such a right was not recognized, but today various state and federal statutes protect employees' ability to engage in collective bargaining.

Specifically, the **National Labor Relations Act** grants employees the right to bargain as a group and to establish, join, or assist labor organizations or unions. It also requires employers to bargain directly with employees' representatives. The Act prevents employers from interfering in employees' efforts to organize, or their efforts to engage in labor or union related activities. Moreover, the Act establishes guidelines for the kinds of activities in which employees and employers may engage, including picketing, strikes, and lockouts. The Act applies to all employers with businesses engaged in interstate commerce.

Like other statutes governing employment relations, the Act establishes an administrative agency, the **National Labor Relations Board** ("NLRB"), to oversee its implementation. The NLRB helps resolve disputes between employees and employers.

## Employment Discrimination

Anti-discrimination laws are aimed at preventing discrimination in the workplace based on age, religion, disability, sex, race, and national origin. One of the primary anti-discrimination laws is **Title VII of the Civil Rights Act of 1964** ("Title VII"), which prohibits employment discrimination based on race, color, religion, sex and national origin. Title VII makes it unlawful to discriminate on such basis in all aspects of employment including hiring, firing, recruiting, and compensation. It also prohibits employers from retaliating against employees in any way for filing a discrimination complaint, or otherwise participating in a proceeding alleging discrimination against the employer. However, there are exceptions to this anti-discrimination rule. For example, if a classification is a **bona fide occupational qualification**, then discrimination may be permitted.

As part of its prohibition against sex discrimination, Title VII also prohibits sexual harassment in the workplace. Title VII not only prohibits intentional incidences of harassment, but also prohibits **"quid pro quo"** practices, whereby an employer requests a sexual favor in exchange for providing an employee with some employment benefit. Sexual harassment also covers working conditions that create a hostile environment, which means an atmosphere where employees are subjected to a pattern of severe or pervasive unwelcome sexual behavior or advances.

The **Equal Pay Act** ("EPA") prohibits differences in wages based on sex for men and women who perform substantially the same work, which is defined as jobs with the same skill, effort, responsibility, and working conditions.

Other laws, passed pursuant to Title VII, prohibit discrimination against particular groups of employees. Thus, the **Age Discrimination in Employment Act** ("ADEA") prevents discrimination against employees who are forty years old or more. The **Americans with Disabilities Act** ("ADA") prohibits discrimination against certain employees with mental or physical disabilities. The ADA also requires that employers make reasonable accommodations for employees who qualify as disabled under the ADA. The **Pregnancy Discrimination Act** prohibits discrimination based on pregnancy or childbirth.

In order to interpret and enforce various employment anti-discrimination laws, Congress created the **Equal Employment Opportunity Commission** ("EEOC"). The EEOC issues rules and guidelines aimed at ensuring the effective implementation of anti-discrimination laws. The EEOC also establishes procedures for employees who believe they are victims of discrimination. Under these procedures, employees can file a claim with the EEOC, and the EEOC must then investigate the claim. If the EEOC determines discrimination has occurred, it will attempt to fashion an appropriate remedy with the employer. If such an attempt is unsuccessful, the EEOC either will bring a suit in federal court, or give notice to the employee indicating that she can bring suit in federal court. If the employee or the EEOC is successful in court, the employee may be awarded a variety of different remedies including back pay and retroactive benefits, reinstatement, and even attorney's fees. The EEOC also can impose fines on an employer that violates anti-discrimination rules.

## 5.7 CREDITORS' RIGHTS

### Meanings of Terms

**Creditor** is a person who extends credit or a loan, and hence the person to whom a debt is owed.

**Collateral** represents the property that is the subject of a security interest.

**Debt** is a specified amount of money owed to the creditor.

**Debtor** is the person who borrows money, and thus who owes a debt.

**Security Interest** is an interest in property or collateral granted in order to ensure payment of a debt or obligation.

**Unsecured Creditor** is a creditor that does not have a security interest in any of the debtor's property or assets.

### Collection Rights

If creditors have a security interest, then they have the right to take possession of collateral in the event of default. The terms of the agreement between the creditor and the debtor will define what constitutes a default as well as what constitutes an event of default enabling a creditor to take possession of collateral. Once a creditor's right to possession has arisen pursuant to that agreement, the creditor may seize the collateral and hold it until repayment is made. The creditor also may sell the collateral in order to recover the debt. The sale must be commercially reasonable and the debtor must be given notice of the sale. Proceeds from the sale are applied first toward any costs associated with the sale, and then must be used to satisfy the debt. If the proceeds are insufficient, then the creditor still has a claim against the debtor. If the creditor receives more proceeds than she needs to satisfy the debt, then she must give the remaining funds to the debtor.

If a creditor has a security interest in real property, that interest is called a **mortgage**. When there is a default under the mortgage, the creditor's right to take possession of the property is called **foreclosure**. Foreclosure generally occurs through a judicial sale pursuant to which a court official sells the property. Until the foreclosure sale, the debtor has the right, referred to as **equity of redemption**, to recover her property by paying the full amount of the debt as well as any costs incurred by the creditor.

Some statutes grant creditors the right to impose a **lien**, which means the right to hold a security interest on a debtor's property. Liens arising by statute include liens to secure payment for taxes, judgments, and mechanics liens. Like other security interests, such liens enable the creditor to take possession of property in the event of a default.

An unsecured creditor does not have any rights to take possession of a debtor's property if the debtor defaults on her obligations.

## Secured Transactions

A **secured transaction** refers to an agreement pursuant to which a creditor receives a security interest in some property or asset in exchange for lending money. In the event of a default, the security interest allows the creditor to take possession of the property or asset in order to recover the value of the loan. Article 9 of the UCC governs secured transactions.

In order to establish a security interest, there must be **attachment**. Without attachment, the creditor's rights in the security interest are not enforceable. Attachment cannot occur unless

(a) the parties agree to create a security interest, which agreement, known as the **security agreement**, must be in writing and signed by the debtor (alternatively, the agreement may be evidenced by the creditor taking possession of the collateral);

(b) the creditor provides money or some other form of consideration for the security interest; and

(c) the debtor must have rights in the collateral such that she can grant them to the creditor.

Often there may be other parties who have or seek to have a security interest in the collateral granted to the creditor. In order for the creditor to ensure that her security interest is given priority, the security interest must be **perfected**. Perfection generally occurs by filing a **financing statement**, which describes the collateral and the creditor's security interests in the collateral. The filing serves as notice of the creditor's security interest to third parties. Perfection also may occur by taking possession or control of the collateral.

Perfection establishes a creditor's right to the collateral as against third parties. Thus, once a security interest is perfected, it takes priority over unperfected security interests. With regard to perfected security interests, the first person to file her security interest has priority. If neither party perfected by filing, then the first person to perfect her security interest has priority.

If a security interest has attached and there is a default under the security agreement, a creditor has the right to take possession of the collateral subject to the security interest. Moreover, if the security interest is perfected and the creditor has priority, then the creditor will be allowed to take possession despite the existence of other secured parties.

## Creditor Rights in Bankruptcy

Creditors have specific rights during bankruptcy proceedings. Federal law under the **United States Bankruptcy Code** ("Code") governs bankruptcy proceedings, and such proceedings occur in federal bankruptcy court. The Code creates procedures for debtors to obtain protection from creditors, and provides for the elimination or reduction of many of their debt obligations. In order to initiate bankruptcy proceedings, a petition must be filed in bankruptcy court. Bankruptcy proceedings may be either voluntary or involuntary. A **voluntarily proceeding** is one initiated by the debtor, while an **involuntary proceeding** is one initiated by the creditor in order to obtain payment for debts. Many debtors voluntarily file for bankruptcy so that they can be protected from a creditor's collection efforts. Once a bankruptcy proceeding is initiated, a creditor may not seek to collect her debts outside of the proceeding. In fact, the filing of a bankruptcy petition generally creates an **automatic stay**, pursuant to which all collection actions must stop. However, some creditors, particularly secured creditors, may get relief from such stays in order to prevent their collateral from declining in value.

There are three primary forms of bankruptcy proceedings. A proceeding under **Chapter 7** of the Code ("Chapter 7") provides for the liquidation of the debtor's assets. In that proceeding, a bankruptcy trustee is appointed to administer the liquidation process. The debtor then transfers her assets to the trustee so that the trustee can sell them and distribute them to creditors. The trustee must make a determination regarding the amount each creditor will be entitled to receive based on the available assets. This generally means that most creditors only receive a fraction of the debt owed to them. However, this process extinguishes the claims of unsecured creditors (although the claims of secured creditors may remain). The purpose of the Chapter 7 proceeding is to enable debtors to gain a fresh start, but the proceedings are only available to debtors once in an eight-year period.

A creditor also can file a petition for bankruptcy under **Chapter 11** of the Code ("Chapter 11"). Chapter 11 provides for a supervised reorganization of the debtor's business. Under this proceeding, a debtor must submit a **plan of reorganization** to the bankruptcy court, which generally provides for termination or reduction of the debtor's debts. However, after 120 days, creditors have the right to submit competing plans for reorganization. The court then must make a determination regarding the most efficient and feasible plan. Acceptance of a reorganization plan discharges creditors' claims, other than the manner in which they are provided for within the plan.

A proceeding under **Chapter 13** of the Code ("Chapter 13") enables debtors to create a repayment plan for certain debts. Under this proceeding, debtors retain their assets, but use the bankruptcy process to help them adjust their debts and devise a plan for repaying them over a specified period.

## 5.8 PRODUCT LIABILITY

**Product liability** represents a general term used to describe the liability imposed on sellers and other persons for compensating people who have been injured as the result of a defective product. Product liability actions can be brought as tort or contract claims. If the liability action constitutes a contract claim, then it is brought as a breach of warranty (see Chapter 8). If the action represents a tort action, then, as the discussion below reveals, many of the traditional tort claims and defenses set forth in Chapter 6 may be applicable.

### Defective Product

In order to form the basis of a product liability suit, a product must be defective. There are three kinds of defects: a **manufacturing defect**, a **design defect**, and an **inadequate warning defect**.

A manufacturing defect occurs when a product is incorrectly manufactured in a way that makes it unreasonably dangerous to consumers. When the plaintiff's suit is based on a manufacturing defect, the plaintiff must be able to demonstrate that an ordinary consumer would view the product as unreasonably dangerous, known as the **consumer expectation test**.

A design defect arises when a product is properly manufactured, but the product's design itself poses a danger to customers. An inadequate warning defect arises when a product fails to provide sufficient warnings concerning its dangers. Such a defect can be construed as a design defect. When an action is based on a design defect, the plaintiff must prove that it would have been economically feasible for the manufacturer to use an alternative or modified design.

## Liability Based on an Intentional Tort

If the defendant intended the product to cause harm or knew that such harm was likely to occur, she can be liable for an intentional tort and be made to pay both compensatory and punitive damages. However, the defendant can raise traditional defenses for intentional torts such as consent (see **Defenses to Intentional Torts** discussed in Section 6.2).

## Liability Based on Negligence

The elements of a prima facie case for negligence associated with product liability are the same as those required for an ordinary negligence action: duty, breach, causation, and damages (see **Negligence** discussed in Section 6.3). A duty arises whenever the defendant is a **supplier**, which means the defendant either supplies, manufactures, or sells the product.

In order to show a breach of the supplier's duty, plaintiffs must demonstrate that the defendant's conduct fell below the appropriate standard of care, and that such failure led to the defective product being supplied. Proof of a breach of duty differs depending on the type of defect. For manufacturing defects, the plaintiff can use **res ipsa loquitor** to establish breach related to a manufacturer (see **Breach of Duty** discussed in Section 6.3). In design defect cases, a breach can be established only if the plaintiff proves that the defendant knew or should have known that the product as designed was dangerous.

General tort causation principles and defenses apply for claims involving negligence.

## Liability Based on Strict Liability

Some product liability actions will impose strict liability (liability without regard to who is at fault) on the defendant. Strict liability will arise if (a) the defendant is a commercial supplier, such as a manufacturer, retailer, assembler or wholesaler, and the product reaches the consumer in the same condition it was supplied, (b) the product is unreasonably dangerous consistent with the standard established for a manufacturing defect or design defect, as applicable, (c) the defect existed when the product left the defendant's control and the defect was a proximate cause of the plaintiff's injury, and (d) the plaintiff suffered actual damages.

The defendant can raise the defense of assumption of risk, but not contributory negligence with regard to a strict liability action. Moreover, disclaimers do not enable the defendant to avoid liability.

# 5.9 CONSUMER PROTECTION

**Consumer protection** is a concept referring to laws and statutes aimed at addressing issues of concern to consumers. Such laws and statutes regulate the relationships between consumers and the entities that sell goods and services. As a result, consumer law covers an array of topics from bankruptcy law to product liability and fraud. Many of the topics that fall within the scope of consumer law, such as antitrust, fraud, and product liability, have been addressed in other areas of this book. Hence, antitrust laws protect consumers from the negative impact of trusts and monopolies, product liability laws enable consumers to bring actions against merchants and other sellers when they purchase defective goods, and tort law provides remedies for services to consumers that fall below the appropriate level of care.

## Federal Trade Commission

The **Federal Trade Commission** ("FTC") is an independent federal agency established to promote consumer protection and reduce unfair competition among businesses. The **Bureau of Consumer Protection** is a division of the FTC that seeks to educate consumers regarding their rights and assist the FTC with the enforcement of consumer protection laws.

## Credit Protections

There are a variety of laws related to credit that are not only designed to promote better and more equitable practices with regard to the extension of credit, but also to ensure the confidentiality of credit information. The

**Fair Credit Reporting Act** regulates consumer credit reporting agencies and provides procedures for regulating the proper use and release of credit reports. It also regulates the kind of information that must be contained in such reports in order to promote accurate credit reporting. The **Equal Credit Opportunity Act** prohibits institutions from discrimination related to credit applications. The **Fair Debt Collection Act** prohibits abusive and unfair debt collection practices, and imposes penalties on debt collectors who engage in such practices. The **Truth in Lending Act** is designed to ensure fair disclosure of credit terms, thereby protecting consumers from inaccurate and unfair billing and credit card practices.

## Privacy Protection

One important aspect of consumer protection involves safeguarding consumer's private and confidential financial information. Thus the **Gramm-Leach-Bliley Act** was enacted to protect consumer's personal information and work with states as well as other federal agencies to generate polices that facilitate those protection efforts. The Act essentially has three components: (a) to safeguard consumer's personal information by ensuring that financial institutions that have access to consumer's private information institute plans to keep such information confidential, (b) to ensure that consumers receive better disclosure regarding a financial institution's policies for sharing a consumer's confidential information, and even allow consumers to restrict such sharing in appropriate circumstances, and (c) to prohibit **pretexting**, which means obtaining information (particularly consumer's private financial information) under false pretenses.

## Unfair Competition

**Unfair competition** refers to the collection of laws dealing with actions that have a negative impact on a business interest, and potentially places businesses at a competitive disadvantage. Tort law represents the primary remedy for actions based on unfair competition. For example, a claim alleging intentional interference with business relations represents an unfair competition claim. In addition to tort remedies, both states and the federal government have adopted rules regulating specific practices. Many of these rules focus on protecting the intellectual property rights of a business. This is because such rights often are important to the success of many businesses. For example, the **Lanham Act** represents a federal statute that prohibits **trademark infringement**, and imposes penalties on those who engage in infringing behavior. A **trademark** is a distinct mark or symbol that identifies a business and its products. Trademark infringement dilutes or otherwise harms the strength of the mark and hence its value to the business.

States have adopted rules protecting **trade secrets**, which are formulas, practices, processes, designs, and similar confidential information that give businesses a competitive advantage in the marketplace. For example, the recipe for various soft drinks constitutes a trade secret. States have developed laws that prohibit the theft and improper disclosure of such secrets. In addition to state laws, many businesses develop their own non-disclosure or non-compete agreements designed to ensure that employees do not disclose trade secrets.

False and deceptive advertising is also construed as unfair competition. Indeed, the FTC specifically regulates such advertising and brings actions against companies believed to be engaging in advertising practices harmful to consumers. In order to demonstrate that advertising is false and deceptive, it must be shown that the advertising is (a) false because it is not true or because there is no evidence to support claims made within the advertising, (b) deceptive because it likely to mislead the reasonable consumer and it is important to the consumer's decision regarding whether to purchase products or services, and (c) likely to cause injury to consumers.

## 5.10 INTERNATIONAL BUSINESS LAW

**International business law** seeks to govern the business relationships and transactions between parties of different countries. It is embodied in various court cases, treatises, and statutes. Under Article II of the Constitution, federal treaties constitute the supreme law of the land, and thus laws that conflict with treaties can be declared unconstitutional.

### Treaties

The Constitution makes treaties the supreme law of the land, and hence gives them a status equivalent to the Constitution and federal statutes. However, in order to achieve that status, treaties must be adopted by the president with the advice and consent of at least two-thirds of the Senate. Thus, if the president or a state executes an agreement with a nation, those agreements are not considered treaties.

Treaties regulate many international business transactions. **Bilateral treaties** refer to treaties entered into between two nations, while **multilateral treaties** refer to treaties among several parties that seek to allocate rights and responsibilities among the parties. **Bilateral investment treaties** refer to treaties between two nations addressing investment concerns. The U.S. has a **Bilateral Investment Treaty program** ("Program") aimed at coordinating its efforts to provide protection for the investment interests of U.S. citizens doing business in foreign countries, and improve investors' access to foreign markets. The Program also seeks to encourage developing companies to create strong and transparent investment policies, and thus contribute to the development of international law. Under the Program, the U.S. negotiates bilateral investment treaties based on a model form. That form includes several important provisions such as ensuring that other nations treat American investors in the same manner that they treat their own citizens, and granting American investors the ability to submit their disputes to international arbitration. The form also seeks to provide more effective remedies for **expropriation**, which means a government's taking of foreign citizen's businesses and assets located in its country, generally without proper compensation.

The United States also enters into bilateral tax treaties aimed at addressing the manner in which taxes imposed on various business operations will be allocated between countries. Such treaties are designed to ensure that the tax treatment of entities doing business in foreign countries is equitable, and does not undermine such entities' ability to compete effectively in the marketplace.

## Commercial Activities and Sovereign Immunity

Under the **Foreign Sovereign Immunities Act**, federal and state courts do not have jurisdiction over cases against a foreign nation. However, when a suit involves certain forms of commercial activity, such nations are not immune from jurisdiction. Thus, foreign nations will not have the protection of immunity when a suit involves (a) commercial activities that occurred in the U.S., (b) actions in the U.S. based on commercial activities abroad, or (c) commercial activities abroad that have a direct impact on the U.S. This Act gives Americans the ability to hold foreign nations liable for commercial activities that have a substantial impact on U.S. interests.

## Trade Regulations

Various statutes regulate **exports**, which are goods created in the U.S. and shipped and sold in other countries. Exports are a crucial component of international trade. In 1982, Congress enacted the **Export Trading Company Act** to encourage the exportation of American goods. The Act established the **Department of Commerce** and charged it with strengthening competitiveness of American products, promoting trade, and ensuring fair trade. By contrast, the **Export Administration Act** ("EAA") regulates exports, including implementing export controls, which restrict the exportation of certain goods based on national security and other concerns. That Act established the **Export Administration Regulations**, known as EAR, which provide a framework for regulating exports and issuing licenses for exports subject to controls. The EAR also impose sanctions for violations of its rules and licensing standards.

Congress also regulates **imports** (goods created elsewhere, but shipped and sold in the U.S.) by imposing **tariffs** or taxes on such imports. Indeed, various tariff acts have been in place since the country's founding. Tariffs and imports are regulated by the **Bureau of Customs and Border Protection** (the "Bureau"), which is also responsible for preventing terrorists and terrorist weapons from entering the U.S. Although the Bureau used to be a division of the Department of Commerce, in 2003 the agency became a part of the Department of Homeland Security. Often, in order to increase trade between America and certain countries, the U.S. will enter into **free trade agreements**, which eliminate or reduce tariff rates on goods being imported from such countries. One such free trade agreement is the **North American Free Trade Agreement**, which promotes trade among the U.S., Canada, and Mexico.

The **World Trade Organization** ("WTO") is an organization that seeks to promote fair trade. Over 150 countries, including the U.S., belong to the WTO, and the WTO serves to bring such countries together to negotiate the development of trading rules and principles. In fact, one of the WTO's primary goals is to produce rules for a fair and equitable trading system. Such rules are based on the 1948 **General Agreement on Tariffs and Trades** ("GATT"), which was the first international agreement on trading rules and standards. These rules help guide the WTO agreements regarding how its members should conduct trade and formulate trade agreements among nations. WTO Agreements are guided by various principles, which include ensuring that nations (a) do not discriminate between trading partners by providing special favors to particular countries or their products, known as **Most Favored Nation treatment**, (b) do not discriminate against foreign products, and thus treat all products within their borders equally, known as **National Treatment**, (c) give beneficial treatment to less developed countries, and (d) make their trade rules more transparent. The WTO also has a system for settling trade disputes among nations.

## Foreign Bribes

In order to regulate improper and illegal business practices in foreign countries, the **Foreign Corrupt Practices Act** prohibits companies from seeking to bribe foreign officials in order to obtain a business advantage in their country.

## Economic Growth and Development

A significant component of international law is providing financial and other assistance to developing countries and emerging markets in order to promote economic growth and stability. The U.S. belongs to various organizations that seek to address these issues. Hence, the **World Bank**, comprised of more than 180 members including the U.S., provides financial assistance to developing countries. Similarly, the **International Monetary Fund**, headquartered in Washington, D.C., provides funds for countries experiencing financial difficulties. The U.S. also belongs to the **Organisation for Economic Co-operation and Development** ("OECD"), which seeks to promote market economics and democratic governments. The OECD provides a forum for addressing economic, social, and other issues that impact the international community so that its members can exchange policy on a range of issues.

# CHAPTER 6
## Torts

# Chapter 6

# TORTS

## 6.1 MEANINGS OF TERMS

### Intentional tort

An **intentional tort** is a tort or civil wrong resulting from some deliberate conduct or from a situation where the conduct is substantially certain to occur. The key elements of an intentional tort are an act, intent, and causation.

### Negligence

**Negligence** is a tort constituting a breach of a duty owed by one person to another that causes harm to the non-breaching party's person or property. The key elements of a negligence claim are duty, breach, causation, and damages.

### Prima Facie

**"Prima facie"** is a Latin term meaning "on its first appearance" or "by first instance." In a tort suit, the plaintiff has the burden of proof, which requires the party to present the essential evidence required to prove her case. This is referred to as presenting the prima facie evidence because it is the first set of required evidence. If the plaintiff fails to present prima facie evidence, then her case will be dismissed without the need for any response from the defendant. However, establishing a prima facie case is not enough to impose liability. Instead, after the plaintiff establishes her prima facie case, the defendant has the opportunity to present defenses.

### Strict Liability

**Strict liability** represents a tort for which a person will be held liable regardless of fault. Thus, if the plaintiff proves the defendant committed an act, the defendant will be liable even if she acted with reasonable care or in good faith.

## Tort

A **tort** is a civil wrong that enables a person to bring a lawsuit.

## 6.2 INTENTIONAL TORTS

### Battery

**Battery** is in essence an improper touching of a person. In order to establish a prima facie case of battery, a plaintiff must prove that:

(a) the defendant acted in a manner that caused some **harmful** or **offensive** contact to the **plaintiff's person**,

(b) the defendant intended to cause such contact, and

(c) the defendant caused the contact or his actions set in motion something that caused the contact, which is referred to as **causation**.

"Contact to a plaintiff's person" includes contact to anything connected to a person, such as her clothing or a bag she may be carrying. While harmful contact refers to contact that creates some physical injury, offensive contact refers to contact that a reasonable person would find objectionable. Thus, if someone who is overly sensitive finds the contact offensive, she will not be able to recover if an average person would not object to the contact.

A defendant will be deemed to have **intent** either (a) if she desired to bring about the contact, in which case the intent is **specific intent**, or (b) if she knew with sufficient certainty that her actions would bring about the contact, in which case the intent is **general intent**. In order to recover for a battery, a plaintiff does not have to show damages and the plaintiff does not have to have knowledge of the contact.

### Assault

An **assault** occurs when one party causes the other to expect that a battery will be committed against her. In order to establish a prima facie case of assault, a plaintiff must prove that:

(a) the defendant acted in a manner that caused the plaintiff a **reasonable apprehension** that she would suffer immediate harmful or offensive contact to her person,

(b) the defendant intended to cause such apprehension, and

(c) there was causation, which means the defendant caused the apprehension or his actions set in motion something that caused the apprehension.

Apprehension in this context refers to an expectation as opposed to fear. A person can have a reasonable apprehension of contact even when she has no fear of the contact. Reasonable apprehension is determined by whether an average person would be apprehensive, and would not apply to someone who is overly sensitive.

Reasonable apprehension will also exist even if the defendant is not capable of performing the actual conduct. The classic example is if A points an unloaded gun at B, but B does not know the gun is unloaded. Even though A is not capable of shooting B, B's apprehension of being shot and hence of some immediate harmful contact, is reasonable.

Words alone are generally insufficient to create apprehension without some overt act such as a raised hand. Threats of some future harm or contact are not enough to create apprehension because the apprehension must be immediate. Also, because assault requires apprehension, the plaintiff must have knowledge of the defendant's act, which differs from battery where the plaintiff's knowledge of the act is not required. Similar to battery, the plaintiff need not prove damages in order to recover for assault.

## Transferred Intent for Assault and Battery

**Transferred intent** occurs when a defendant intends to commit a tort against one party but (a) commits the tort against a different person, (b) commits a different tort against the same person, or (c) commits a different tort against a different person. Transferred intent applies to assaults and batteries. Thus, if A intends to commit a battery against B, but instead commits an assault against C, intent will still exist for the tort committed against C. In fact, in such a case, because no battery occurred, transferred intent also would allow B to recover for assault because the attempted battery caused B to be in reasonable apprehension of a battery. In this regard, transferred intent enables a defendant's intent to be transferred from one victim to another or from one act to another.

## Intentional Infliction of Emotional Distress

**Intentional infliction of emotional distress** occurs when a person causes extreme emotional distress to another person. In order to establish a prima facie case of intentional infliction of emotional distress, the plaintiff must prove that:

(a) the defendant engaged in extreme and outrageous conduct,

(b) the defendant either intended to cause the plaintiff to suffer severe emotional distress, or recklessly disregarded the probability that her conduct would cause such distress,

(c) there was causation because the defendant or something he set in motion caused the distress, and

(d) the plaintiff suffered damages.

To qualify as **emotional distress**, the plaintiff must demonstrate that a reasonable person would find the defendant's conduct outrageous, shocking, and beyond the bounds of decency. This means that emotional distress is an objective standard. However, if the defendant is aware that a person is particularly vulnerable or sensitive, and intentionally seeks to cause distress to that person, the defendant may be liable even if an ordinary person may not consider the defendant's behavior to be outrageous.

In order to recover for intentional infliction of emotional distress, a plaintiff must suffer damages in the form of severe and extreme emotional distress. However, the plaintiff need not prove that he suffered any physical injury.

## Defenses to Intentional Torts

The defendant can raise a number of defenses to avoid liability for an intentional tort. First, if the plaintiff gives her consent to the defendant's act, the defendant will not be liable. Consent can be express or implied. Consent will be implied if a reasonable person would believe that the plaintiff had consented. Consent also may be implied by law in situations where a person is incapable of giving consent, but where the action is necessary to prevent death or serious injury to a person or property. For example, consent will be implied in situations where a doctor provides medical assistance to an unconscious patient because it is an emergency situation and the assistance is both necessary and something to which a reasonable person would consent.

Second, if the defendant's actions constituted **self-defense**, then she may avoid liability. Self-defense represents situations in which a person reasonably believes her actions are necessary to protect herself from physical harm. When a person takes such an action, she only can use the amount of force that is reasonably necessary to protect herself from harm, and if more force is used, then she will not be able to establish a case of self-defense.

Thus, while a person can use deadly force to protect herself, she only can use such force if she is confronted with deadly force. Self-defense excuses or justifies intentional acts.

A third defense is **defense of others**. A person may use this defense if her actions were designed to protect another person, and the other person could have acted in self-defense. In other words, if a person defends another person using actions that the other person could have used in self-defense, then her actions will be justified.

# 6.3 NEGLIGENCE

A prima facie case of negligence requires the plaintiff to prove that (a) the defendant owed a duty to the plaintiff, (b) the defendant breached the duty, (c) the breach was the actual and proximate cause of the plaintiff's injury, and (d) the plaintiff suffered damage to her person or property.

## Duty

Whenever a person acts, she is under a duty to act in the manner that an ordinary prudent person would act under the circumstances. The person's actions must be consistent with the **standard of care** that a person is required to exercise. The general standard of care is a **"reasonable person"** standard, which is an objective standard and requires that a person act in a manner that an average prudent person exercising reasonable care would act. However, a different standard of care applies for some people. The standard of care for professionals requires them to act with the knowledge or skill consistent with their profession (see **malpractice** discussed in Chapter 5). Moreover, the standard of care for children requires them to act with the care that is reasonable for a child of a similar age, intelligence, and experience.

As a general matter, people are not under an affirmative duty to act. If someone is in danger, there is generally no duty to help the person avoid danger. However, once someone acts for the benefit of another, that person is under a duty to perform her actions with reasonable care. In other words, even if someone is acting to benefit another, her actions must be consistent with the appropriate standard of care. For example, suppose A is walking down the street and sees that a bus is going to hit B. A has no obligation to warn or help B. However, if A decides to help B by pushing B out of harm's way, she can be held liable for negligence if she used unreasonable force when pushing B. To avoid this result, some states have enacted "**good samaritan**" statutes that allow people who voluntarily aid others to avoid liability for negligence unless their actions fall significantly below the appropriate standard of care.

## Breach of Duty

A defendant will have breached her duty when she fails to exercise the standard of care applicable to her actions.

In some cases, a breach of duty will be established by the principle of **Res Ipsa Loquitor**. Res Ipsa Loquitor is a Latin term meaning "the thing speaks for itself," and is used in circumstances where a particular action generally occurs as a result of a breach of someone's duty. In order to use Res Ipsa Loquitor, a plaintiff must establish that (a) the harm would not ordinarily occur without someone's negligence, (b) the instrument creating the harm was under the sole and complete control of the defendant at the time the harm occurred, and (c) the harm did not result from the plaintiff's own conduct.

## Causation

Causation involves two factors: actual cause and proximate cause. **Actual cause** refers to a finding that the plaintiff's injury was the "**cause-in-fact**" or the "**but-for**" cause of the defendant's actions. In other words, the plaintiff must demonstrate that "but for" the defendant's actions, the plaintiff would not have suffered harm.

**Proximate cause** is essentially a foreseeability test, and operates to limit actual cause to those consequences that a plaintiff can prove represented a foreseeable result of the defendant's actions. In some circumstances, an event will occur after a defendant's actions that will contribute to a plaintiff's harm. Such an event is known as an **intervening cause** or **intervening force**. If such a force is a foreseeable consequence of the defendant's actions, then the defendant will be liable for the harm created by the force as long as the harm is also foreseeable.

## Damages

The plaintiff must demonstrate that she suffered actual harm or injury as a result of the defendant's actions. A plaintiff may recover for all of her injuries, even if the extent of the injuries was not foreseeable. The plaintiff also may recover for damages to her property. Moreover, if the defendant's conduct was willful or reckless, then the plaintiff may be able to recover punitive damages. However, the plaintiff has a duty to mitigate, and hence will not be able to recover those damages that could have been avoided with the exercise of reasonable care.

## Defenses

**Contributory negligence** is a defense to negligence that refers to situations in which the plaintiff's own negligence has contributed to her harm. Years ago, a plaintiff's contributory negligence represented a complete defense to the plaintiff's claim, and allowed the defendant to avoid all liability for negligent actions. Today, however, most states have adopted a **comparative negligence** standard. Comparative negligence means that a plaintiff's damage award will be reduced by the amount reflecting the plaintiff's contribution to her harm.

The defendant also can avoid liability by establishing a defense based on **assumption of risk**. Assumption of risk refers to a situation in which the plaintiff has knowledge of a risk of injury and voluntarily engages in an action despite the risk. Assumption of risk can be explicit, because a person specifically agrees to the risk of such behavior, or implicit, such as when a person engages in behavior knowing of the risk. A typical case involving implicit assumption of risk occurs when a person agrees to engage in an inherently dangerous activity (such as skydiving) or to participate in a risky sport (such as boxing). Assumption of risk allows the defendant to avoid all liability for her actions. Assumption of risk is not available as a defense to intentional torts.

Additionally, most states that apply a comparative negligence standard do not allow assumption of risk to bar a plaintiff's suit. Instead, only if the plaintiff's conduct is unreasonable or the plaintiff expressly assumed the risk will the defendant be able to use the assumption of risk doctrine to avoid liability.

## 6.4 STRICT LIABILITY

**Strict liability** is established when (a) someone has an absolute duty of care, (b) that duty is breached, (c) the breach constitutes the actual and proximate cause of the plaintiff's injury, and (d) the plaintiff or her property is harmed. An absolute duty of care arises either by statute or imposed by the court when a defendant is engaged in an **ultrahazardous activity**, such as using explosives or caring for wild animals. There are generally no defenses to torts that involve strict liability.

## 6.5 HARMS TO REPUTATION OR ECONOMIC INTERESTS

### Defamation

A prima facie case of **defamation** is established by showing that (a) the defendant used **defamatory language**, which is language that has a negative impact on someone's reputation, (b) the language was **"of or concerning"** the plaintiff, which means a reasonable person understands it refers to the plaintiff, (c) there was a **publication** of the language, which means it was communicated to a third party, and (d) the defamatory language damaged the plaintiff's reputation.

A plaintiff's obligation to prove damages depends on the type of defamation at issue. **Libel** constitutes defamatory language that is written or permanently recorded, while **slander** involves spoken defamatory language. Damages are presumed for libel, while slander generally requires proof of damages. However, slander relating to a person's business or profession, or indicating that a person (a) suffers from a loathsome disease, (b) is guilty of a crime of moral turpitude, or (c) that a women has engaged in unchaste behavior, does not require proof of damages. Both consent and truth constitute complete defenses for defamation, and thus enable the defendant to avoid all liability.

### Interference with Business Relations

**Interference with business relations** constitutes an action against someone who deliberately interferes with someone else's economic relationship. A prima facie case requires the plaintiff to demonstrate that: (a) there was a valid business relationship or expected relationship between the plaintiff and a third party, (b) the defendant knew of the relationship, (c) the defendant intentionally interfered with the relationship in a manner that caused its breach or termination, and (d) the plaintiff was damaged as a result of the interference. The relationship at issue does not have to be a current relationship. Instead, so long as the plaintiff reasonably expected that his relationship with another person would give rise to some future economic benefit, he will be able to recover.

## 6.6 VICARIOUS LIABILITY

**Vicarious liability** refers to situations where one person is liable for the torts of another. The doctrine of **respondeat superior** makes employers liable for the torts of their employees when they are committed within the scope of the employment relationship.

This doctrine applies even if an employee engages in personal business while carrying out acts of the employer so long as the personal business is minor in terms of time and geographic area. Substantial deviations from the employee's primary business obligations will be deemed outside of the scope of the employment relationship, and the employer will not be liable for actions that occur during those deviations. This doctrine is known as **frolic and detour**. For example, suppose an employee decides to visit a relative during a business trip and commits a tort while on her way to her relative's house. The employer may still be liable for the tort if the trip to the employee's relative's house did not take a long time and did not take the employee significantly out of the way from her employment-related destination.

Notwithstanding the vicarious liability doctrine, an employer is generally not liable for intentional torts committed by an employee. However, if an act is done in furtherance of the employer's business, then the employer will be held liable for the intentional tort. In these cases, the tort is explicitly or implicitly authorized such as, for example, if an employee is a bodyguard and pushes rowdy fans out of her employer's path.

# CHAPTER 7

## Agency, Partnerships and Corporations

# Chapter 7

# AGENCY, PARTNERSHIPS AND CORPORATIONS

## 7.1 AGENCY

### Creation of the Agency Relationship

**Agency** is a relationship where one person, known as the **principal**, intends for another person, known as the **agent**, to act on her behalf.

An agency relationship ordinarily is created (a) by an agreement, express or implied, between the principal and the agent, (b) by **estoppel**, which means the principal indicates to a third party that someone has the ability to act as her agent, (c) by **ratification**, which means that the principal agrees to be held liable for the actions of a third party, even when those actions were not originally authorized by the principal, and (d) by necessity, which means that a principal (who is usually responsible for another) will be held responsible for the agent's acts during an emergency situation. For example, if a child receives medical treatment while away from home, the parent can be held liable for the child's treatment because the relationship will be viewed as an agency relationship created by necessity.

Generally a written agreement is not necessary to create an agency relationship. However, some states may require a written agreement when the relationship involves contracts covered by the Statute of Frauds.

### Duties of the Agent

An agent owes three fiduciary duties to her principal and may be held liable for breaching any of those duties. The agent has a fiduciary **duty of loyalty** to the principal, which means that the agent cannot act in ways that benefits herself to the detriment of the principal. The duty of loyalty also means that the agent may not take for herself an opportunity that belongs to the principal. Thus, the agent may not secretly make profits from a transaction that she is engaged in on behalf of the agent, nor can the agent enter into a transaction that would conflict with a transaction that she has entered into on behalf of the principal.

An agent also has a **duty of obedience**, pursuant to which she must obey all reasonable instructions from the principal. In addition, an agent owes the principal a **duty of care**, which means that the agent must carry out her duties on behalf of the agent in good faith and with reasonable care.

## Liability of Principal

A principal will be held liable for actions of an agent so long as the agent acted with **authority**. There are two forms of authority, **actual authority** and **apparent authority**. Actual or apparent authority will be sufficient to bind the principal to a given action by the agent.

**Actual authority** represents authority that the agent reasonably believes she has based on her interactions with the principal. Actual authority can be created by express agreement between the principal and the agent, known as **express actual authority**, or it can be implied.

**Implied actual authority** may arise from an express agreement between the agent and the principal when it is reasonable for the agent to believe that an agreement implies the authority to carry out actions necessary to the accomplishment of the express agreement. For example, if the principal gives the agent the authority to act as her cashier, but does not give her any further instructions, it is reasonable for the agent to believe that she has the implied actual authority to accept cash or checks from the principal's customers. Implied actual authority also may arise based on custom because an agent can act consistent with customs. Implied actual authority can also arise based on **acquiescence**. Hence, if the agent has performed an action in the past on behalf of the principal and the principal had notice of the performance, but failed to object to it within a reasonable amount of time, the principal will be deemed to have acquiesced to the agent's performance. However, it must be reasonable for the agent to believe that the principal acquiesced.

If actual authority exists, an agent's act will bind the principal unless the authority has been **terminated** prior to the act. Actual authority can be terminated upon (a) the expiration of a specified time or event, or after a reasonable time period, (b) a change of circumstances that would cause the agent to reasonably believe that the relationship had been terminated, (c) the agent's breach of her duty, (d) notification from either party of their desire to terminate the relationship, or (d) the death or loss of capacity of either party.

**Apparent authority** arises when the principal leads a third party to reasonably believe that the agent has the authority to act on her behalf. At times, apparent authority may arise based on the title a principal bestows on her agent. Thus, if the principal hires an agent to act as her cashier, then by bestowing such a title on her, the principal has given third parties the reasonable impression that the agent has the ability to act on the principal's behalf in a manner consistent with a cashier's responsibility. Thus, the agent can act in a manner consistent with custom as it relates to cashiers. In this example, however, there is both actual and apparent authority because both the agent and the third party have a reasonable impression regarding the agent's ability to act. However, suppose the principal tells the cashier that she cannot accept checks from customers. If the agent nevertheless accepts checks from customers, she will not have actual authority. However, she may have apparent authority because (a) it is still reasonable for the third party to believe that the agent can act on the principal's behalf in a manner consistent with a cashier's responsibility, and (b) accepting checks is a customary aspect of a cashier's duty.

If apparent authority exists, an agent's act will bind the principal unless the third party receives **notice** of the lack of authority prior to the act. Thus in the cashier example, if the principal notifies the third party that the agent cannot accept checks, then the cashier's acceptance of the check will not bind the principal.

If a person purports to act as an agent on behalf of another without authority, the purported agent may bind the other party as a principal if the purported principal ratifies the actions. In that case, the **ratification** will serve as actual authority for the transaction. Such ratification can occur by an express agreement from the principal or based on the principal's conduct, pursuant to which the principal either accepts the benefits of the purported agent's actions or does not object to such actions within a reasonable amount of time. In order for the ratification to be valid, however, the principal must have knowledge of all material facts regarding the action.

## Liability of Agent

If the agent does not have authority to act, then the agent will be liable for any transactions in which she enters.

If an agent *does* have the authority to act, then the agent generally will not have any liability for her actions. However, liability will be imposed in some circumstances. Those circumstances depend on whether the principal was disclosed or undisclosed. If a principal is **disclosed**, which means her existence *and* identity are known to the third party, then the agent will have no liability unless the parties intend otherwise. A principal is **partially disclosed** if a third party has knowledge of her existence, but not her identity, while an **undisclosed principal** is one whose identity and existence are not known to the third party. If a principal is partially disclosed, then both the agent and the principal are liable for the transaction. However, if a principal is undisclosed and the transaction has been completed, then only the agent is liable. These situations reveal that the failure to completely identify the principal to a third party may expose the agent to liability for contracts made on the principal's behalf.

## Termination

An agency relationship can be terminated in the same manner that actual authority may be terminated.

# 7.2 PARTNERSHIPS

## Creation of the Partnership

A **partnership** is an association of two or more people who enter into business together for the purpose of making a profit. If one person enters a business in order to make a profit, the resulting business entity is referred to as a **sole proprietorship**.

A partnership may be created without any formalities, and need not be in writing. It can arise by an express agreement or it can be implied based on the conduct of the parties. When determining if a partnership has arisen based on the parties' conduct, the **sharing of profits** is prima facie evidence of a partnership, unless the profits were shared as payment for a debt, wages, or a loan. Courts also will consider the extent to which parties have joint responsibility for a given endeavor, which includes shared ownership and management rights. Because it can be created without any agreement or other formal requirements, a partnership is considered to be a **default** form of business.

A **partnership by estoppel** arises when a person indicates to a third party that he is a partner, when in fact he is not. In such a circumstance, the person will be "estopped" from denying his status as a partner, and will be held liable to the third party for any harm created by his misrepresentation. However, the other purported partners will not have any liability.

Because a partnership represents a consensual relationship, unless there is a contrary agreement, the consent of all partners is necessary for anyone to become a partner in the partnership.

All property originally brought into the partnership, or subsequently acquired for the account of the partnership, is **partnership property**. Unless there is a contrary agreement, property acquired with partnership funds is also partnership property.

## Relations Between Partners

Unless there is a contrary agreement, all partners share equally in the profits and losses of the business. In addition, unless there is an agreement for other arrangements, all partners have equal rights to manage the affairs of the partnership. This is true even if the partners do not share equally in the profits of the business. Generally, each partner has one vote and actions are decided by majority vote.

Partners owe each other the highest fiduciary duty of care and loyalty. This means that partners must carry out their duties using reasonable care and must act to benefit the partnership. Thus, a partner cannot use the partnership's property or assets to benefit himself; rather all acts on behalf of the partnership must benefit the partnership as a whole. In addition, partners cannot take an opportunity that rightfully belongs to the partnership. A partner will be liable to the other partners if he breaches his partnership duty.

## Tax Structure

A partnership is subject to **flow-through** tax treatment. This means that the partnership itself is not taxed. Instead, each partner is taxed on his share of the partnership profits, whether or not such profits have been distributed. In other words, the tax "flows" through the partnership to the individual partners. This flow-through tax treatment represents one of the primary benefits of organizing a partnership because it ultimately enables the partnership to retain more of its funds.

## Liability

A partnership is an agency relationship. Each partner's actions will bind the partnership so long as the partner acts with either actual or apparent authority. Actual authority may arise from the partnership agreement or a majority vote of the partnership, unless the agreement or a statute requires a different vote for accomplishing particular actions.

Each partner is *personally* liable for the debts and obligations of the partnership. This is distinct from a corporation whose shareholders have limited liability (see **Corporations** discussed in Section 7.3), as well as other partnership and business entities where at least some of the participants have limited liability (see **Comparison with other Business Entities** discussed below). In order to distinguish it from other partnerships, when a partnership's participants have personal liability it is sometimes referred to as a **general partnership**.

In general, partners are jointly and severally liable for a partner's wrongful acts and breaches of trust, while partners are jointly liable for all other obligations. However, in some states, partners are jointly and severally liable for all partnership obligations.

A partner's liability changes if he leaves the partnership or is admitted to the partnership after formation. Thus, a newly-admitted partner is personally liable only for the debts and obligations that arose after he became a member of the partnership. A retiring partner is personally liable only for those debts and obligations that arose prior to his withdrawal from the partnership, as long as he provides notice of his withdrawal.

## Dissolution and Termination

Under the Uniform Partnership Act, **dissolution** represents a change in the relation of the partners caused by any partner ceasing to be associated with the partnership. A dissolution can arise by (a) a specific period of time as outlined in the partnership agreement, (b) the express desire of any partner, if the partnership has no specific period, (c) the mutual agreement of all the partners, (d) the expulsion of any partner, (e) the death of any partner, (f) the bankruptcy of any partner or the partnership, or (g) court decree.

As a general matter, dissolution terminates the actual authority of all partners to act on behalf of the partnership, except to perform acts necessary for **winding up** the affairs of the partnership. In order to terminate apparent authority, the partnership must provide notice to third parties who have had dealings with the partnership. If, however, partners elect to continue the business and such election occurs, then authority will not be terminated.

Once a partnership's affairs have been wound up, its remaining assets must be distributed. After such distribution, the partnership will be deemed terminated. Partnership assets must be distributed in the following order:

1. Creditors of the partnership,

2. Any partners who have made loans to the partnership,

3. Partners, as return for their capital contribution, and

4. All partners equally, or consistent with the terms of the partnership agreement.

## Comparison of Limited Partnerships and Other Business Entities

There are a variety of different business entities from which a person can choose to organize her business. Like the partnership, each of the business entities discussed below (in addition to the sole proprietorship) have flow-through tax treatment and thus only the participants in the entity are taxed, as opposed to the entity itself.

One prominent business entity is the **limited partnership**. Unlike the general partnership, in order to create a limited partnership, a certificate must be filed with the secretary of state or an equivalent state office.

The principle difference between a limited partnership and a general partnership is that the limited partnership has two different types of partners with different rights and responsibilities. A limited partnership must have one or more **limited partners** and one or more **general partners**.

The general partner's role in the limited partnership is similar to the role of a partner in a general partnership. The general partner has *personal liability* for all the debts and obligations of the limited partnership. Also, the general partner has the ability to manage the affairs of the limited partnership.

The limited partner has a more restricted role. The limited partner does not have personal liability. Instead, his liability is limited to the capital he has contributed to the entity. The limited partner does not participate in managing the affairs of the business. If he does, he may lose his protection of limited liability, and be held personally liable for the debts and obligations of the limited partnership.

A **limited liability partnership** or LLP is an entity that has all of the features of a general partnership, except with regard to formation and liability. Thus, a filing is required to create an LLP. Also, in an LLP, personal liability only extends to partners who commit a wrongful act or who are responsible for supervising people who commit such an act. Such liability is called **supervisory liability**. Unlike the general partnership, partners in an LLP may have limited liability.

A **limited liability company** or LLC is an entity in which the people who have made a financial investment in the company, known as **members**, do not have personal liability. Moreover, people who choose to organize as an LLC have the option of choosing one of two management structures. All members of the LLC can participate in the management of the LLC similar to a general partnership, which is referred to as a **member-managed** LLC. Alternatively, only a few members, known as **managers**, may be authorized to manage the affairs of the LLC. Such a structure is referred to as a **manager-managed** LLC. A manager-managed LLC has a management style similar to a corporation (see **Corporations** discussed in Section 7.3). Like the LLP and the LP, the LLC requires a filing to be formed.

Table 7-1 at the end of this chapter provides a comparison of some of the key features of the corporation and the various other business entities.

# 7.3 CORPORATIONS

## Creation of the Corporation

A **corporation** is an artificial entity created by law and viewed as having an existence distinct from its owners and managers. A corporation has continued or **perpetual existence**.

In order to form a corporation, a certificate must be filed with the secretary of state or an equivalent state office. The process of filing such certificate is known as **incorporation**. The certificate is generally referred to as the **articles of incorporation**, the **articles of organization** or the **charter**. The articles of incorporation must contain the name of the corporation, its purpose and powers, the amount of shares the corporation is authorized to issue, and the name of the **incorporators** or the initial directors. Incorporators represent people who prepare, sign and file the articles of incorporation. A corporation comes into existence upon the filing of the articles of incorporation or, in some states, when a **certificate of incorporation** is issued revealing acceptance of the articles of incorporation.

Once a corporation comes into existence, an initial meeting must be called in order to organize the corporation. At the meeting, directors and officers will be elected and other transactions will be approved that will enable the corporation to carry on its business. Importantly, **bylaws** will be adopted. Bylaws essentially represent the operating agreement for the corporation, and set forth the corporation's rules and procedures including the functions of various officers, how meetings must be conducted, and voting requirements. While state law requires that each corporation adopt bylaws, the bylaws do not have to be filed.

The laws of the state of incorporation govern the relationships among the parties in the corporation. This is known as the **internal affairs doctrine**.

## Relations of Parties

**Shareholders** are viewed as owners of the corporation because they own the stock (see discussion below) issued by the corporation. Shareholders then vote to elect members of the **board of directors** who have the authority to manage the corporation's affairs. These directors elect or appoint **officers** who operate the corporation on a day-to-day basis.

**Corporate Parties**

```
┌─────────────────────┐
│    Shareholders     │
└─────────────────────┘
           │
           ↓
┌─────────────────────┐
│     Directors       │
└─────────────────────┘
           │
           ↓
┌─────────────────────┐
│     Officers        │
└─────────────────────┘
```

## Shareholders

Although shareholders are viewed as the owners of the corporation, they do not have the right to manage the corporation. Instead, shareholders' rights are limited to a few distinct matters. First, shareholders have the right to vote in proportion to the number of shares they hold. Shareholders vote to elect the members of the board of directors. Shareholders also vote on fundamental matters such as to amend the articles of incorporation, to dissolve the corporation, or to sell all of the corporation's assets.

Second, shareholders may bring suits against the corporation. Such suits can take the form of a **direct** suit or a **derivative** suit. A direct suit is a suit brought because the corporation or its officers or directors need to remedy a harm inflicted on an individual shareholder. A derivative suit is a suit brought by a shareholder on behalf of the corporation usually alleging that officers or directors have breached their fiduciary duty and caused harm to the corporation and its shareholders. Derivative suits were created to allow shareholders to bring actions that corporate officers and directors may be reluctant to bring because such actions involve suing themselves or one of their colleagues. However, because the derivative suit is brought on behalf of the corporation, any damages must be paid directly to the corporation. State laws impose strict requirements for bringing a derivative suit, including that shareholders must first demand that corporate directors bring suit, unless the demand is excused. Only shareholders have the right to bring a derivative action.

## Directors and Officers

Shareholders elect the members of the board of directors who manage the corporation. Actions by the board are decided by majority vote. A board can delegate its authority to one or more **committees**, which are comprised of members of the board of directors. These committees generally oversee various corporate functions from compensation schemes to financial matters. Some common committees are the nominating committee (responsible for overseeing the nomination of candidates for directors), the audit committee (responsible for overseeing a company's financial affairs and auditing process), and the compensation committee (responsible for setting compensation for executives and other officers). Such committees are required for public companies. The board also has the ability to elect or appoint officers who operate the day-to-day affairs of the modern corporation. Such officers typically include a president, vice president, secretary, and treasurer. These officers then hire the corporation's employees.

Officers and directors have a fiduciary **duty of care** to carry out their duties in good faith, with reasonable care and in a manner they believe to be in the corporation's best interests. Courts apply the **business judgment rule** to determine if officers and directors have breached this duty. The business judgment rule is a presumption that officers and directors are well-intentioned and perform their duties in good faith. Thus, in order to demonstrate a breach of the duty of care, this presumption must by overcome. It can be overcome by showing that officers and directors (a) engaged in fraud or illegality, (b) were grossly negligent or uninformed, or (c) had no rational basis for their actions. It is generally very difficult to overcome the presumption of the business judgment rule and hold directors or officers liable for breaching their duty of care.

Directors and officers also have a fiduciary **duty of loyalty**, which governs transactions in which directors or officers have a conflict of interests. Directors and officers do not receive the business judgment rule presumption for such transactions. Thus, they must prove that such transactions are fair to the corporation.

## Stocks and Dividends

A share or stock represents a proportionate interest in the corporation. Shares can be divided into classes, which are generally **common** shares and **preferred** shares. Common shares represent the basic class of shares issued to shareholders, and typically come with the right to vote and receive **dividends**, when and if directors declare them, and in the amounts set by directors (see **dividends** discussed below). Preferred shares represent shares with some type of preference, such as the ability to receive dividends prior to common shareholders, the ability to receive specific amount of dividends, or the ability to receive assets in liquidation prior to common shareholders.

A **dividend** reflects a distribution by the corporation to shareholders issued in proportion to their share ownership. Other than selling their shares, dividends represent one of the primary means by which shareholders receive a return on their investment. The board has the discretion to determine if and when the corporation will issue dividends to the shareholders, as well as the discretion to determine the amount of the dividend, unless it is set by agreement. Typically, the amount of dividends to be paid to preferred shareholders is set. However, the board still retains the discretion to determine when the corporation will pay such dividends. Then too, state law prohibits board members from paying dividends if such payment would leave the corporation without the ability to pay its obligations.

## Tax Structure

A corporation is not subject to flow-through tax treatment. This means that the corporation itself is taxed. In addition, each shareholder is taxed when the corporation issues a dividend. Because there are two levels of tax applied to a corporation, some refer to its tax treatment as a form of

**"double taxation."** Such taxation represents one of the principle differences between a corporation and other business entities and makes a corporation's tax structure less advantageous than such entities.

## Liability

The corporation is responsible for its debts and obligations. Thus, all of the parties within the corporation enjoy **limited liability**, which means that they are not personally responsible for the debts and obligations of the corporation. This limited liability is a principle feature of the corporation, distinguishing it from partnerships, where some or all of the partners have personal liability. However, under certain circumstances, a court will disregard the corporation for liability purposes, and **"pierce the corporate veil"** to hold officers, directors, or shareholders liable for corporate debts. Courts pierce the corporate veil reluctantly, and only to prevent fraud, illegality, or provide relief in circumstances where corporate actors have operated the corporation improperly and in a manner that harms third parties.

## Termination

A corporation terminates by **dissolution** and **liquidation**. A corporation may be dissolved either voluntarily or by the court. In order for a corporation to be voluntarily dissolved, there must be approval by the board and a majority of the shareholders. The corporation then must file a **certificate of dissolution** or **article of dissolution** with the secretary of state or its state equivalent office. A court also may order dissolution of a corporation on specified grounds, such as when the majority of the board has acted illegally or wasted corporate assets. However, courts are extremely reluctant to dissolve profitable corporations. After a corporation is dissolved, its business continues, but solely for the purpose of winding up its affairs. The corporation then liquidates, distributing out its remaining assets to creditors and to shareholders.

**Table 7-1. COMPARISON OF BUSINESS ENTITIES**

|  | GP | LLP | LP | LLC | Corporation |
|---|---|---|---|---|---|
| Ownership | 2 or more general partners | 2 or more general partners | At least one general partner and one limited partner | Most states allow one member | At least one shareholder |
| Formation | No filing required | Filing required | Filing required | Filing required | Filing required |
| Management | Each general partner has an equal right to manage and control the partnership | Each general partner has an equal right to manage and control the LLP | Only general partners have the rights to manage and control the LP; limited partners may not participate in management | Two types: Member-managed—all members manage  Manager-managed—only persons who are managers manage the LLC | Directors and officers manage; shareholders control through share ownership |

*(Continued)*

**Table 7-1. COMPARISON OF BUSINESS ENTITIES** *(Continued)*

| | GP | LLP | LP | LLC | Corporation |
|---|---|---|---|---|---|
| Authority | All general partners have authority to bind the partnership | All general partners have authority to bind the LLP | Only general partners have authority to bind the LP | Two types:<br><br>Member-managed—all members have authority<br><br>Manager-managed—only persons who are managers have authority | Directors and officers have authority to bind the corporation |
| Liability | All general partners have personal liability | General partners are personally liable only if they or persons they supervise commit wrongful acts | All general partners have personal liability; limited partners are liable only if they participate in control of the LP | All members have limited liability | Directors, officers, and shareholders have limited liability |

*(Continued)*

**Table 7-1. COMPARISON OF BUSINESS ENTITIES** *(Continued)*

| | GP | LLP | LP | LLC | Corporation |
|---|---|---|---|---|---|
| Withdrawal Rights/ Dissolution | All general partners can withdraw at any time without the consent of other general partners; withdrawal triggers dissolution | All general partners can withdraw at any time without the consent of other general partners; withdrawal triggers dissolution | If no agreement, limited partners can withdraw upon 6 months' notice; limited partners' withdrawal does not trigger dissolution. General partners can withdraw at any time; withdrawal triggers dissolution unless there is at least one other general partner. | Members can dissociate at any time without the consent of other members; dissociation does not trigger dissolution; specified percentage of members must vote to dissolve | Shareholders can transfer shares at any time without the consent of other shareholders, officers, or directors; dissolution needs approval by board and majority of shareholders |

# CHAPTER 8
## Sales

# Chapter 8

# SALES

Sales represent contracts for goods. Thus, many of the common law rules governing contracts may apply to such sales. This Chapter identifies some of those circumstances where the rules governing contracts for sales differ from the common law rules for other forms of contracts.

## 8.1 MEANINGS OF TERMS

Article 2 of the UCC governs all transactions for the sale of goods. All of the terms defined below are based on UCC definitions.

**Buyer** is a person who buys or enters into a contract to buy goods

**Goods** represent things that are movable at the time of the contract

**Merchant** is a person who ordinarily deals in goods of the kind sold or otherwise by her occupation holds herself out as having the knowledge or skill relevant to the goods involved in the transaction

**Sale** is a contract pursuant to which a buyer purchases goods from a seller for a price

**Seller** is a person who sells or enters into a contract to sell goods

## 8.2 FORMATION OF UCC CONTRACTS

### Offer and Acceptance Under the UCC

When two parties have exchanged written communications related to a sale of goods, the UCC establishes rules for determining whether an offer and acceptance has occurred. Often, these written communications will be in the form of preprinted forms. Hence, the process of assessing whether an offer and acceptance has occurred is often referred to as **battle of the forms**.

The UCC does not define an offer and thus follows the common law's definition (see Section 4.2 of Chapter 4). However, the UCC modifies the rule regarding option contracts. Under the common law, an offeror may revoke an offer unless she receives consideration to keep it open, creating an option contract. However, under the UCC, if a *merchant* signs a written offer agreeing to hold an offer open, the offer will be irrevocable for the period stated in the offer or for a reasonable amount time if no period is stated.

The UCC also provides guidance on the types of communications that constitute an acceptance. Consistent with current law, the UCC rejects the mirror image rule. Instead, a buyer's definite and timely expression of acceptance will be construed as an acceptance, even if it contains terms that are different or in addition to those contained in the offer. However, if the acceptance is conditioned on the seller's consent to the new terms, then there is no acceptance. Instead the buyer's communication will be treated as a rejection and a counteroffer.

## Buyer's Acceptance

The UCC creates additional rules regarding the conduct that will constitute an acceptance. Thus, under the UCC, a buyer will be deemed to have accepted goods if

(a) after a reasonable opportunity to inspect the goods, the buyer indicates to the seller that (i) the goods are conforming, or (ii) she will take them even though they do not conform,

(b) after a reasonable opportunity to inspect the goods, the buyer fails to notify the seller that she objects to the goods within a reasonable time, or

(c) the buyer acts in a manner that is inconsistent with the seller's ownership of the goods.

## Buyer's Rejection Right

With regard to most common law contracts, a minor defect in performance will be treated as substantial performance and hence a party cannot reject the performance. However, under the UCC, a buyer can reject goods that fail to conform in any respect to the contract terms. This is known as the **"perfect tender"** rule. Under that rule, unless the sale relates to an installment contract, when goods fail in any respect to conform to the contract, the buyer has the right to (a) reject all of them, (b) accept all of them, or (c) accept any commercial units and reject the rest. However, the buyer's right of rejection changes when the sale relates to an **installment contract**, which is defined as a contract that allows goods to be delivered in separate installments or lots. With regard to such a contract, the buyer may reject goods *only* if the nonconformity substantially impairs the value of that installment and cannot be **cured** by the seller (see **cure** discussed below).

In order for a rejection to be effective, the buyer must timely notify the seller of her intention to reject within a reasonable time after the goods have been delivered or tendered.

## Seller's Cure Right

The perfect tender rule is subject to the seller's right to **cure**. Ordinarily, if the buyer rejects goods because they are non-conforming and the seller has delivered the goods before the time provided under the contract, the seller may notify the buyer of her intention to cure within a reasonable period of time, and cure by delivering new conforming goods, within the time provided under the contract. If this occurs, the buyer must accept the conforming goods. However, if the time for delivery has passed, then the seller can cure within a reasonable time *only* if she has reasonable grounds to believe that the buyer would adjust the price to take any non-conformity into account. In all other circumstances, the seller cannot cure after the time for delivery has passed.

The seller's right to cure changes if there is an installment contract. The UCC provides that the buyer cannot reject goods in an installment contract if the seller can cure. Any rejection under these contracts constitutes a breach. Moreover, if the goods in an installment contract are properly rejected, the seller has the same right to cure that she had with respect to goods under other UCC contracts.

## Buyer's Ability to Revoke Acceptance

Once a buyer accepts goods, she is obligated to pay the price of the goods. However, the buyer's acceptance may be revoked if (a) the goods are nonconforming and the nonconformity substantially impairs the value of the goods and (b) the buyer had accepted the goods either (i) on the reasonable assumption that the nonconformity would be cured and they have not been timely cured or (ii) without discovering the nonconformity, if such nonconformity was difficult to discover.

Revocation is not effective until the buyer notifies the seller of the revocation. In addition, revocation must occur (a) within a reasonable time after the buyer knew or should have known the basis for revocation, and (b) before there has been any substantial change in the condition of the goods. When an acceptance is properly revoked, it is treated like a rejection.

## Meanings of UCC Contracts

When the buyer's acceptance includes additional terms, such terms are treated as **proposals** for inclusion in the contract. If *both* parties are not merchants, then the seller must specifically agree to the proposals in order for them to be included in the contract. In other words, if one of the parties is not a merchant, the contract will include only the terms contained in the seller's offer. However, if both parties are merchants, the proposals become part of the contract unless (a) the offer expressly limits acceptance to its terms, (b) the proposals materially alter the contract, or (c) the seller previously has rejected the proposals or rejects the proposals within a reasonable time after acquiring notice of it.

In essence, the UCC rules related to additional terms have two components. First, regardless of the buyer's identity, an expression with additional terms will be construed as an acceptance. Second, if both parties are merchants, then the proposals will be deemed automatically accepted upon the occurrence of one of the three instances mentioned above. However, if both parties are not merchants, then the proposals must receive the consent of the seller.

When the buyer's acceptance includes different terms, courts disagree regarding the impact of the terms. Some courts apply the same rules governing additional terms. Other courts conclude that any different terms must be **disregarded**. This means that when there are different terms, the terms contained in the seller's offer will govern the contract. Still other courts apply the **knockout** rule. This rule treats the different terms as canceling or "knocking" each other out so that neither term is included in the contract. As a result, courts will be required to imply a term.

When the parties to a contract fail to establish a contract, their conduct will be sufficient to establish a contract, if the conduct recognizes the existence of a contract. In such a situation, only those terms on which the parties' agree will be included in the contract; any different or additional terms will be excluded. Courts will then imply any open terms necessary to effectuate the agreement.

## Modification and Consideration

An agreement under the UCC may be modified without consideration so long as the modification is in good faith.

## Statute of Frauds

Under the Statute of Frauds, contracts for the sale of goods for the price of $500 or more must be in writing and signed by the party to be bound. As a general rule, if such contracts are not in writing, then they will not be enforceable. However, if payment has been made and accepted or goods have been delivered and accepted, then the UCC contract is enforceable to the extent of such payment or delivery (see Section 4.8 of Chapter 4).

# 8.3 WARRANTIES

## Express Warranties

An **express warranty** is an agreement made by the seller to the buyer that goods will conform to such agreement. The warranty can be created by words, description, sample, or model. However, the warranty must be an expression of fact and not opinion. Thus, a statement such as "Those shoes are great," represents an opinion that does not create an express warranty. By contrast, a statement such as "those shoes are the best of their kind," does represent a statement that could give rise to an express warranty claim because it can be verified. An express warranty can only be waived by language consistent with the warranty.

## Implied Warranty of Merchantability

An **implied warranty of merchantability** exists in every sale of goods if the seller is a merchant. Such a warranty represents an assurance that the goods will pass without objection in the trade and are fit for their ordinary use. In other words, the goods must be acceptable to people within the industry. Such a warranty may be waived if it is in writing, conspicuous, and mentions the word "merchantability."

## Implied Warranty of Fitness for a Particular Purpose

An **implied warranty of fitness for a particular purpose** arises when a seller has reason to know that a buyer is (a) purchasing goods for a particular purpose, and (b) relying on the seller's skill or judgment in purchasing the goods. A waiver of this warranty must be in writing and conspicuous.

## 8.4 REMEDIES

### Buyer's Damages

Generally, the buyer's remedy when the seller fails to deliver goods or when goods have been properly rejected will be expectation damages. Such damages will represent the difference between the contract price and the market price at the time the buyer learned of the breach, together with any incidental and consequential damages, but less any expenses saved as a result of the breach. If the buyer chooses, he may **cover** by making a reasonable purchase of substitute goods. If the buyer chooses to cover, the seller must pay the buyer the difference between the cost of cover and the contract price, together with any incidental and consequential damages, but less any expenses saved as a result of the breach.

The buyer can recover damages for accepted goods that are non-conforming, so long as he notifies the seller of the nonconformity within a reasonable time period. The damages will be the difference between the value of the goods delivered and their value if they had conformed to the contract, plus any incidental and consequential damages.

Damages for breach of warranty are the difference between the value of the goods accepted at the time and place of acceptance, and the value they would have been if they had conformed to the warranty.

### Seller's Withhold Right and Damages

When the buyer fails to make payment, the seller can withhold delivery of goods. When the buyer wrongfully rejects the goods, the seller may recover damages. In that case, the seller can resell the goods and recover the difference between the contract price and the resale price together with incidental damages, but less any expenses saved as a result of the buyer's breach. The resale must be made in good faith and in a commercially reasonable transaction. If the seller does not resell the goods, he may recover the difference between the contract price and the market price at the time and place for delivery, together with incidental damages, but less any expenses saved as a result of the buyer's breach.

### Specific Performance

As under common law, specific performance is only awarded in limited circumstances. Thus, courts will award specific performance when the goods are unique or in any other proper circumstance.

# PRACTICE
# TEST 1

This test is also on CD-ROM in our special interactive TEST*ware*® for the CLEP Introductory Business Law exam. It is highly recommended that you first take this exam on computer. You will then have the additional study features and benefits of enforced time conditions, individual diagnostic analysis, and instant scoring.

# CLEP INTRODUCTORY BUSINESS LAW

## PRACTICE TEST 1

**(Answer sheets appear in the back of this book.)**

**TIME:** 90 Minutes
100 Questions

---

**DIRECTIONS:** Each of the questions or incomplete statements below is followed by five possible answers or completions. Select the best choice in each case and fill in the corresponding oval on the answer sheet.

---

1.  Theories that ethics should be judged based on duties rather than consequences are known as

    (A)  utilitarianism

    (B)  consequentialism

    (C)  deontological

    (D)  due process

    (E)  imperatives

2.  An agreement to require a buyer to resell products to a particular manufacturer is known as

    (A)  a production quota

    (B)  a tie-in agreement

    (C)  a market division transaction

    (D)  an exclusive dealing agreement

    (E)  a horizontal agreement

3.  In an action for an intentional tort, a defendant may raise which of the following defenses?

    (A) Assumption of risk

    (B) Consent

    (C) Undue influence

    (D) Mistake

    (E) *Res ipsa loquitor*

4.  Paula was crossing the street without using the crosswalk in violation of a state law. Simon, who was driving above the speed limit in violation of state law, hit Paula causing her serious injury. If Paula sues Simon, most courts would hold that

    (A) Paula cannot recover because she contributed to her injuries

    (B) Paula cannot recover because she assumed the risk

    (C) Paula cannot recover because her actions represented implied consent

    (D) Paula can recover because Simon was more at fault than Paula

    (E) Paula can recover but only for damages related to Simon's conduct

5.  Nancy saw Cynthia selling cookies on the corner for $1 each. Nancy took $3 out of her pocket and gave it to Cynthia, who gave Nancy three cookies, which Nancy promptly ate. Which of the following best describes this transaction?

    (A) A promise

    (B) A contract

    (C) A unilateral contract

    (D) An executed exchange

    (E) A quasi contract

6. On receiving a summons, a defendant can do which of the following?

   I. File a demurrer

   II. Make a motion to dismiss for lack of subject matter jurisdiction

   III. File a response raising claims against the plaintiff

   (A) I only

   (B) II only

   (C) III only

   (D) I and II only

   (E) I, II, and III

7. Fifteen-year-old Stacy entered into a contract to purchase a motorcycle from Roy. A week after purchasing the motorcycle, Stacy turned 16, the age of majority in her state. One day later, Stacy was in an accident and the motorcycle was destroyed, though Stacy survived with minimal injuries. Right after the accident, Stacy contacted Roy to get her money back for the motorcycle. In a suit between Stacy and Roy, a court is most likely to hold that

   (A) Stacy can disaffirm the contract because she was a minor at the time she entered into the contract.

   (B) Stacy can disaffirm the contract because she disaffirmed within a reasonable time.

   (C) Stacy cannot disaffirm the contract because she cannot return the motorcycle to Roy.

   (D) Stacy cannot disaffirm the contract because she was almost 16 when she purchased the motorcycle.

   (E) Stacy cannot disaffirm the contract because a motorcycle is a necessity.

8. Which of the following is true of the Superfund program?

   (A) It was established to locate and clean up hazardous waste sites.

   (B) It was established to improve trade with developing nations.

   (C) It was established to supplement employees' retirement benefits.

   (D) It was established to help companies pay off their debts in bankruptcy.

   (E) It was established to improve economic markets in developing countries.

9. Which of the following functions could NOT be performed by a judge of a trial court?

   (A) Delivering a verdict

   (B) Making rulings on the evidence

   (C) Granting motions for discovery

   (D) Providing instructions to the jury

   (E) Conducting pretrial hearings

10. The ability of a buyer to purchase substitute goods in the event of a seller's breach is known as

   (A) cure

   (B) waiver

   (C) cover

   (D) promissory estoppel

   (E) revocation

11. Emma, the owner of a pizza shop, was engaged in discussions with Todd regarding the possibility of his being her delivery driver. However, Sharon convinced Todd to work for her instead. If Emma sues Sharon, the court is most likely to hold that

    (A) Emma cannot recover because Emma and Sharon are not partners.

    (B) Emma cannot recover because Emma and Sharon do not have a contract with one another.

    (C) Emma cannot recover because Emma and Todd never entered into a contract.

    (D) Emma can recover if she can prove that Sharon knew of her relationship with Todd.

    (E) Emma can recover if she can prove that Sharon's actions were not motivated by good faith.

12. If a corporation wants to sell its securities to sophisticated investors without registering them, the corporation would most likely rely on which of the following provisions of the Securities Act?

    (A) Regulation S

    (B) Regulation D

    (C) Rule 10b-5

    (D) Rule 701

    (E) Section 11

13. Which of the following best defines a quasi contract?

    (A) Promise made by one party

    (B) Incomplete promise

    (C) Promise implied in fact

    (D) Transaction that allows recovery for reliance damages

    (E) Transaction that allows recovery for unjust enrichment

14. Ruby wants to print a newsletter that critiques the local and state governments' efforts regarding the economy. The state wants to review the newsletter to make sure it agrees with the critique. If Ruby sues the state to prevent it from reviewing her newsletter, which of the following standards of review will a court use?

    (A) Strict scrutiny, because it involves regulation of content

    (B) Intermediate scrutiny, because this is a restriction of time, place, and manner

    (C) Intermediate scrutiny, because this does not involve a suspect classification

    (D) Rational basis test, because the state has an interest in the type of speech at issue

    (E) Rational basis test, because this involves commercial speech

15. Lucy needs to take some time off from work to care for her mother who is seriously ill. Which of the following requires her employer to give her time off?

    (A) The Fair Labor Standards Act

    (B) The Family Medical Leave Act

    (C) The National Leave Act

    (D) The National Labor Relations Act

    (E) Worker's compensation

16. A court applies the rule of reason to analyze which of the following?

    (A) Negligence

    (B) Securities fraud

    (C) Restrictions on trade

    (D) Product liability actions

    (E) Investment contracts

17. Edward sold Ivan an alarm clock. Under the agreement, the alarm clock was sold "as is." When Ivan took the clock home and tried to set it, the alarm did not work. If Ivan sues Edward, which of the following is true?

    (A) Edward cannot be held liable because Ivan agreed to the purchase "as is."

    (B) Edward cannot be held liable because he did not make any representations about the clock.

    (C) Edward cannot be held liable unless Ivan can prove that he relied on Edward's skill and judgment.

    (D) Edward can be held liable unless the "as is" language was in writing and conspicuous.

    (E) Edward can be held liable unless the "as is" language was in writing, conspicuous, and mentions "merchantability."

18. Eric and Len are partners in a general partnership that sells ice cream. Eric decided that he also wants to sell sandwiches. For the next three weeks, Eric sells sandwiches in Len's presence. Assuming Len never expressly consented to the selling of sandwiches, which of the following is true?

    (A) Eric has no actual authority for his actions because Len never consented to them.

    (B) Eric has no actual authority for his action because there is no written agreement to them.

    (C) Eric has actual authority because Len's failure to object means he acquiesced.

    (D) Eric has actual authority because both partners have equal rights to manage the business.

    (E) Eric has actual authority unless the customers have notice that there is no such authority.

19. In general, a defendant claiming self-defense must show that

   (A) the defendant feared for her life

   (B) the defendant attempted to retreat

   (C) the defendant did not intend to cause harm

   (D) the defendant reasonably believed her actions were necessary to protect herself

   (E) the defendant reasonably believed her actions would not cause harm

20. John has been receiving abusive and threatening phone calls from a collection agency. If John wanted to sue the agency, which of the following would form the basis of his claim?

   (A) The Fair Debt Collection Act

   (B) The Fair Credit Reporting Act

   (C) The Equal Credit Opportunity Act

   (D) The Truth in Lending Act

   (E) The Consumer Protection Act

21. Which of the following is a distinction that can be drawn between assignment and delegation?

   (A) Assignment involves a transfer of an interest in a contract, and delegation does not.

   (B) Assignment involves a contract that benefits a third party, and delegation does not.

   (C) Assignment transfers a right, and delegation transfers a duty.

   (D) Assignment relates to a tort claim, and delegation relates to a contract claim.

   (E) Assignment terminates the rights of all parties who do not consent to it, and delegation does not.

22. If a contract falls within the Statute of Frauds, which of the following statements is true?

    (A) The contract cannot be used as evidence to explain the agreement between the two parties.

    (B) The contract must be in writing and signed by the party sought to be bound.

    (C) The contract is voidable if it was for the sale of goods valued at less than $500.

    (D) The contract must be in writing and signed by both parties.

    (E) The contract does not have to be in writing to be enforceable.

23. A material breach allows the nonbreaching party to take which of the following actions?

    I.   Suspend performance and terminate the contract

    II.  Suspend performance and await cure

    III. Suspend performance and bring suit for the full contract price

    (A) I only

    (B) II only

    (C) III only

    (D) I and III only

    (E) I, II, and III

24. Which of the following applies if the defendant in a product liability action did not know and could not have known that a product had a design defect?

    (A) The defendant does not have liability for negligence.

    (B) The defendant does not have liability negligence unless she is a supplier.

    (C) The defendant does not have liability for any action involving product liability.

    (D) The defendant does have liability unless the product had clear disclaimers.

    (E) The defendant does have liability if the plaintiff can prove that the defect caused her injuries.

25. Julie's boss told her that she would receive a promotion only if she performed sexual favors for him. If Julie sues her boss, which of the following would form the basis of her claim?

    (A) Negligence

    (B) The Due Process Clause

    (C) The National Labor Relations Act

    (D) Title VII

    (E) The Equal Employment Act

26. On taking possession of a debtor's property, a creditor may take which of the following actions?

    I.   Hold the property until repayment is made

    II.  Sell the property in a commercially reasonable sale

    III. Occupy the property until repayment is made

    (A) I only

    (B) II only

    (C) III only

    (D) I and II only

    (E) I, II, and III

27. Article I of the Constitution establishes the

    (A) executive branch

    (B) judicial branch

    (C) legislative branch

    (D) Bill of Rights

    (E) Supreme Court

28. Renée told Daryll that he could purchase her new car if he promised to pay her $50,000. Unbeknownst to Daryll, Renée was playing a practical joke on him and did not intend to sell her car. When Daryll told Renée that he was willing to pay her the $50,000 for her car, Renée immediately told Daryll that she was just joking and that the car was not for sale. If Daryll sues Renée to purchase the car, the court will probably find that Daryll is

    (A) not entitled to purchase the car because Renée told Daryll she was just joking before Daryll made any payment

    (B) not entitled to purchase the car because Renée told Daryll she was joking immediately after he told her he would pay

    (C) not entitled to purchase the car because the fact that Renée was joking reveals that she did not intend to be bound by any contract

    (D) entitled to purchase the car because $50,000 is a reasonable price for a car

    (E) entitled to purchase the car because Renée's words reveal an intent to be bound

29. The ability of a party to bring a lawsuit is called

   (A) jurisdiction

   (B) standing

   (C) venue

   (D) domicile

   (E) attachment

30. Ideas Inc. has agreed to a merger with Money Corp. Which of the following statements is true?

   (A) The merger agreement must be analyzed under the business judgment rule.

   (B) The merger agreement constitutes a vertical agreement.

   (C) The merger agreement must be approved under the Hart-Scott-Rodino Act.

   (D) The merger agreement must be approved under the Robinson-Patman Act.

   (E) The merger agreement must be approved under the Sarbanes-Oxley Act.

31. Which of the following best defines the frolic and detour doctrine?

   (A) An employer can be held liable for all an employee's actions during the course of her employment except those that are substantial deviations from her employment responsibilities.

   (B) An employer can be held liable for an employee's actions only when the employee does not deviate from her employment responsibilities.

   (C) An employer can be held liable for an employee's personal actions if the employer consents to them.

   (D) An employer can be held liable for an employee's personal actions if the employer ratifies them.

   (E) An employer can be held liable for all an employee's actions during the course of her employment even when they constitute detours.

32. In general, the Supreme Court grants a writ of certiorari in which of the following cases?

    (A) Cases involving error in a lower-court decision

    (B) Cases involving federal statutes

    (C) Cases involving foreign citizens

    (D) Cases involving conflicts between state courts on important questions of law

    (E) Cases involving mistakes in factual findings

33. A contract that keeps an offer open for a period of time is called

    (A) a quasi contract

    (B) an executory contract

    (C) a unilateral contract

    (D) a bilateral contract

    (E) an option contract

34. All of the following can form the basis of personal jurisdiction EXCEPT

    (A) presence

    (B) residency

    (C) venue

    (D) minimum contacts

    (E) consent

35. On Monday Leslie mailed an acceptance to Peter's offer. On Tuesday Leslie changed her mind and mailed a rejection to Peter's offer. Which of the following will apply if Peter receives the rejection before he receives the acceptance?

    (A) No contract will result because the two different responses negate Leslie's assent.

    (B) No contract will result because rejection is effective upon receipt.

    (C) No contract will result because the rejection was received prior to the acceptance.

    (D) A contract will result because acceptance is effective upon dispatch.

    (E) A contract will result because when two communications are sent, the mailbox rule does not apply.

36. Which of the following is true of the World Trade Organization?

    (A) It is an administrative agency that facilitates free trade.

    (B) It is an organization that helps create rules for fair trading practices.

    (C) It is a trade agreement among most of the largest countries in the world.

    (D) It is an organization that provides financial assistance for world trading activities.

    (E) It is an organization that investigates improper trading activities.

37. Virginia entered into a contract with Tammy, that states that it cannot be assigned. Assuming there is no other provision related to assignment, which of the following statements is correct?

   (A) An assignment by Virginia would be unenforceable.

   (B) An assignment by Virginia requires Tammy's consent.

   (C) An assignment by Virginia would entitle Tammy to terminate the contract.

   (D) An assignment by Virginia requires Virginia to give Tammy notice before the assignment.

   (E) An assignment by Virginia would entitle Tammy to sue Virginia for breach of contract.

38. Which of the following decisions could NOT be heard in state court?

   (A) Decisions involving a federal treaty

   (B) Decisions involving an important state statute

   (C) Decisions involving citizens of a foreign county

   (D) Decisions involving an amount in controversy exceeding $75,000

   (E) Decisions involving an international business dispute

39. Ron entered into an agreement with Noah in which Noah promised to pay Ron $3,000 if Ron built Noah a basketball court. Ron began building the basketball court, but Noah changed his mind. If Ron sues Noah, a court will probably hold that

   (A) Noah must allow Ron to complete performance

   (B) Noah must pay Ron $3,000 in damages immediately

   (C) Noah can revoke the contract because it is illusory

   (D) Noah can revoke the contract because there is no longer mutual assent

   (E) Noah can revoke the contract because Ron has not yet accepted

40. The state of California wants to build a bike path that crosses through Holly's backyard. If Holly wants to challenge their actions, which of the following constitutional provisions would most likely impact her challenge?

    (A) The First Amendment

    (B) The Second Amendment

    (C) The Fifth Amendment

    (D) The Equal protection clause

    (E) The Commerce clause

41. Under the Uniform Commercial Code (UCC), if an offeree expresses the intent to accept an offer but the acceptance contains terms that are additional to those contained in the original offer, which of the following is true?

    (A) The expression will be construed as an acceptance, but the additional terms will be rejected based on the knockout rule.

    (B) Unless both parties are merchants, the expression will be construed as a rejection.

    (C) The expression will be construed as a rejection based on the mirror-image rule.

    (D) The expression will be construed as an acceptance, and the additional terms will be viewed as proposals for inclusion in the contract.

    (E) The expression will be construed as a counteroffer that must be accepted within a reasonable period.

42. A method of establishing a breach of duty based on a finding that an act does not generally occur without negligence is called

    (A) proximate cause

    (B) transferred intent

    (C) *res ipsa loquitor*

    (D) *prima facie*

    (E) *respondeat superior*

43. Which of the following defendants can file for a writ of habeas corpus?

    (A) A defendant who has been summoned to appear in court

    (B) A defendant who is in custody after her judgment is deemed final

    (C) A defendant who has been denied a jury trial

    (D) A defendant in a civil case who has exhausted all remedies

    (E) A defendant in a civil case when her petition for review has been denied

44. Ordinarily a buyer is liable for which of the following?

    (A) Only goods she has explicitly indicated are acceptable

    (B) Goods she fails to reject after a reasonable opportunity to inspect

    (C) All goods delivered within a reasonable time

    (D) All goods she fails to reject after a reasonable time except those that are nonconforming

    (E) All goods delivered except those that are significantly nonconforming

45. The business judgment rule is based on a judgment that

    (A) judges should understand business concepts

    (B) judges should review officers' and directors' conduct under strict scrutiny

    (C) officers and directors are free to use any judgment when operating the business

    (D) officers and directors are disciplined by the market

    (E) officers and directors are well intentioned and act in good faith

46. Which of the following is NOT an essential element of a strict liability claim for product liability?

    (A) The defendant must be a commercial supplier.

    (B) The defendant must be a seller of goods.

    (C) The product must be unreasonably dangerous.

    (D) The defect must have been in existence when the product left the defendant's control.

    (E) The defendant's actions must be a proximate cause of any injury.

47. Which of the following establishes a minimum wage and policies for overtime?

    (A) The Fair Labor Standards Act

    (B) Worker's compensation

    (C) The Social Security Act

    (D) The Equal Pay Act

    (E) The National Labor Relations Act

48. Which of the following is a distinction that can be drawn between a trial court and an appellate court?

    (A) A trial court does not have a judge, and an appellate court does.

    (B) A trial court hears cases between plaintiffs and defendants, and an appellate court hears cases brought by the prosecution.

    (C) A trial court has a grand jury, and an appellate court has a petit jury.

    (D) A trial court conducts trials, and an appellate court does not.

    (E) A trial court can hear oral arguments, and an appellate court cannot.

49. A court will presume damages for slander for all of the following EXCEPT

    (A) slander suggesting that a person has a loathsome disease

    (B) slander relating to a person's profession

    (C) slander relating to a person's children

    (D) slander suggesting that a person has committed a crime of moral turpitude

    (E) slander suggesting a woman has engaged in unchaste behavior

50. Amy owes Mary $500. Amy has contracted with Ian to walk his dogs, and in exchange Ian has agreed to pay Mary $500. Which of the following describes Mary's relationship to Ian and Amy?

    (A) Mary is an assignee.

    (B) Mary is a creditor beneficiary.

    (C) Mary is a promisor.

    (D) Mary is an incidental beneficiary.

    (E) Mary is an obligor.

51. Which of the following is a goal that expectation damages are designed to achieve?

    (A) Prevent unjust enrichment

    (B) Punish the breaching party

    (C) Give the nonbreaching party the benefit of the bargain

    (D) Return the parties to their original positions

    (E) Refund any expense of the nonbreaching party

52. The principle that judges must make decisions that are consistent with prior case law is known as

    (A) *stare decisis*

    (B) precedent

    (C) federalism

    (D) checks and balances

    (E) domicile

53. Valerie purchased a used computer from Tim for $1,000. Tim told Valerie that the computer was in "A plus" condition. A week later the computer crashed, and a specialist told Valerie that it was beyond repair. If Valerie sues Tim, a court is likely to hold that

    (A) Tim cannot be held liable because he is not a merchant.

    (B) Tim cannot be held liable because the computer was used.

    (C) Tim can be held liable because he did not warn Valerie of any potential defects.

    (D) Tim cannot be held liable because his statement was just an opinion.

    (E) Tim can be held liable because his statement can be verified.

54. Christina is extremely afraid of green vegetables. Knowing of her fear, Brittney placed broccoli and peas all over Christina's car floor and seats. Because Christina had no other choice, she cleaned the vegetables out of the car, but the cleaning caused her extreme distress. If Christina sues Brittney, a court will most likely hold that

    (A) Brittney is liable for intentional infliction of emotional distress

    (B) Brittney is liable for negligence

    (C) Brittney is not liable for intentional infliction of emotional distress because Christina assumed the risk when she cleaned the car

    (D) Brittney is not liable for negligence or intentional infliction of emotional distress because they both depend on the reasonable-person standard

    (E) Brittney is not liable for intentional infliction of emotional distress because her conduct would not be considered extreme by an average person

55. The process of establishing a security interest is known as

    (A) perfection

    (B) attachment

    (C) foreclosure

    (D) redemption

    (E) collateral

56. Which of the following generally forms the basis for an exception to the rule of *respondeat superior*?

    (A) An option contract

    (B) An intentional tort

    (C) Unfair competition

    (D) Slander

    (E) Vicarious liability

57. On Monday Wendy offered to sell Fred her house. On Tuesday Fred drove by Wendy's house and noticed that a "Sold" sign had been put out front. After noticing the sign, Fred quickly called Wendy on his cell phone and told her he was accepting her offer. However, Wendy informed Fred that the house had already to been sold. If Fred sues Wendy to enforce her offer, a court will probably hold that

    (A) Wendy must honor the offer because she did not revoke it in time

    (B) Wendy must honor the offer because only an intended offeree can accept an offer

    (C) Wendy does not have to honor the offer because Fred appeared to have knowledge that the house had been sold prior to trying to accept Wendy's offer

    (D) Wendy does not have to honor the offer to Fred because she made the offer to two people

    (E) Wendy does not have to honor the offer because it has lapsed

58. Which of the following acts protects consumers' financial information?

    (A) The Consumer Protection Act

    (B) The Truth in Lending Act

    (C) The Gramm-Leach Bliley Act

    (D) The Fair Credit Reporting Act

    (E) The Equal Credit Opportunity Act

59. Law that is formed by judges deciding decisions on a case-by-case basis is known as

    (A) common law

    (B) civil law

    (C) judicial law

    (D) code law

    (E) contract law

60. Cerina has entered into a contract with Justin pursuant to which she has paid Justin to mow her mother, Elizabeth's, lawn. Cerina does not owe Elizabeth any money. If Justin fails to mow Elizabeth's lawn, a court will likely hold that

    (A) Elizabeth cannot recover against anyone because she is a donee beneficiary

    (B) Elizabeth cannot recover against anyone because she is an incidental beneficiary

    (C) Cerina can recover against Justin because Elizabeth is a creditor beneficiary

    (D) Elizabeth can recover against Cerina because Elizabeth is a donee beneficiary

    (E) Elizabeth can recover against Justin because she is an intended beneficiary

61. Pretexting means

    (A) obtaining private information to use in an improper manner

    (B) obtaining private information to use in a tort proceeding

    (C) obtaining private information to use in a securities trade

    (D) obtaining private information under false pretenses

    (E) obtaining private financial information under false pretenses

62. Donna wants to place an advertisement for the opening of her store in the newspaper. The ad will announce that her company "sells the best sports apparel in the land." The state of New York wants to prevent Donna from placing the ad. In an action between Donna and the state, a court would probably hold that

    (A) Donna cannot place the ad because advertising is not protected speech

    (B) Donna cannot place the ad if the state can prove that it is false and misleading

    (C) Donna cannot place the ad if the state can prove it would give her a competitive advantage

    (D) the state cannot prevent Donna from placing the ad because it would violate her freedom of speech

    (E) the state cannot prevent Donna from placing the ad because it would constitute an unfair restriction on her trade

63. Which of the following promises would be enforceable by the majority of courts?

    (A) Molly promises to give Linda $500 if Linda promises to stop speeding.

    (B) Linda offers to pay Molly $20; in exchange Molly can either wash Linda's car or "take the money and run."

    (C) Molly washes Linda's car. When Linda returns, Linda promises to pay her.

    (D) Linda announces over the loud speaker in a grocery store that she will pay the first person who agrees to wash her car for a reasonable price. Molly immediately agrees to wash her car for $20.

    (E) Molly agrees to wash Linda's car for $20. Later, Molly tells Linda that she needs $5 extra to wash Linda's car. Linda agrees.

64. Although Michael was not at fault, a lion in his care broke out of his cage and harmed several people. In this case, Michael will most likely be liable for

    (A) negligence

    (B) assault

    (C) strict liability

    (D) battery

    (E) intentional infliction of emotional distress

65. A document containing information that must be delivered to investors before their purchase of a security is called a(n)

    (A) registration statement

    (B) prospectus

    (C) proxy statement

    (D) proxy

    (E) investment contract

66. Carl entered into a contract with Adam to sell him a car. Later Carl discovered that Adam was a minor. As a result, Carl refused to sell Adam the car. If Adam sues Carl, a court would most likely hold that

    (A) the contract is enforceable because Adam has not disaffirmed it

    (B) the contract is unenforceable because Adam is a minor

    (C) the contract is unenforceable because a car is not a necessity

    (D) the contract is unenforceable because no performance has yet been given

    (E) the contract is enforceable so long as Adam looks to be over the age of majority

67. Title VII regulates all the following conduct EXCEPT

    (A) discrimination in promotions based on age

    (B) discrimination in hiring based on sex

    (C) discrimination in firing based on national origin

    (D) discrimination in recruiting based on religion

    (E) discrimination in compensation based on color

68. An agreement among business competitors to restrict the supply of a particular product to increase the price is known as

    (A) price fixing

    (B) production quotas

    (C) exclusive dealing

    (D) exclusive distributor

    (E) exclusive production

69. Which of the following represents a reason to demand assurance?

    (A) Cure

    (B) Cover

    (C) Retraction

    (D) Reasonable uncertainty

    (E) Hindrance

70. A bankruptcy proceeding in which a person transfers all her assets to a trustee so they can be distributed to creditors is called

    (A) a distribution

    (B) a reorganization

    (C) a liquidation

    (D) an adjustment

    (E) an assignment

71. Which of the following is the standard of care for lawyers?

    (A) A lawyer must act as a reasonable person would act.

    (B) A lawyer must act with the knowledge and skill consistent with lawyers in the profession.

    (C) A lawyer must act with the care of lawyers of similar age and intelligence.

    (D) A lawyer must act in the best interests of others.

    (E) A lawyer must do no harm.

72. All of the following are essential elements of a defamation action EXCEPT

    (A) the language at issue must be communicated to a third party

    (B) the language at issue must have a negative impact on the plaintiff's reputation

    (C) the language at issue must concern the plaintiff

    (D) the language at issue must be permanently recorded or written

    (E) the language at issue must damage the plaintiff's reputation

73. On February 1, Reggie entered into a contract to purchase a cake from Connor to be delivered on February 14. On February 3 Reggie had a tragic accident and was judged mentally incompetent by a court. On February 10 Reggie's representative called Connor and informed him that Reggie would not be bound by the contract. If Connor sues Reggie, a court will likely hold that

   (A) Reggie can avoid the contract because a court determined that Reggie was mentally incompetent

   (B) Reggie can avoid the contract because Reggie was not at fault for his accident

   (C) Reggie cannot avoid the contract because the contract terms were fair

   (D) Reggie cannot avoid the contract because Reggie did not disaffirm the contract within a reasonable time

   (E) Reggie cannot avoid the contract because Reggie was mentally competent at the time he entered into the contract

74. A business in which one person has personal liability and the ability to manage the business, while the other person's liability is limited to an investment is called a

   (A) sole proprietorship

   (B) limited liability company

   (C) limited partnership

   (D) limited liability partnership

   (E) general partnership

75. If Brad transfers to Carol his obligation to paint Fatima's house, Brad is called a

   (A) a promisor

   (B) an assignor

   (C) a delegator

   (D) an obligor

   (E) a real party in interest

76. As Ryan was walking down the street, he fainted and hit his head on the pavement, creating a large cut. Gina, a doctor, noticed Ryan's fall and rushed to help Ryan, who was unconscious as a result of the fall. Gina was able to clean and bandage the cut before Ryan regained consciousness. If Gina sues Ryan to recover the cost of her medical services, which of the following would be the basis for recovery?

    I.   Unjust enrichment

    II.  Quasi contract

    III. Breach of contract

    (A) I only

    (B) II only

    (C) III only

    (D) I and II only

    (E) I, II, and III

77. Which of the following statements concerning the Employee Retirement Income Security Act is true?

    (A) It regulates retirement and Social Security.

    (B) It requires employers to appoint an administrator for benefit plans.

    (C) It requires employers to maintain employee benefit plans.

    (D) It requires employees to contribute to employee benefit plans.

    (E) It requires employers to withhold contributions from employees' salaries.

78. All of the following are related to antitrust law EXCEPT

    (A) the Superfund program

    (B) the Sherman Act

    (C) the Clayton Act

    (D) a monopoly

    (E) price discrimination

79. Paul told Mary that if she exercised every day for a month, Paul would pay Mary $500. Mary exercised for a month, but Paul refused to pay Mary. If Mary sues Paul, a court will probably hold that

    (A) Paul is liable because two promises were exchanged

    (B) Paul is not liable because he did not benefit from Mary's actions

    (C) Paul is liable because Mary agreed to do something she was not obligated to do

    (D) Paul is not liable because Mary did not refrain from doing anything

    (E) Paul is liable because Mary has substantially performed

80. Which of the following best defines the duty to mitigate?

    (A) It is an absolute duty to avoid incurring additional costs after a breach.

    (B) It is a duty owed by defendants to make alternative arrangements for the plaintiff in the event of a breach.

    (C) It is a duty owed by the defendant to make substitute arrangements if a breach is anticipated.

    (D) It is not a duty at all, but allows the plaintiff to compel the defendant to make substitute arrangements after a breach.

    (E) It is not a duty at all, but the plaintiff's damages will be reduced if she fails to make reasonable efforts to avoid incurring additional costs after a breach.

81. Ordinarily, an appellate court reverses the judgment of a trial court for

    (A) necessary and proper reasons

    (B) lack of personal jurisdiction

    (C) a clear abuse of discretion

    (D) evidence of judicial errors

    (E) evidence of plaintiff's misstatements

82. Which of the following will apply if a contract represents a full, final, and complete record of the parties' agreement?

    (A) Evidence regarding a condition may be admitted.

    (B) Written evidence of prior commitments may be used to define the agreement.

    (C) Written evidence of prior commitments may be used to define the agreement so long as the evidence is consistent with the agreement.

    (D) Evidence regarding a mistake or fraud may not be admitted.

    (E) Evidence regarding custom or trade usage may not be admitted.

83. All of the following can trigger dissolution of a general partnership EXCEPT the

    (A) bankruptcy of a partner

    (B) end of the partnership term

    (C) expulsion of a partner

    (D) withdrawal of a partner

    (E) admission of a partner

84. Exercising jurisdiction over a person based on that person's minimum contacts within the state is known as

    (A) general jurisdiction

    (B) limited jurisdiction

    (C) consensual jurisdiction

    (D) long-arm jurisdiction

    (E) subject matter jurisdiction

85. James has purchased a product that was manufactured differently from other products. If James sues the manufacturer, which of the following is true?

    (A) James must prove that the product could have been designed to eliminate the danger without impairing its function.

    (B) James must prove that the average customer would view the product as unreasonably dangerous.

    (C) James must prove he is a bona fide purchaser.

    (D) James must prove the product lacked sufficient warning.

    (E) James must prove that the product could have been designed more safely.

86. Jack entered into a contract with Phil stating that Jack would pay Phil's band $10,000 to play at his graduation party so long as Jack had received RSVPs from at least 30 percent of his guests within a week. Jack sent his invitations late. As a result, Jack only had received 10 percent of the RSVPs at the end of the week. Which of the following regarding the contract between Jack and Phil is true?

    (A) If Jack refused to allow Phil to perform, Phil could sue Jack for breach of contract.

    (B) If Jack refused to allow Phil to perform, Phil could sue Jack for specific performance.

    (C) Neither Jack nor Phil has an obligation to perform under the contract.

    (D) Phil has an obligation to perform so long as he reaffirms his intention to pay Jack.

    (E) Phil has an obligation to wait a reasonable period of time to determine if more people will RSVP.

87. Which of the following takes a contract out of the Statute of Frauds?

    I.   Admission

    II.  Performance

    III. Consent

    (A) I only

    (B) II only

    (C) I and II only

    (D) I and III only

    (E) I, II, and III

88. Cindy was fired from her job through no fault of her own. Which of the following statements is true?

    (A) Cindy is not entitled to any compensation.

    (B) Cindy is not entitled to any compensation unless she contributed to a benefits plan.

    (C) Cindy will be compensated under the Equal Pay Act.

    (D) Cindy will be compensated under her state's unemployment compensation program.

    (E) Cindy will be compensated under her state's Workers Compensation program.

89. Which of the following represents a basis for excusing a condition?

    (A) One party has interfered with the other party's ability to perform the condition.

    (B) The party who is obligated to perform the condition informs the other party of the intention not to perform within a reasonable time.

    (C) It becomes difficult to satisfy the condition.

    (D) Performance has begun, even if it is not substantial.

    (E) The condition is not material.

90. Which of the following is an essential element of battery?

    (A) Severe physical injury

    (B) Knowledge of the battery

    (C) Reasonable fear of harm

    (D) Duty of care

    (E) Intent to cause contact

91. Barry and Sarah have decided to sell cookies together for a profit. They do not have a written agreement but have orally agreed that Barry will receive 60 percent of the profits. Which of the following best defines their relationship?

    (A) Limited liability partnership

    (B) Limited partnership

    (C) General partnership

    (D) Limited liability company

    (E) Sole proprietorship

92. The prosecution in a criminal case must prove the case

    (A) beyond a doubt

    (B) beyond a reasonable doubt

    (C) by a plurality of the evidence

    (D) by a preponderance of the evidence

    (E) by a majority of the evidence

93. Calvin and Ricky both have a security interest in a piece of property. In determining whose interest gets priority, which of the following statements is true?

    (A) If Ricky was granted his interest first, then he has priority.

    (B) If the interest relates to land, a court must determine who gets priority.

    (C) If Ricky took possession first, he has priority.

    (D) If Ricky filed evidence of his interest first, he has priority.

    (E) If Ricky took possession prior to learning of a filing by Calvin, Ricky has priority.

94. Which of the following regulates imports and tariff rates?

    (A) The Federal Communications Commission

    (B) The Department of Commerce

    (C) The National Labor Relations Board

    (D) The Bureau of Customs and Border Patrol

    (E) The Federal Trade Commission

95. If a plaintiff has contributed to her own negligence, which of the following is true?

    (A) Her remedy will be reduced by the amount of damages caused by her own negligence.

    (B) Her remedy will be reduced to the cost of bringing suit.

    (C) She will be barred from any recovery.

    (D) She will be barred from recovery unless her actions were reasonable.

    (E) She will be barred from recovery, but only if she is bringing an action based on an intentional tort.

96. Brian has contracted with Sherry to build Sherry a new home. After the house is complete, Sherry notices that the tiles in the bathroom shower are a different color from the tiles she requested. If Sherry refuses to pay Brian, a court is likely to hold that

    (A) Sherry is not entitled to withhold her performance because construction has been completed

    (B) Sherry is not entitled to withhold her performance because Brian has substantially performed

    (C) Sherry is entitled to withhold her performance because once construction is complete, the breach becomes total

    (D) Sherry is entitled to withhold her performance because Brian did not get her consent to change the tiles

    (E) Sherry is entitled to withhold her performance because Brian breached by failing to perform in accordance with the contract

97. A motion made after the plaintiff has presented her case and before the defendant presents her defense or claims is known as

    (A) demurrer

    (B) summary judgment

    (C) directed verdict

    (D) motion to strike

    (E) judgment n.o.v.

98. A buyer has accepted a contract, but added additional terms. If both parties are merchants, the terms will be part of the contract EXCEPT if

    (A) the offer was limited to acceptance of its terms

    (B) the additional terms materially alter the contract

    (C) the additional terms are inconsistent with custom

    (D) the seller rejects the additional terms within a reasonable time

    (E) the seller previously rejected the additional terms

99. Which of the following was the first international agreement on trading rules?

    (A) The Uniform Commercial Code

    (B) The Export Trading Act

    (C) The General Agreement on Tariffs and Trades

    (D) The North Atlantic Free Trade Agreement

    (E) The World Trade Organization

100. Elton owns a bakery shop and has entered into an agreement with John in which he has agreed to buy all the cookies John makes for the next year. This agreement is

    (A) an illusory promise

    (B) void because it lacks mutual obligation

    (C) void for lack of consideration

    (D) void because its terms are uncertain

    (E) valid and enforceable

# CLEP INTRODUCTORY BUSINESS LAW PRACTICE TEST 1

## ═══ **Answer Key** ═══

| | | | |
|---|---|---|---|
| 1. (C) | 26. (D) | 51. (C) | 76. (D) |
| 2. (D) | 27. (C) | 52. (A) | 77. (B) |
| 3. (B) | 28. (E) | 53. (E) | 78. (A) |
| 4. (E) | 29. (B) | 54. (A) | 79. (C) |
| 5. (D) | 30. (C) | 55. (B) | 80. (E) |
| 6. (E) | 31. (A) | 56. (B) | 81. (C) |
| 7. (B) | 32. (D) | 57. (C) | 82. (A) |
| 8. (A) | 33. (E) | 58. (C) | 83. (E) |
| 9. (A) | 34. (C) | 59. (A) | 84. (D) |
| 10. (C) | 35. (D) | 60. (E) | 85. (B) |
| 11. (D) | 36. (B) | 61. (D) | 86. (A) |
| 12. (B) | 37. (E) | 62. (B) | 87. (C) |
| 13. (E) | 38. (A) | 63. (D) | 88. (D) |
| 14. (A) | 39. (A) | 64. (C) | 89. (A) |
| 15. (B) | 40. (C) | 65. (B) | 90. (E) |
| 16. (C) | 41. (D) | 66. (A) | 91. (C) |
| 17 (E) | 42. (C) | 67. (A) | 92. (B) |
| 18. (C) | 43. (B) | 68. (B) | 93. (D) |
| 19. (D) | 44. (B) | 69. (D) | 94. (D) |
| 20. (A) | 45. (E) | 70. (C) | 95. (A) |
| 21. (C) | 46. (B) | 71. (B) | 96. (B) |
| 22. (B) | 47. (A) | 72. (D) | 97. (C) |
| 23. (B) | 48. (D) | 73. (E) | 98. (C) |
| 24. (A) | 49. (C) | 74. (C) | 99. (C) |
| 25. (D) | 50. (B) | 75. (C) | 100. (E) |

# DETAILED EXPLANATIONS OF ANSWERS

## PRACTICE TEST 1

1.    **(C)**   Deontological theories are based on the notion that ethical behavior is guided by duties or obligations. Although "categorical imperative" refers to an ethical concept based on the deontological theory created by Immanuel Kant, "imperatives" (E) is not an ethical theory. In contrast, to deontological theories, consequentialism (B) views ethical behavior in terms of its consequences. Utilitarianism (A) is a consequentialist theory that maintains that actions should be judged on whether they maximize the good of everyone. Due process (D) refers to the notion, based on constitutional provisions, that people should receive a fair and just process.

2.    **(D)**   An agreement requiring a buyer to sell or resell products to a particular manufacturer is referred to as an exclusive dealing agreement and is a potential violation of antitrust rules. Because the agreement is between a buyer and a seller, it is a vertical agreement. Horizontal agreements (E) are agreements between business competitors. Similarly, a production quota (A) and a market division transaction (C) are forms of horizontal agreements. Although a tie-in (B) is a form of vertical agreement, it refers to an agreement in which a seller agrees to sell a product to a customer but only on the condition that the customer purchases a different product.

3.    **(B)**   The available defenses for intentional torts are consent, self-defense, and defense of others. Because it involves a deliberate act designed to cause some harm, assumption of risk (A) is not an available defense for intentional torts. Both undue influence (C) and mistake (D) are incorrect because they are defenses to the enforcement of contracts. *Res ipsa loquitor* (E) is not a defense but a method of establishing a breach of duty in a negligence action.

4. **(E)** Paula would likely bring suit against Simon for negligence because he was driving above the speed limit and therefore violating his duty of reasonable care. One of the defenses to negligence focuses on the extent to which a plaintiff has contributed to her own injuries, which is the case here since Paula also violated her duty to exercise reasonable care by crossing without using the crosswalk. Historically, a plaintiff's negligence barred her recovery and hence it was an absolute defense. Such a total bar was known as contributory negligence. However, most modern courts allow a comparative negligence defense that reduces a plaintiff's recovery based on the extent of her negligence. Thus, (E) is correct, while (A) is incorrect. (D) is also incorrect because in a comparative negligence regime, Paula's negligent actions will be taken into account and thus she will not likely recover for all of her damages. Unless she behaved unreasonably, most jurisdictions that apply a comparative negligence standard do not allow assumption of risk (B) to bar a plaintiff's recovery. The notion that Paula implicitly consented to her action is similar to a claim of implied assumption of risk because it suggests that Paula knowingly engaged in behavior despite its danger, thereby implicitly consenting to the risk of that behavior. When that occurs, there is an implicit assumption of risk, making (C) incorrect for the same reasons that (B) is incorrect.

5. **(D)** Whenever an exchange is completely instantaneous, such that each party has fully performed and does not make any promises, the transaction is not a contract but an executed exchange. Both (B) and (C) are incorrect because they are actual contracts. A promise (A) is a commitment to act and because the transaction occurred instantly, neither Nancy nor Cynthia made a commitment. A quasi contract (E) is not a contract but a transaction that gives rise to an award for unjust enrichment. Since no party has received a benefit that she did not deserve, (E) is also incorrect.

6. **(E)** A summons is a notice that the defendant is being sued. Each option represents an action that a defendant may take on receiving a summons.

7. **(B)** A contract with a minor is voidable by the minor during the time she is a minor and for a reasonable period after she reaches majority. Stacy disaffirmed the contract one day after she reached majority. Although there is no specific rule regarding what constitutes a reasonable time, it is likely that a court would hold that one day is reasonable. (A) is incorrect because it suggests that any contract a minor enters into will be enforceable. There are exceptions for items of necessity as well as the limit for contracts in which

a person enters into but does not disaffirm once she reaches majority. In a contract with a minor, the minor has the responsibility to return anything in her possession. However, if it has been destroyed, the minor can still avoid the contract and have no further obligations. Thus (C) is incorrect. The rule with regard to contracts with minors is absolute, and so long as a person is a minor at the time of the contract (D), she will have the opportunity to avoid. (E) is incorrect because although a minor cannot avoid contracts for necessities, necessity is usually defined as something necessary for a person's livelihood, and it is not likely that a motorcycle falls into that category.

8.   **(A)**   The Superfund program was established by the Comprehensive Environmental Response Compensation and Liability Act, known as CER-CLA, to help clean up hazardous waste. Thus, (A) is correct. (B), (C), (D), and (E) are incorrect.

9.   **(A)**   In a trial court, juries deliver the verdict, while judges preside over the trial. Answer choices (B), (C), (D), and (E) reflect functions that a trial judge undertakes in order to facilitate the trial process.

10.   **(C)**   The Uniform Commercial Code ("UCC") provides additional damage remedies for buyers and sellers of goods. For instance, the UCC grants a buyer the ability to make reasonable purchases of substitute goods in the event of a breach, a process known as cover. "Cure" (A) refers to a buyer's ability to replace nonconforming goods with goods that satisfy the contract term. (B) is incorrect because the buyer does not waive or give up any rights when engaging in cover. "Promissory estoppel" (D) represents the ability to enforce a contract without consideration when a party has justifiably relied on it. "Revocation" (E) refers to the right to terminate or take back something and in this context it refers to the right to terminate acceptance.

11.   **(D)**   Emma will likely sue Sharon based on the tort of interference with business relations because Sharon interfered in Emma's potential economic relationship with Todd. Tort requires that the defendant have knowledge of the business relationship. It does not require that the plaintiff and defendant have a relationship with each other, but rather that the defendant interfere in a relationship that the plaintiff has with someone else. Thus both (A) and (B) are incorrect. In addition, the tort of interference applies to formal relationships as well as expected relationships. It does not matter that Emma and Todd did not execute a contract (C), so long as there is a genuine expected relationship when there is a reasonable expectation of a financial

benefit. (E) is incorrect because Sharon's good faith is irrelevant—Emma need only prove that she deliberately interfered, even if she did so for a good reason.

12. **(B)** The Securities Act requires registration of any sale of securities, unless there is an exemption. Regulation D is an exemption that allows corporations to sell their securities to certain sophisticated investors, known as accredited investors. Regulation S (A) refers to an exemption for offerings that occur primarily outside the United States. Rule 10b-5 (C) is an anti-fraud provision that prohibits deceptive practices associated with securities offerings. Moreover, it is a provision of the Securities Exchange Act. Rule 701 (D) relates to an exemption for certain offerings to employees. Section 11 (E) imposes liability for material misstatements or omissions in a registration statement.

13. **(E)** A quasi contract is not a contract at all, but a transaction that allows a plaintiff to recover damages when she has relied to her detriment on a promise that is not supported by any consideration. Since they do not capture the true meaning of a quasi-contract, (A) and (B) are not the best responses. Quasi-contracts are sometimes referred to as contracts that are "implied in law" to refer to the notion that a court implies the contract for purposes of providing some legal remedy. A contract that is implied in fact (C) is an actual contract that is implied based on the facts and circumstances of a given situation. While damages will be awarded when there has been some justified reliance on a person's promise, the recovery for a quasi-contract is not reliance damages (D).

14. **(A)** Because it implicates Ruby's speech rights, the state's actions must be reviewed to determine if they are prohibited by the First Amendment. The state's review of Ruby's newsletter is clearly designed to regulate its content—by making sure the content is consistent with the state's views. When a government action is aimed at regulating the content of speech, it is subject to strict scrutiny. Time, place, and manner restrictions (B) refer to restrictions regarding processes, such as those requiring that a person speak only during certain times or in certain locations. The state's actions do not reflect such procedural-based restrictions. (C) is incorrect because a suspect classification does not just relate to classification by race or color, but includes laws that impact a fundamental right, such as the freedom to speak. (D) is incorrect because while a state must demonstrate (depending on the scrutiny applied) a compelling or important reason for its act in order for the court to uphold the restriction, a state's rationale for engaging in a

particular act does not impact the type of scrutiny a court uses. (E) is incorrect not only because this does not appear to be commercial speech but also because restrictions on commercial speech merit strict review when they focus on content.

15. **(B)** The Family Medical Leave Act requires employers to give their employees time off for certain family and medical emergencies, which includes caring for family members. The Fair Labor Standards Act (A) establishes minimum wage and overtime. The National Leave Act (C) does not exist. The National Labor Relations Act (D) regulates collective bargaining matters. Worker's compensation (E) provides compensation for work-related injuries.

16. **(C)** The rule of reason refers to a standard of analysis used to determine if agreements violate the Sherman Act's prohibition on restrictive trade practices or monopolies. Since none of the other responses refer to trade practices or monopolies, they are incorrect.

17. **(E)** Since the sale of the clock constitutes a sale of goods, it is regulated by the UCC. The UCC implies various warranties in every sale, including the warranty of merchantability. That warranty creates an implicit promise that the goods will be fit for their ordinary use. Because an alarm clock's ordinary use is to provide an alarm, Edward's sale appears to have violated this warranty. The UCC provides that the warranty can be waived if it is in writing, conspicuous, and mentions merchantability. Selling a good "as is" (A) is not enough to waive the warranty—it must comply with these other UCC requirements. (B) is incorrect because Edward can be held liable based on implied warranties under the UCC. (C) is incorrect because Ivan only needs to show that the goods were not fit for their ordinary purpose to prove a violation of the warranty. Reliance on Edward's skill and judgment is an element necessary for the implied warranty of fitness of a particular purpose, not the warranty of merchantability. Similarly, (D) is incorrect because it does not state the requirement of mentioning merchantability.

18. **(C)** A partnership relationship is an agency relationship and is therefore governed by the principles of authority. Actual authority can arise by acquiescence when a principal knows about an agent's actions but does not object to them. Because Len knew of Eric's actions but did not object to them, he is deemed to have acquiesced and given Eric implied actual authority. With regard to implied actual authority, a partner's acquiescence is viewed as implicit consent. Thus Len's express consent was not necessary and (A)

is incorrect. Authority can be given without a written agreement, making (B) incorrect. While partners have equal management rights (D), that fact alone does not confer authority. Because actual authority involves the relationship between the principal and the agent—and in the case of partnerships, between the partners—it does not matter what third parties believe (E). Instead, third parties' beliefs implicate apparent authority.

19. **(D)** Self-defense is a defense a defendant can raise to avoid liability for intentional torts. A defendant's use of force cannot be excessive, which means she may use only the amount of force that is reasonably necessary to protect herself. A defendant must believe that her actions are necessary to protect herself from harm, but she does not have to fear for her life (A). While older doctrine required that a defendant attempt to retreat (B) before using self-defense, modern courts do not have a retreat requirement. When the defendant uses force, the only requirement is that it should be reasonable. Hence a defendant can both intend to cause (C) and cause harm (E).

20. **(A)** The Fair Debt Collection Act prohibits abusive and unfair collection practices. The Fair Credit Reporting Act (B) regulates credit report agencies. The Equal Credit Opportunity Act (C) and the Consumer Protection Act (E) do not exist. The Truth in Lending Act (D) ensures that there is fair disclosure of credit terms.

21. **(C)** An assignment represents a transfer of a right, while delegation represents a transfer of a duty. Both assignment and delegation relate to contracts that transfer a right as well as benefiting a third party. Thus (A), (B), and (D) are incorrect. Neither assignment nor delegation terminates the rights of parties who do not consent to them. For example, the obligor in an assignment continues to have rights and obligations under the contract, even though her consent is not required for the assignment. Thus (E) is not a correct response.

22. **(B)** The Statute of Frauds requires contracts that fall within its coverage to be in writing and signed by the person sought to be bound. Thus, (B) is the correct response, while (D) and (E) are incorrect. The Statute of Frauds has no impact on rules of evidence. Instead, the rule regarding the kinds of information that can be admitted into evidence is the Parol Evidence Rule, making (A) incorrect. Contracts involving the sale of goods for *more than* $500 fall within the Statute of Frauds. A contract that is less than that amount (C) does not.

23. **(B)**  A material breach allows a nonbreaching party to suspend performance and await cure. However, the party cannot terminate the contract. Moreover, while the nonbreaching party can sue for damages, she cannot sue for the full contract price because the contract has not yet been terminated.

24. **(A)**  In a design defect case, in order to show a breach of duty for negligence, it must be established that the defendant knew or should have known that the design was defective. (B) is incorrect because a defendant's liability in negligence actions does not depend on her status. A products liability action also can be brought as an intentional tort or under strict liability. In order to prove liability for an intentional tort, it must be shown that a defendant intended to cause harm or knew that it was likely to occur. Thus, a defendant's lack of knowledge may bar an intentional tort claim as well. However, strict liability imposes liability regardless of fault so the defendant may still be held liable despite her lack of knowledge, so (C) is incorrect. (D) is incorrect because disclaimers do not allow defendants to avoid product liability actions based on strict liability. While strict liability is imposed without fault, it does require that the product was unreasonably dangerous and that the defect existed when it left the defendant's control. Thus, (E) is incorrect.

25. **(D)**  Title VII of the Civil Rights Act prohibits employment discrimination based on sex and other specified criteria. This includes a prohibition on quid pro quo, which is requesting favors in exchange for some employment benefit. Because Julie's circumstances represent quid pro quo, she would bring a claim under Title VII. Since Julie's boss's statement is more properly characterized as a violation of Title VII, she would not bring a negligence action (A). The Due Process Clause (B) only applies to establishing a fair process whenever someone may be deprived of life, liberty, or property. The National Labor Relations Act (C) regulates collective bargaining matters. The Equal Employment Act (E) does not exist.

26. **(D)**  Creditors have various collection rights, including the right to take possession of a debtor's property. When a creditor takes possession of the property, she can either hold it until repayment is made or sell it to recover the money owed. However, the creditor does not have the right to occupy the property.

27. **(C)**  Article I of the Constitution establishes the legislative branch. Article II establishes the executive branch (A), while Article III establishes the judiciary (B). The Bill of Rights (D) represents the first 10 amendments

of the Constitution. The Supreme Court (E), as part of the judiciary, was established by Article III.

28. **(E)** To form a contract, there must be mutual assent, but mutual assent is an objective standard. This means that mutual assent will be determined based on whether a reasonable person could construe the words and conduct of the parties as assent, rather than based on the subjective or secretive intent of the parties. Thus, the fact that Renée was joking suggests that she did not have a subjective intent to enter into a contract. However, subjective intent does not matter because Renée failed to tell Daryll that she was joking. Instead, an objective assessment of her words indicated that she intended to enter into a contract. (A) and (B) are incorrect because at best Renée's disclosure to Daryll that she was joking is an attempt at revocation. However, Daryll's promise to pay $50,000 represented acceptance. Thus, if it is a revocation, her disclosure is too late to terminate the offer. Then too, with regard to (A), it does not matter that Renée told Daryll before he made payment because a contract has been formed based on Daryll's promise to make payment. (C) is incorrect because mutual assent is an objective standard and Renée cannot avoid the contract just because she secretly was pretending to make an offer if a reasonable person would believe that her words objectively demonstrated an intent to make an offer. (D) is not the best answer because the validity of a contract does not turn on the adequacy of consideration.

29. **(B)** Whether or not a party can bring a lawsuit depends on whether the party has standing, which means a legally recognizable claim that reveals an injury in fact. Jurisdiction (A) represents the ability of a court to hear a case, while venue (C) relates to determining whether the defendant has selected the appropriate court within a given geographic area. Domicile (D) refers to the place that is considered to be a person's or entities' permanent residence. Attachment (E) does not relate to court procedures at all but to a secured transaction and the process by which a security interest is established.

30. **(C)** Section 7A of the Clayton Act, known as the Hart-Scott-Rodino Act, regulates monopolies and unfair competition. In connection with that regulation, parties who want to merge must get approval from the U.S. Justice Department under the Hart-Scott-Rodino Act. The business judgment rule (A) refers to a standard of analysis for determining if directors or officers have breached their fiduciary duty. A vertical agreement (B) is an agreement between a buyer and a seller, not a potential merger.

The Robinson-Patman Act (D) regulates price discrimination. The Sarbanes-Oxley Act (E) does not relate to monopolistic power but is an act that amends provisions of the federal securities laws to improve certain disclosures and increase accountability.

31. **(A)** The doctrine of *respondeat superior* makes employers liable for their employees' actions that are taken within the scope of business. However, the frolic and detour doctrine maintains that when an employee substantially deviates from the course of her employment duties, an employer will avoid liability. (B) is not as strong an answer because an employer will be held liable for actions taken in the course of small deviations. Because an employer will be held liable regardless of her consent, (C) is not the best answer. Moreover, while ratification may create liability, frolic and detour does not focus on issues of ratification. (E) is incorrect because frolic and detour pinpoints exceptions to the general rule of employer liability.

32. **(D)** The Supreme Court will only grant a writ of certiorari in rare circumstances. One of those situations includes questions of importance, such as conflict among states on important questions. The Supreme Court generally does not grant *certiorari* for errors or mistakes. Hence, (A) and (E) are incorrect. The Supreme Court also does not grant certiorari just because cases involve federal statutes (B) or foreign citizens (C).

33. **(E)** When an offeree pays the offeror to keep an offer open, she creates an option contract. The option contract makes the offer irrevocable for the period of the option. A quasi contract (A) is not a contract at all. An executory contract (B) is one in which both parties continue to have performance obligations. It is not a term used to define contracts at formation. A unilateral contract (C) is one in which, at the time of formation, there is only one performance duty remaining. In contrast, a bilateral contract (D) refers to a contract where there are two promises remaining at the time of contract formation.

34. **(C)** Personal jurisdiction refers to the ability of a court to exercise power over the parties to a case. It can be created in four ways: a person's physical presence, residency or domicile, consent, or minimum contacts. Venue refers to the proper court within a particular geographic area in which an action must be litigated. Thus, venue cannot be used to establish jurisdiction.

35. **(D)** Under the mailbox rule, acceptance is effective on dispatch. Thus, (D) is correct because the first thing Leslie mailed was an acceptance, and this mailing creates a contract at the point it is sent. (A) is incorrect because Leslie's assent will be determined based on which communication is deemed to be effective first. (B) is incorrect because although rejection is effective on receipt, acceptance is effective on dispatch and the acceptance was mailed first. (C) is incorrect because acceptance is effective on dispatch so it does not matter if the acceptance was received after the rejection was received. (E) is incorrect. The mailbox rule is not effective when a rejection is sent before an acceptance is sent. However, when two communications are sent, but the acceptance is sent first, the mailbox rule applies, and the acceptance will be effective.

36. **(B)** The World Trade Organization ("WTO") is an organization of more than 100 countries that seeks to promote fair trade by facilitating dialogue between countries and generating agreed-on trading rules. Thus (B) is correct, and both (A) and (C) are incorrect. The WTO does not provide financial assistance (D). Financial assistance is provided by such entities as the World Bank and the International Monetary Fund. The WTO has no investigative powers (E).

37. **(E)** Courts interpret contracts that contain a provision prohibiting assignment as a restriction on delegation. This means that such a provision does not invalidate assignments. Instead, any assignment made pursuant to such an agreement is valid and enforceable, but it constitutes a breach of contract. (A) is incorrect because the assignment is valid. In addition, an assignment can occur without the obligor's consent, which means that (B) is incorrect. Because the assignment is valid, Tammy cannot terminate the contract (C). Finally, while an obligor must be given notice after the assignment so she can know to whom she owes a performance duty, notice does not have to be given before assignment (D).

38. **(A)** State courts are courts of general jurisdiction, which means they can hear any case that is not specifically reserved to the federal courts. The only cases specifically reserved to the federal courts—that is, where the federal courts have exclusive jurisdiction—are cases arising under the Constitution, federal laws, or federal treaties. All other cases are decisions that state courts can hear. This includes cases over which federal courts can exercise diversity jurisdiction, such as cases involving citizens of a foreign country for matters exceeding $75,000.

39. **(A)** Ron and Noah have entered into a unilateral contract because Ron's performance and acceptance are the same action. Ordinarily, an offer can be revoked any time before acceptance. However, under a unilateral contract, the offeror—in this case Noah—must give the offeree the opportunity to complete performance once performance has begun. Thus, (A) is correct, and by extension (E) is incorrect. Noah does not have to pay Ron until Ron's performance has been completed or there has been some breach by Noah, so (B) is not the best answer. The contract is not illusory (C) because a promise has been exchanged for a performance. (D) is incorrect because mutual assent is judged at the time of contract formation and the contract was already formed.

40. **(C)** The Fifth Amendment restricts the government from taking private property without sufficiently compensating the owner of the property. Courts have construed this prohibition to include actions that amount to actual possession of property as well as actions that undermine the value of a person's property. Because the state's action could be considered "taking," (C) is the correct response. The First Amendment (A) relates to the freedom of speech, assembly, and religion. The Second Amendment (B) covers the right to keep and bear arms. The Equal Protection Clause (D) relates to nondiscrimination. The Commerce Clause (E) gives Congress the right to regulate interstate commerce.

41. **(D)** Under the UCC, the buyer's expression will be viewed as an acceptance coupled with a proposal for inclusion. The knock-out rule (A) is applied when the buyer's expression includes different terms. The UCC provides a different rule regarding additional terms when the contracting parties are merchants. However, the rule does not impact acceptance. Instead, regardless of the buyer's identity, an expression with additional terms will be construed as an acceptance. Thus (B) is incorrect. Both modern law and the UCC have rejected the mirror-image rule (C), which required replies to match the offer exactly to be construed as an acceptance. Under common law, a reply with materially different terms is treated as a rejection and a counteroffer. However, the UCC changes this rule; thus (E) is incorrect.

42. **(C)** *Res ipsa loquitor* is Latin for "the thing itself speaks" and is a doctrine for establishing breach of a duty. Proximate cause (A) is one of the required elements of negligence. Transferred intent (B) refers to the notion that a defendant's intent to commit an intentional tort can be transferred either from one party to another or from one action to another. *Prima facie* (D) refers to the elements a plaintiff must prove to establish

her case. *Respondeat superior* (E) represents a doctrine that makes employers liable for the actions of their employees that occur within the scope of employment.

43. **(B)** The writ of habeas corpus refers to a defendant's request for a new proceeding to challenge an unlawful detention. (B) is correct because habeas corpus can only be used by people in custody. This means (A) and (C) are incorrect. Defendants in civil cases are not eligible for habeas corpus review because they are not taken into custody, making (D) and (E) incorrect.

44. **(B)** Under the UCC, all goods will be deemed as accepted if a buyer fails to reject them within a reasonable time after having the opportunity to inspect them. This means that a buyer will be liable for goods even when she does not explicitly indicate her acceptance. Thus, (A) is incorrect. (C) and (D) are incorrect because the UCC gives buyers time to reject goods within a reasonable period after delivery. (E) is incorrect because the buyer's acceptance covers all goods, even those that are nonconforming.

45. **(E)** The business judgment rule represents the idea that directors and officers are in the best position to make decisions and gives directors the presumption that their decisions are made in good faith. The business judgment rule views directors and officers, and not judges, as in the best position to make business decisions. Thus (A) is not correct. (B) is also not correct because the business judgment rule gives directors and officers significant discretion in their conduct. (C) is not correct because the business judgment rule presumes that directors and officers use good business judgment. (D) is incorrect because the rule does not relate to market pressures.

46. **(B)** A products liability claim based on strict liability requires that the defendant be a commercial supplier, that the product reach the consumer in the same condition it was supplied, that the product be unreasonably dangerous, that the defect be in existence when the product left the defendant's control, and that the defect was the proximate cause of injury. (B) is the correct response because it is not one of these elements.

47. **(A)** The Fair Labor Standards Act sets a federal minimum wage and overtime policies. Workers' Compensation (B) relates to compensation for work-related injuries. The Social Security Act (C) provides retirement benefits, and the Equal Pay Act (D) prohibits discrimination in pay

based on sex. The National Labor Relations Act (E) governs collective bargaining and not wages.

48. **(D)** An appellate court reviews decisions of the lower courts and thus does not hold trials. Although the trial judge does not render a verdict, both trial and appellate courts have judges which means (A) is not correct. Criminal cases are brought by the prosecution, while civil cases involve both a plaintiff and defendant. However, both trial courts and appeals courts hear civil and criminal cases, so (B) is incorrect. A grand jury decides whether a criminal case should go to trial and, once at trial, a petit jury hears the evidence. Thus (C) is not correct. Because an appellate court hears oral arguments, (E) is incorrect.

49. **(C)** A court presumes damages for slander, which is oral defamation, in all the situations other than slander regarding a person's child.

50. **(B)** Amy and Ian have entered into a contract that benefits a third party, Mary. When the beneficiary (Mary) is owed a debt that the contract is designed to repay, the beneficiary is known as a creditor beneficiary. Because Amy owes Mary money, Mary is a creditor beneficiary. An assignee (A) is the person to whom a right is assigned under an assignment. The promisor (C) is the person who must give performance under a third party beneficiary contract to a third party. In this case, the promisor is Ian, who is going to pay money to Mary. An incidental beneficiary (D) is someone who is not an intended beneficiary and has no rights under the agreement. An obligor (E) is the person who has an obligation to perform on behalf of the assignee in an assignment.

51. **(C)** Expectation damages are designed to give the nonbreaching party what was "expected" under the contract. Thus, (C) is correct because expectation damages are designed to provide the benefit of the bargain. (A) is incorrect because unjust enrichment damages are awarded through restitution. (B) is incorrect because contract damages are aimed at compensation, not punishment. (D) is incorrect because expectation damages seek to approximate where the parties would have been if performance had occurred. (E) is incorrect because reliance damages, not expectation damages, seek to refund any expenses incurred.

52. **(A)** *Stare decisis* is the principle that compels judges to follow prior decisions. Precedents (B) are the prior decisions that must be followed. Federalism (C) is the notion that the state and federal governments share power.

Checks and balances (D) refers to the notion that each of the three branches of government balance the authority of the other branches. Domicile (E) refers to permanent residency.

53. **(E)** The UCC applies when there is a sale of goods valued at more than $500, which is the case with regard to this computer. Pursuant to the UCC, there are both implied and express warranties. In this case, Tim's comment regarding "A plus" condition may be construed as an express warranty because it suggested that the computer was in top condition and could be verified. The UCC applies to all sellers of goods, and thus (A) is incorrect. Indeed, it does not matter that the goods are not new (B). Because warning does not serve to waive an express warranty, (C) is not correct. It is possible that one could attempt to construe Tim's words as an opinion (D), but since the words suggest a high quality and are verifiable (E), it is more likely that courts will hold that they constitute a warranty.

54. **(A)** Ordinarily, intentional infliction of emotional distress and negligence require application of a reasonable-person standard. Hence, overly sensitive people may not be able to prove their claims unless their claims would be consistent with a rational person. However, when a defendant knows of a person's sensitivity and exploits it, the defendant may be held liable. In this case Brittney knew of Christina's fear and intentionally preyed on it. As a result, it is likely Brittney will be held liable for intentionally causing Christina emotional distress. (B) is not the best response because Christina did not suffer any physical harm, which is required by negligence. (C) is not the correct response because assumption of risk is not a defense for an intentional tort. Again, (D) is not the best response because this situation likely represents an exception to the reasonable person standard. (E) is not correct because it is essentially the same rationale as (D).

55. **(B)** To establish a security, there must be attachment. Perfection (A) refers to the process of ensuring that the creditor's interest receives priority. (C) is incorrect because foreclosure is the process of taking possession of real property that is subject to a mortgage. Redemption (D) refers to the creditor's right to pay the full amount of her debt and recover her foreclosed property. Collateral (E) is the property in which a security interest is granted.

56. **(B)** Ordinarily, an employer is held liable for the actions of an employee within the regular course of business. However, when an employee commits an intentional tort, the employer is generally not liable. The doctrines

specified in (A), (C), and (D) do not apply to this context. (E) is incorrect because vicarious liability is the general doctrine that one person will be held liable for another person's torts, so it is not an exception to *respondeat superior*.

57. **(C)** An offer can be revoked before acceptance. Revocation can be direct or indirect. An offer is revoked indirectly when the offeree has knowledge of reliable information that the offeror has taken actions inconsistent with a continued offer. Thus (C) is the correct answer because Fred appears to have knowledge that Wendy took actions inconsistent with his offer. In this respect, Wendy's revocation occurred before Fred's acceptance. (A) is incorrect because Wendy did revoke in time, even though her revocation was indirect. (B) is incorrect because while only an intended offeree can accept an offer, Fred is no longer the only intended offeree when Wendy makes an offer to someone else. If Wendy makes an offer to two people (D) in a manner suggesting that each person has the ability to accept, then both people have offers that can form the basis of a contract. The fact that Wendy has apparently made two offers does not determine which contract she must honor. (E) is not correct because there are no facts to indicate that the offer has lapsed. An offer lapses after a reasonable time has passed, and in this case there is only one day between the offer and acceptance.

58. **(C)** The Gramm-Leach Bliley Act protects consumers' personal information. The Consumer Protection Act (A) and the Equal Credit Opportunity Act (E) do not exist. The Truth in Lending Act (B) ensures that there is fair disclosure of credit terms. The Fair Credit Reporting Act (D) regulates credit reporting agencies.

59. **(A)** Common law is law formed through judicial decision making. Civil law (B) refers to law that is made with reference to a code. Judicial law (C) does not exist. Code law (D) is another term for civil law. Contract law (E) refers to the law that governs contracts.

60. **(E)** In a third-party beneficiary contract, only intended donees can recover. Elizabeth is an intended beneficiary because her right to performance is recognized by the contract between Cerina and Justin. However, there are two forms of intended beneficiaries, donee beneficiaries and creditor beneficiaries. Elizabeth is a donee beneficiary because she has not been made a beneficiary in order for Cerina to repay her money that is owed her. A donee beneficiary can bring suit against the promisor but not the promisee. This means Elizabeth can bring suit against Justin because he is the promisor. Thus

(E) is correct and (A) is incorrect. (B) is also incorrect because Elizabeth is an intended beneficiary and not an incidental beneficiary, who is someone that is not recognized and does not have rights under the contract. Because Elizabeth is not a creditor beneficiary, (C) is not correct. A donee beneficiary cannot recover against the promisee, making (D) incorrect.

61. **(D)** Pretexting refers to obtaining private information under false pretenses, and the information does not relate solely to financial information, nor does it need to be obtained for a particular use. For this reason, all of the other responses are incorrect.

62. **(B)** While the First Amendment protects the freedom of speech, it does not protect speech that may be false or misleading. The Federal Trade Commission regulates false and deceptive advertising and even brings actions against companies that engage in improper advertising. (B) is the best response because if Donna's ads are false or deceptive, the state can regulate them. (A) is not the best response because advertising is protected under the First Amendment so long as it is truthful. (C) is incorrect because speech cannot be regulated to prevent competition. (D) is incorrect because courts recognize the ability of states to restrict some speech, such as speech that is false or misleading. (E) is incorrect for the same reason as (C), that is, speech is not regulated with reference to competition concerns.

63. **(D)** Each of these scenarios focuses on the kind of actions that would constitute consideration or some other issue involving contract formation. An offer must intend to invite acceptance. Although Linda's offer was to a large number of people (and thus looks like only an invitation to make an offer), it invites acceptance by stating that the first person to respond could accept. This kind of statement is sufficient to form the basis of an offer. Moreover, while the terms appear too indefinite to create mutual assent, most courts will enforce a contract for a "reasonable" offer because it reflects an offer to accept terms that fall within an acceptable range. Thus (D) is likely an enforceable contract. The promise in (A) lacks consideration, because speeding is illegal and thus Linda has not promised to refrain from doing something she has a right to do. (B) is incorrect because it also is lacking in consideration. When a person is offered alternative performances to which she can respond, both of the alternatives must be supported by consideration. The "take the money and run" proposal is not supported by consideration because Molly does not have to do anything for the money. As a result, both that promise and the entire transaction lack consideration. (C) is also incorrect. Since Molly washed Linda's car before Linda made her promise, the promise lacked con-

sideration. Indeed, the promise represented past consideration. With respect to (E), Linda's agreement to the extra $5 lacks consideration because Molly had a preexisting duty to perform. Thus, (E) is incorrect.

64. **(C)** Strict liability is imposed when someone has an absolute duty of care and is therefore liable without regard to fault. This duty often arises when a person is engaged in an ultra-hazardous activity, which includes caring for wild animals. The fact that an animal in his care harmed others may be enough to hold Michael liable under strict liability. (A) is not as strong a claim. Because the other responses require some intentional actions they are not the best responses.

65. **(B)** A prospectus must be delivered to investors. A registration statement (A) contains both the prospectus and information not required to be delivered to investors. A proxy statement (C) refers to a document that must be delivered to shareholders whenever the corporation solicits their vote, while a proxy (D) is essentially the shareholder's ballot. An investment contract (E) is a type of security.

66. **(A)** A contract with a minor is only voidable by the minor. Thus, as long as a minor does not disaffirm the contract, it is valid. (B) is incorrect because Adam's status as a minor does not automatically make the contract void. In general a minor cannot disaffirm contracts for a necessity (C). However, that doctrine is not relevant here because Adam is not seeking to disaffirm the contract. A contract arose at the point that two promises are exchanged. Thus, the lack of performance (D) does not make the contract unenforceable. Generally, the fact that a minor looks older (E) has no impact on the capacity doctrine because that doctrine depends only on whether a party is under the age of majority, regardless of appearance.

67. **(A)** Title VII regulates all forms of discriminatory behavior in the workplace as it relates to sex, national origin, religion, race, and color. It does not regulate discrimination based on age.

68. **(B)** Production quotas refer to restricting the supply of products to increase their products. Price fixing (A) refers to an agreement to set particular prices. (C) is incorrect because it refers to an agreement that requires a buyer to resell her products to particular manufacturers. (D) is incorrect because it involves granting a company the exclusive right to manufacture a product within a given area. Exclusive production (E) is not a recognized antitrust term.

69. **(D)** A party can demand assurances when she has reasonable uncertainty regarding the other party's intention to perform. Cure (A) is the ability to supply conforming goods, and cover (B) is the ability to buy substitute goods following a breach. A retraction (C) is the ability to terminate or take back a statement of repudiation. Hindrance (E) refers to a person's interference with the fulfillment of a condition.

70. **(C)** A liquidation refers to a total distribution of assets. Distribution (A), adjustment (D), and assignment (E) are not bankruptcy proceedings. A reorganization (B) is a bankruptcy proceeding, but it involves restructuring the business.

71. **(B)** In most negligence actions, the standard of care is the reasonable-person test. However, with regard to professionals, that standard changes. (B) is correct because it imposes a standard of care that is consistent with the professional standard. (A) is not correct, as a professional is not judged by the traditional reasonable-person test. (C) is not correct because it reflects the standard of care for minors. Similarly, neither (D) nor (E) reflects the proper standard of care for lawyers.

72. **(D)** Defamation requires showing that the defendant used language that had a negative impact on the plaintiff's reputation, the language must have concerned the plaintiff, it must have been communicated to a third party, and there must be some damages. (D) is the correct response because the language can either be written or oral so long as it is communicated.

73. **(E)** A mentally incompetent person or her representative can avoid a contract. However, the person must be incompetent at the time of the contract formation. (A) is incorrect because Reggie was judged incompetent after the contract was formed. (B) is incorrect, because the reason for Reggie's incompetence is not important to the question of capacity for purposes of contract avoidance. Like a minor, a mentally incompetent person can avoid a contract even if the terms are fair (C). (D) is incorrect because Reggie is bound on other grounds.

74. **(C)** A limited partnership has at least one limited partner with limited liability and at least one general partner with general liability. (A) is incorrect because it involves only one person. (B) is incorrect because a limited liability partnership protects all its members from liability. (D) is incorrect because liability is based on whether a person commits an act or

supervises someone who commits an act. (E) is incorrect because all partners in a general partnership have personal liability.

75. **(C)** The person who transfers an obligation is referred to as a delegator, thus (C) is correct because Brad transferred his obligation. A promisor (A) is the person who will render performance to a third-party beneficiary. An assignor (B) is the person who assigns her right in an assignment. An obligor (D) is the person who has a continuing obligation in an assignment. A real party in interest (E) is someone who, after transfers, is entitled to rights under a contract.

76. **(D)** Gina does not actually have a contract with Ryan. Thus, her recovery would need to be on some basis. In this case a court is likely to refer to the transaction as a quasi contract because Gina provided her services in a context where it was likely that Ryan would have consented if he had been given the chance. Thus the contract will be implied in law. A quasi contract allows a person to cover to avoid unjust enrichment. Since there was no contract between Gina and Ryan, responses that include III are incorrect.

77. **(B)** The Employee Retirement Income Security Act ("ERISA") regulates retirement benefit plans. It requires that employers appoint an administrator for their plans. (A) is not correct because ERISA only relates to benefit plans. ERISA does not require that companies maintain benefit plans, so (C) is incorrect. ERISA also does not require employees to contribute to the benefit plan, either through direct contribution or contributions through withholding. Thus (D) and (E) are incorrect.

78. **(A)** The Superfund program was established to assist with the clean-up of hazardous waste; it does not relate to antitrust. The other responses are either terms that relate to antitrust or are statutes that regulate practices that are deemed to restrict trade.

79. **(C)** The agreement between Paul and Mary is a valid contract because Mary has performed an act that she was not legally required to perform. (A) is not correct because two promises were not exchanged; rather there was a promise (payment of money) for a performance. Because consideration does not require that the promisor benefit, (B) is incorrect. (D) is incorrect because consideration requires either an act or a forbearance, and in this case there was an act. (E) is incorrect because Mary did not substantially perform; rather, she fully performed.

80. **(E)** The duty to mitigate is not a duty because it does not require a party to act. Instead, it provides that when a party fails to take steps to mitigate a loss, the damager's remedy will be reduced. The duty to mitigate is not an absolute obligation (A). (B) and (C) are incorrect because the duty does not impact defendants but rather affects plaintiffs. (D) is incorrect because the duty does not allow for a specific performance award.

81. **(C)** Ordinarily the appeals court gives great deference to trial court judgments. Thus, (C) is correct because judges overturn decisions based on a clear abuse of the discretion doctrine. "Necessary and proper" (A) is not a standard of review but a clause in the Constitution that gives Congress additional powers. A court will not reverse for lack of personal jurisdiction (B) because it is waived if it is not challenged at the first available opportunity. Given the appeals courts deference, mere evidence of judicial errors (D) or of plaintiff's misstatements (E) do not generally form the basis for reversal.

82. **(A)** A contract that represents a full, complete, and final record of the parties' agreement is a complete integration. Under the Parol Evidence Rule, when a contract is completely integrated, neither written nor oral evidence can be admitted to define the meaning of the agreement. However, there are exceptions. Thus, evidence may be admitted to prove that the agreement is subject to a condition. Neither (B) nor (C) is correct. (C) represents the rule for partially integrated agreements. (D) and (E) are incorrect because evidence of mistake, fraud, or custom are other exceptions to the general rule barring evidence for completely integrated contracts.

83. **(E)** A partnership can be created without any formal requirements and can be dissolved in much the same way. The death, withdrawal, bankruptcy, or expulsion of a partnership will trigger dissolution. So too will the end of the partnership term. However, the admission of a new partner does not trigger dissolution.

84. **(D)** Jurisdiction based on minimum contacts is also referred to as long-arm jurisdiction. General jurisdiction (A) refers to courts that can hear a broad array of cases. Limited jurisdiction (B) refers to courts that can hear only a particular subset of cases. Consensual jurisdiction (C) does not exist. Subject matter jurisdiction (E) refers to a court's ability to exercise jurisdiction over the matters within a particular case.

85. **(B)** A manufacturing defect relates to a defect that arises when something has been made improperly, and does not reflect a defect in the design of the product. A plaintiff must prove that the product as incorrectly manufactured was dangerous, and the courts apply a customer expectation test. (C) is incorrect because there is no requirement that a purchase be "bona fide." (A), (D), and (E) are incorrect because they relate to claims that must be made in connection with a design defect.

86. **(A)** Jack and Phil's contract is subject to a condition. Therefore neither party has an obligation to performance unless the condition has been met or excused. Here, the condition has not been met because the appropriate number of RSVPs have not been sent in. However, if one party to a contract hinders a contract, then the condition will be excused. In this case Jack has arguably hindered the condition by failing to send them out on time. As a result, the condition will be deemed excused, and if Phil desired to perform, he would have a right to perform. Once the condition is waived, both parties have an obligation to perform, and if Jack does not allow performance, the contract will be breached. Although there will be a breach, courts are reluctant to compel specific performance (B), so Phil is not likely to get specific performance. (C) is incorrect because, since the condition has been excused, both parties have an obligation to perform. (D) is incorrect because there is no need for Phil to affirm his desire to fulfill the contract. (E) is incorrect because if a condition is not met, Phil has no obligation to wait and see if it will be met.

87. **(C)** A contract will be taken out of the Statute of Frauds when there has been performance, at least to the extent of the performance. Admission in court or in court documents will take a contract out of the Statute of Frauds. However, consent is not sufficient. Therefore responses that include consent are incorrect.

88. **(D)** Unemployment compensation programs compensate employees who are fired without fault. Unemployment compensation is conferred for eligible employees and does not require contribution. Thus (A) and (B) are incorrect. (C) is incorrect because the Equal Pay Act prohibits discrimination in pay based on sex and is not applicable to employee compensation. (E) is incorrect because worker's compensation relates to compensation for work-related injuries.

89. **(A)** If a contract is subject to a condition, it must be met or excused. However, if one party hinders the condition through interference, then the

condition will be excused. (B) is incorrect because a condition cannot be excused merely by one person expressing an intent not to fulfill the condition; such an expression may be viewed as a breach. (C) is incorrect because mere difficulty in performing the contract condition does not excuse it. (D) is not correct because substantial performance must occur before a condition will be excused. (E) is not correct because a condition cannot be excused simply because it is perceived as being immaterial.

90. **(E)** Battery is an intentional touching. (E) is correct because intent is necessary. The other choices are elements of battery and are all incorrect.

91. **(C)** Because Barry and Sarah have entered into a business together to make a profit without filing anything or signing an agreement, they have created a general partnership. This is true even if they have a different profit-sharing arrangement. (A), (B), and (D) are incorrect because they require some form of filing and written agreement. (E) is incorrect because a sole proprietorship involves only one person.

92. **(B)** A criminal case requires that the evidence against the defendant be proven beyond a reasonable doubt. (D) is the standard for civil cases. All the remaining responses are not standards for either civil or criminal trials.

93. **(D)** In order to establish priority in a security interest, it must be perfected. The first person who perfects by filing has priority over other claims. When a person is granted the interest, (A) has no impact on issues of perfection. An interest in land (B) may be perfected in the same manner that all other security interests may be perfected. While perfection can arise through possession (C), the person who files first has priority. It is only when neither person has filed that the person who takes possession first has priority. (E) is incorrect because a person's possession does not take priority over a prior filing.

94. **(D)** The Bureau of Customs and Border Patrol ("Bureau") regulates imports and tariff rates. The Federal Communications Commission (A) regulates radio, television, and other forms of communications. The Bureau superseded the Department of Commerce (B). The National Labor Relations Board (C) regulates collective bargaining. The Federal Trade Commission (E) regulates unfair trade.

95. **(A)** Although older rules barred recovery when a plaintiff contributed to her own injuries, modern rules allow recovery but reduce the damage award. (B) is incorrect because the plaintiff receives more than just legal costs. (C) is incorrect because it reflects the older rule. (D) is incorrect because the plaintiff will not be barred from receiving compensation. (E) is incorrect because contributory negligence is not a defense in intentional torts.

96. **(B)** Substantial performance refers to performance that is basically complete but has some minor defect. When there has been substantial performance, the other party is not entitled to withhold performance. Brian's actions would likely constitute substantial performance because he built an entire house of which the shower tiles are a relatively minor part. If Brian's performance had had significant defects, the fact that he has completed would not prevent Sherry from recovery (A). Here the defects are not serious, so Sherry cannot withhold her performance. (C) is incorrect because it is an incorrect formation of when a breach becomes total. (D) is incorrect because Sherry's consent does not impact whether a material or trivial breach has occurred. (E) is incorrect, because while there has been a breach, it is not material, so Sherry cannot withhold.

97. **(C)** A directed verdict comes at the end of the plaintiff's presentation of the case. A demurrer (A) comes prior to filing the defendant's response. (B) and (D) are incorrect because they can be made before a trial starts. (E) is incorrect because it comes at the end of the entire trial.

98. **(C)** Once additional terms have been proposed, under the UCC they will be incorporated if both parties are merchants, except in limited circumstances. Each of the provisions sets forth those circumstances except for the requirement that the terms be consistent with custom.

99. **(C)** The General Agreement on Tariffs and Trades ("GATT") was the first agreement on trade. The Uniform Commercial Code (A) governs contracts. (B) is incorrect because it is an agreement regarding exports. The North Atlantic Free Trade Agreement (D) is a recent agreement that seeks to promote free trade among the United States, Mexico and Canada. Although the World Trade Organization (E) sets trading rules, GATT predated it.

100. **(E)** Elton's agreement with John is a requirements contract because John is providing Elton with all his requirements. Although it first appears as if there is no consideration, in fact Elton is agreeing to purchase cookies and John is agreeing to sell them to Elton. (A), (B), and (C) are incorrect because they each suggest that the contract fails to be supported by consideration. Yet courts have indicated that consideration in these cases does exist. (D) is incorrect because although the agreement does not specify the exact number of cookies to be sold, courts imply a reasonableness standard based on prior dealings or custom.

# ▼
# PRACTICE
# TEST 2

This test is also on CD-ROM in our special interactive TEST*ware*® for the CLEP Introductory Business Law exam. It is highly recommended that you first take this exam on computer. You will then have the additional study features and benefits of enforced time conditions, individual diagnostic analysis, and instant scoring.

# CLEP INTRODUCTORY BUSINESS LAW

## PRACTICE TEST 2

**(Answer sheets appear in the back of this book.)**

**TIME:** 90 Minutes
100 Questions

---

**DIRECTIONS:** Each of the questions or incomplete statements below is followed by five possible answers or completions. Select the best choice in each case and fill in the corresponding oval on the answer sheet.

---

1. A consumer purchased a defective product. If the consumer wanted to sue because of an injury caused by the product, which of the following would form the basis of the suit?

   I. Negligence

   II. Express warranty

   III. Intentional tort

   (A) I only

   (B) II only

   (C) III only

   (D) I and II only

   (E) I, II, and III

2.  Recovering on a theory of unjust enrichment is known as

    (A) promissory estoppel

    (B) reliance

    (C) restitution

    (D) liquidated damages

    (E) legal capacity

3.  Which of the following motions can be made after a jury has entered a verdict?

    (A) Directed verdict

    (B) Summary judgment

    (C) Judgment n.o.v.

    (D) Demurrer

    (E) Lack of venue

4.  Which of the following governs contracts for the sale of goods?

    (A) Parol Evidence Rule

    (B) Statute of Frauds

    (C) Uniform Commercial Code

    (D) Restatement of Contracts

    (E) Law of Promissory Estoppel

5.  Alice entered into a contract with May stating that she will give Alice swimming lessons for $500 so long as the pool is open in the summer. Which of the following statements about the contract is true?

    (A)  If the pool is closed, neither May nor Alice will have an obligation to perform.

    (B)  If the pool is closed in the summer, May can require Alice to give her lessons during the winter.

    (C)  If Alice has purchased a swimsuit and goggles in reliance on May's promise to give her swimming lessons, May must give her swimming lessons even if the pool is closed in the summer.

    (D)  If the pool is closed, there has been a material breach of the contract.

    (E)  If the pool is closed, both May and Alice have substantially performed.

6.  Which of the following requires reasonable accommodations?

    (A)  The Family Medical Leave Act

    (B)  Americans with Disabilities Act

    (C)  Title VII

    (D)  Age Discrimination Act

    (E)  Pregnancy Discrimination Act

7.  Which of the following applies if a third party reasonably believes that an agent has the authority to act on behalf of a principal?

    (A)  The agent is liable if the principal did not expressly authorize her actions.

    (B)  The agent is liable unless the principal ratifies her actions.

    (C)  The principal is not liable if the agent did not have express authority from the principal.

    (D)  The principal is not liable unless the principal acquiesced to the agent's actions after the fact.

    (E)  The principal is liable unless the third party had notice of the agent's lack of authority.

8.  Under the Uniform Commercial Code (UCC), if an offeree expresses an intent to accept an offer but the acceptance contains terms that are different from those contained in the original offer, which of the following statements are true?

    I.   The expression will be construed as an acceptance, and the different terms will be disregarded.

    II.  The expression will be construed as an acceptance, and the different terms will be viewed as proposals for inclusion.

    III. The expression will be construed as an acceptance, but if the parties' terms conflict, they will cancel each other out.

    (A) I only

    (B) II only

    (C) III only

    (D) I and II only

    (E) I, II, and III

9.  Which of the following is NOT an exception to the Statute of Frauds?

    (A) An admission that a contract was made

    (B) Part performance of a contract that cannot be performed within a year

    (C) Part performance of a contract for the sale of land

    (D) Part performance of a contract for the sale of goods

    (E) Promissory estoppel

10. Which of the following best defines the Supreme Court's review of an appeals court decisions?

    (A) Great deference is given to all determinations.

    (B) Great deference is given to interpretations of the law.

    (C) Great deference is given to factual finds unless they contain errors.

    (D) Great deference is given to factual finds, but interpretations of the law are reviewed anew.

    (E) Great deference is given to factual findings and interpretations of the law, but any claims of error are newly reviewed.

11. Randy is a director at AI Co. Randy purchased shares of AI Co. and a week later sold them for a profit. Randy's transaction is known as

    (A) a private placement

    (B) a public offering

    (C) investment profits

    (D) short-swing profits

    (E) insider trading

12. Gary swung a hollow bat at Frank's head and missed. Assuming the bat looked like a regular bat, what act did Gary most likely commit?

    (A) Battery

    (B) Defamation

    (C) Assault

    (D) Negligence

    (E) Intentional infliction of emotional distress

13. Donald lives next door to Meredith and decides to prune Meredith's bushes for her. If he sues Meredith for the cost of his services, which of the following statements is true?

    (A) Meredith will not be held liable because pruning Meredith's bushes will be construed as a gift.

    (B) Meredith will not be held liable because there was no written agreement between Donald and Meredith.

    (C) Meredith will be held liable because she has received the benefit of Donald's services.

    (D) Meredith will be liable because pruning someone's bushes is not a customary gift.

    (E) Meredith will be liable because Donald suffered a detriment by pruning Meredith's bushes.

14. An employee believes he has been passed over for promotion because of his religion. With which of the following agencies must he file a claim?

    (A) Consumer Protection Agency

    (B) The Equal Employment Opportunity Commission

    (C) The National Labor Relations Board

    (D) The Federal Trade Commission

    (E) The Workers Protection Agency

15. Alvin's corporation issued securities without properly registering them. Which of the following provisions of the Securities Act will likely be used to hold the corporation liable?

    (A) Section 11

    (B) Section 12(a)(1)

    (C) Section 12(a)(2)

    (D) Section 4

    (E) Section 5

16. Danny and Nadia have entered into a contract pursuant to which Danny has agreed to pay Nadia $500 and Nadia has agreed to give Danny a set of tennis clubs. Two days later, Nadia transfers her right to payment to Frank. This subsequent transfer is best described as

    (A) a third-party beneficiary contract

    (B) a delegation

    (C) an assignment

    (D) a unilateral contract

    (E) a bilateral contract

17. Which of the following qualifies as consideration?

    (A) A gift

    (B) Past consideration

    (C) An agreement to perform a preexisting duty

    (D) An agreement to extinguish a debt

    (E) An illusory promise

18. Which of the following regulates the cleanup of historical hazardous waste sites?

    (A) The National Environmental Policy Act

    (B) The Environmental Protection Agency

    (C) The Clean Water Act

    (D) The Resource Conservation and Recovery Act

    (E) The Comprehensive Environmental Response, Compensation, and Liability Act

19. Which of the following bankruptcy codes regulates proceeds for debtors who want to design a repayment plan?

    (A) Chapter 5

    (B) Chapter 7

    (C) Chapter 11

    (D) Chapter 13

    (E) Chapter 15

20. A company that is registered under the Securities Exchange Act of 1934 is called

    (A) a private company

    (B) a reporting company

    (C) an investment company

    (D) a securities company

    (E) a statutory company

21. The doctrine of substantial performance means

    (A) a party has substantially breached the contract

    (B) a party has substantially performed under the contract but has committed a material breach

    (C) a party has substantially performed under the contract but has committed a minor breach

    (D) a party has substantially performed under the contract and has not committed any breach

    (E) a party is obligated only to substantially perform the contract

22. Which of the following is true of the common-law system?

    (A) It is judge-made law.

    (B) It is based on a system that references a comprehensive code.

    (C) It has its roots in the Roman Empire.

    (D) It is a system followed by the majority of the countries in the world.

    (E) It is based on a system that references a set of common laws.

23. Corporate actions that consider all corporate constituents is known as

    (A) shareholder primacy

    (B) fiduciary responsibility

    (C) corporate charitable giving

    (D) corporate social responsibility

    (E) public welfare

24. Anthony entered into a contract with Tanya to wash her car. Later that day Tanya got into a car accident and, though she did not get hurt, her car was totaled. Which of the following doctrines is most likely to support Tanya's claim to avoid the contract?

    (A) Frustration of purpose

    (B) Unilateral mistake

    (C) Unconscionability

    (D) Duress

    (E) Promissory estoppel

25. The process of examining the decisions of federal and state governments to make sure they do not violate the Constitution is called

    (A) judicial examination

    (B) judicial review

    (C) constitutional examination

    (D) federalism

    (E) precedent

26. Andy yelled "gun" in the middle of a crowded train station. If the government sues Andy, a court will likely hold that

    (A) Andy will be held liable because his speech is subject to strict scrutiny

    (B) Andy will be held liable because his speech violated time, place, and manner restrictions

    (C) Andy will be liable because his speech represents a clear and present danger

    (D) Andy will not be liable because he was exercising his freedom of speech

    (E) Andy will not be liable because he was exercising his freedom of association

27. Which of the following guarantees a criminal defendant a fair trial?

    (A) Takings Clause

    (B) Due Process Clause

    (C) Equal Protection Clause

    (D) Supremacy Clause

    (E) Proper Procedure Clause

28. Which of the following is effective on dispatch?

    (A) An offer

    (B) An acceptance

    (C) A rejection

    (D) A counteroffer

    (E) A revocation

29. Which of the following is true about misstatements in a registration statement?

    (A) An issuer can avoid liability if he can prove that he had a reasonable basis to believe that the misstatements were true.

    (B) Experts are liable for any misstatements.

    (C) All defendants are equally liable.

    (D) Directors will be liable if they fail to investigate all the information in the registration statement.

    (E) Directors must have a reasonable basis to believe that the misstatements are true.

30. Dora has entered into a contract with Benny to pay Benny $1,000 to paint her portrait. Which of the following is NOT true?

    (A) Benny cannot transfer his obligation to paint Dora without Dora's consent because it involves the performance of a personal service.

    (B) Benny must notify Dora if he transfers his right to receive payment.

    (C) Dora must consent to Benny's transfer of his right to receive payment.

    (D) If Dora pays Benny before he has notice of a transfer by Dora, Benny will have no further responsibility.

    (E) If Dora pays Benny after he has notice of her transfer to another party, Benny may be liable to that party.

31. In an entity with flow-through tax treatment, which of the following is true?

    (A) Shareholders are taxed only on their portion of the entity's profits.

    (B) Employees are taxed based on the entity's profits.

    (C) Partners are taxed on their share of the entity's profits.

    (D) Tax "flows through" the entity such that no partner is liable for any of the entity's taxes.

    (E) Tax "flows through" the entity so that all executives and employees are equally liable for taxes.

32. The Parol Evidence Rule stipulates the

    (A) all oral agreements must be in writing

    (B) all oral agreements are invalid if they cannot be performed within a year

    (C) written and oral evidence of prior commitments are not admissible if a contract is integrated

    (D) oral evidence is not admissible if a contract is integrated

    (E) oral and written evidence of a prior commitment is not admissible if a contract is partially integrated

33. Vicki was driving 20 miles per hour above the speed limit and hit a pole. The pole hit Kim, who was standing next to the pole, and Kim suffered severe injuries. If Kim sues Vicki, a court will probably hold that

    (A) Vicki is liable because Kim's injuries resulted from foreseeable actions

    (B) Vicki is liable because she is the "but for" cause of Kim's injuries

    (C) Vicki is not liable because Kim's injuries were caused by the pole

    (D) Vicki is not liable because she owes no duty to strangers

    (E) Vicki is not liable unless the extent of the damages was foreseeable

34. Ordinarily, a plaintiff must demonstrate which of the following before bringing a suit into court

    I.   Subject matter jurisdiction

    II.  Personal jurisdiction

    III. Proper venue

    (A) I only

    (B) II only

    (C) III only

    (D) I and II only

    (E) I, II, and III

35. Which of the following is an essential element of an investment contract?

    (A) Fraud

    (B) A common enterprise

    (C) A mutual agreement

    (D) A written agreement

    (E) Justifiable reliance

36. On December 1, Wendy orally agreed to sing at the next five New Year's Eve parties that Edward hosted. On December 31, Wendy performed at the first New Year's Eve party hosted by Edward. Two days later Edward informed Wendy that he would not honor the contract. If Wendy sues Edward, a court is likely to hold that

    (A) the contract is enforceable because Wendy has partially performed under the contract

    (B) the contract is enforceable because Wendy began performing under the contract within a year of its execution

    (C) the contract is enforceable because contracts for services are not covered by the Statute of Frauds

    (D) the contract is not enforceable because a contract must be signed by both parties to be enforceable

    (E) the contract is not enforceable because the contract could not be performed within a year

37. An action to permanently reduce the risk associated with a hazardous waste site is known as

    (A) removal

    (B) remediation

    (C) perfection

    (D) attachment

    (E) cleanup

38. Which of the following is true of the Securities and Exchange Commission?

    (A) It is an administrative agency.

    (B) It is a securities review board.

    (C) It is an investment fund.

    (D) It is a national security exchange.

    (E) It is a public commission.

39. Monica has just moved into the neighborhood. Joe has lived in the neighborhood for 30 years. Joe stopped by Monica's house and told her that if she did not agree to allow him to walk her dogs, he would expose embarrassing personal details about her to all the neighbors. If Monica entered into a contract with Joe providing for him to walk her dogs, it would be

    (A) valid and enforceable because it represented a bargained-for exchange

    (B) valid and enforceable because Joe's actions were not illegal

    (C) unenforceable because it lacked mutual assent

    (D) unenforceable because it was entered into under duress

    (E) unenforceable because it violates public policy

40. Which of the following is an essential element of interference with a business relationship?

    (A) The defendant had knowledge of the business relationship.

    (B) The defendant was seeking to benefit from the interference.

    (C) The plaintiff suffered severe economic loss.

    (D) The plaintiff did not have a reasonable time to cure the interference.

    (E) The plaintiff had a long-standing relationship with the third party.

41. A business in which the only partners with personal liability are those who are liable for the complained action and those whom they supervise is called

    (A) a limited partnership

    (B) a limited liability partnership

    (C) a limited liability company

    (D) a corporation

    (E) a general partnership

42. A security interest will be unenforceable if

    (A) the creditor does not take possession of the security

    (B) the creditor does not file notice of the security interest

    (C) the creditor does not provide some form of consideration

    (D) the creditor does not sign the agreement establishing the security interest

    (E) the creditor does not give the debtor notice of intention to enforce the security interest

43. Which of the following falls within the scope of the Supremacy Clause?

    (A) State constitutions

    (B) Decisions of state supreme courts

    (C) Ordinances

    (D) Federal treaties

    (E) Agreements between a state and a foreign country

44. All of the following agreements are per se illegal EXCEPT

    (A) price fixing

    (B) group boycotts

    (C) production quotas

    (D) market division

    (E) tie-ins

45. Ordinarily, which of the following motions must be made at the first available opportunity to avoid waiver?

    (A) Summary judgment

    (B) Lack of personal jurisdiction

    (C) Directed verdict

    (D) Lack of subject matter jurisdiction

    (E) Judgment n.o.v.

46. Kelly has a contract with Lawrence under which she has agreed to pay Lawrence $200 when he delivers her pool table on Monday at 5 p.m. Monday morning Lawrence calls to inform Kelly that he cannot deliver by 5 p.m. If Kelly sues Lawrence for breach, a court will likely hold that

(A) Lawrence is not liable because he still had time to perform

(B) Lawrence is not liable because he notified Kelly of his intention not to perform

(C) Lawrence is not liable unless Kelly can show that she changed her position in reliance on his call

(D) Lawrence is liable because he did not notify Kelly within a reasonable amount of time

(E) Lawrence is liable because he informed Kelly of his intention not to perform

47. Which of the following is not an essential element of mutual mistake?

(A) The mistake must be mutual.

(B) The mistake must relate to a basic assumption of the contract.

(C) The mistake must be outside the parties' control.

(D) The party seeking to bring the action must not have borne the risk of the mistake.

(E) The mistake must be material.

48. All of the following are usual functions of an appeals court EXCEPT

(A) reviewing the transcript of the trial court

(B) hearing oral arguments

(C) re-examining witnesses

(D) modifying a decision of the trial court

(E) setting aside the judgment of the trial court

49. Vicarious liability means

    (A) an employer is liable for an employee's torts only if they occurred within the scope of employment

    (B) an employer is liable for an employee's torts

    (C) an employer is liable for an employee's contracts only if they occurred within the scope of employment

    (D) an employer is liable for an employee's contracts and intentional actions

    (E) an employer is liable for an employee's actions only if the employee obeyed the employer's reasonable instructions

50. Peter and Michael have entered into a contract. Michael has agreed to play the piano at Peter's wedding, and Peter has agreed to pay Michael $6,000. If Michael dies before Peter's wedding, which of the following will apply to the contract?

    (A) Unconscionability

    (B) Impossibility

    (C) Frustration of purpose

    (D) Mutual mistake

    (E) Duress

51. Carl contracted with Danny to paint Danny's house on Thursday morning. On Tuesday Danny called Carl to inform him that he would not be able to start painting until Friday. If Danny calls Carl back Tuesday evening to let him know that he can in fact begin on Thursday, a court would probably hold that

    (A) Carl can refuse Danny's offer because it is a counteroffer

    (B) Carl can refuse Danny's offer because Danny has already breached the contract

    (C) Carl can refuse Danny's offer if it was not in writing

    (D) Carl must allow Danny to perform because he has now indicated his willingness to perform

    (E) Carl must allow Danny to perform because a contract can never be breached before performance time

52. When a plaintiff relies on *res ipsa loquitor,* which of the following is true?

    (A) The plaintiff's injury is something that normally occurs as a result of negligence.

    (B) Both parties are equally at fault.

    (C) Both parties engaged in negligent behavior.

    (D) There has been some unjust enrichment.

    (E) A defendant intends to commit some action against one person, but commits the action against someone else.

53. Jill contracted to build Florence a custom doghouse. When it was complete, Florence noticed that the dog's feeding dish was round and not square as she had requested. Because the dish was built into the floor of the house, it would cost almost twice the amount of the original construction to replace the round dish. If Florence sues Jill, a court is likely to hold that

    (A) Jill is not liable because the contract related to an animal

    (B) Jill is not liable because she has substantially performed

    (C) Jill is liable for the costs associated with Florence advertising for someone to build a new doghouse

    (D) Jill is liable for the costs of reconstructing the doghouse with the proper bowl

    (E) Jill is liable for the difference between the value of the doghouse now and its value as properly constructed

54. Roger owes Lisa $10,000. To satisfy this debt, Roger entered into a contract with Chris pursuant to which Roger agreed to paint Chris's house, and in exchange Chris agreed to pay Lisa $10,000. If Chris refuses to pay Lisa, which of the following is NOT true?

   (A) Lisa has an enforceable claim against Chris because she is an intended beneficiary.

   (B) Lisa has an enforceable claim against Roger because she is a creditor beneficiary.

   (C) Roger has an enforceable claim against Chris.

   (D) Chris does not have to pay Lisa if he can prove that Roger breached his agreement to paint Chris's house.

   (E) Chris does not have to pay Lisa if he can prove that Roger does not owe Lisa any money.

55. In general, which of the following statements about a jury verdict in a civil trial is true?

   (A) It must be unanimous.

   (B) It must be based on evidence beyond a reasonable doubt.

   (C) It can be overturned only for clear errors of facts.

   (D) It must be made without directions from the judge.

   (E) It must be made in consultation with the judge.

56. Max entered into a contract with Kevin pursuant to which Max loaned Kevin $5,000. At the time of the contract, Kevin appeared confused, disoriented, and complained of hearing voices. Two weeks after the contract, Max learned from Kevin's legal guardian that Kevin is mentally incompetent. Kevin's guardian is seeking to disaffirm the contract, although Kevin has spent all but $1,000 of the money Max loaned him. Which of the following statements is the most accurate?

   I.   Kevin cannot disaffirm the contract unless he can pay Max the remaining $4,000 under the contract.

   II.   Kevin can disaffirm the contract because Max had reason to know of Kevin's incompetence.

   III.   Kevin cannot disaffirm the contract unless he can show that the contract terms were unfair.

(A) I only

(B) II only

(C) III only

(D) I and II only

(E) I and III only

57. The Fair Labor Standards Act provides for all of the following EXCEPT

(A) establishing minimum wages

(B) prohibiting employers from hiring children under age 14

(C) establishing labor procedures

(D) establishing overtime pay for full-time workers

(E) establishing overtime pay for part-time workers

58. Jan works for Fairfax Co., which has offices in three states. Jan has never been to the headquarters of Fairfax Co. because it is in a different state from the one in which she works. If Fairfax Co. sued Jan in the state of its headquarters, a court would probably hold that

    (A) Jan could dismiss for lack of subject matter jurisdiction because she has never been in the state

    (B) Jan could dismiss for lack of personal jurisdiction because she has never been in the state

    (C) Jan could dismiss for lack of personal jurisdiction and lack of subject matter jurisdiction unless she gives her consent

    (D) Jan could not dismiss for lack of personal jurisdiction because she has enough contacts with the state

    (E) Jan could not dismiss for lack of subject matter jurisdiction because she has enough contacts with the state

59. The city of Sandy Springs has passed a law banning men from driving on Thursdays. If Bob challenges the law, which of the following standards would apply to the court's review?

    (A) Strict scrutiny

    (B) Intermediate scrutiny

    (C) Rational basis test

    (D) Rule of reason test

    (E) Time, place, and manner test

60. Which of the following clauses of the Constitution grants Congress the power to pass laws consistent with its legislative responsibilities?

    (A) The Supremacy Clause

    (B) The Due Process Clause

    (C) The Necessary and Proper Clause

    (D) The Legislative Powers Clause

    (E) The Commerce Clause

61. A contract in which a third party assumes all the obligations of a previous contract and extinguishes all the rights and obligations associated with it is known as

    (A) assignment

    (B) novation

    (C) accord and satisfaction

    (D) rescission

    (E) an executory contract

62. Albert is 17 years old, but looks 24 because he wears a beard. On Monday Albert entered into a contract with Ben, the owner of a grocery store, to purchase milk and bread for his wife. On Wednesday Albert turned 18. On Thursday Albert returned to the store and demanded his money back from Ben. The age of majority in Albert's state is 18. Ben may be able to enforce the contract against Albert for all of the following reasons EXCEPT

    (A) the bread and milk purchased by Albert constitutes a necessity

    (B) Ben believed Albert was an adult

    (C) Albert is married

    (D) Albert did not disaffirm the contract within a reasonable time after he turned 18

    (E) Albert deliberately misrepresented his age

63. Which of the following best defines the doctrine of piercing the corporate veil?

    (A) Directors and officers can be held liable for the corporation's debts when they become due.

    (B) Directors and officers can be held liable for the corporation's debts when they breach their fiduciary duty.

    (C) Directors and officers can be held liable for the amount of their investment in the corporation.

    (D) Directors and officers can be held liable for the corporation's debt to prevent fraud or illegality.

    (E) Directors and officers can be held liable for the obligations of shareholders.

64. On Monday, Gina and Alice entered into a contract in which Gina agreed to sing at Alice's birthday party for $5,000. On Tuesday, the city in which Gina and Alice lived banned singing. Which of the following is true?

    (A) There is no contract because there is no longer consideration.

    (B) There is no contract because it would be impossible for Gina to perform.

    (C) There is no contract because there is no longer a mutual obligation.

    (D) The contract is valid and enforceable.

    (E) The contract is valid so long as Alice reaffirms it.

65. Ordinarily, which of the following government contracts gives rise to an intended beneficiary?

    (A) Any contract that confers a private right of enforcement

    (B) Any contract that intends to benefit a particular group in society

    (C) Any contract in which a member of the public has no other remedy

    (D) Any contract that the government believes to be important

    (E) Any contract that involves employment matters

66. Which of the following statements regarding an administrative agency is true?

    (A) An agency's rules and regulations cannot be overturned.

    (B) An agency's actions are entitled to strict confidentiality.

    (C) All agency actions are given great deference.

    (D) All administrative remedies must be exhausted before an agency's decisions can be appealed.

    (E) An agency's actions can be appealed only to an administrative review board.

67. A contract will be unenforceable under all the following circumstances EXCEPT if

    (A) the promisor lacked capacity to enter into the contract

    (B) the subject matter of the contract is illegal

    (C) the contract was an oral promise made in consideration of marriage

    (D) the promisor was convinced to enter into the contract by use of force

    (E) the promisor discovers that the contract is difficult to perform

68. Ben picked up a rock and threw it at Kevin, who had his back turned. Although Ben intended to hit Kevin, the rock hit Kevin's backpack. If Kevin sues Ben, a court is likely to hold that

    (A) Kevin is liable for battery because the rock hit Kevin's backpack

    (B) Kevin is liable for assault because the rock hit Kevin's backpack

    (C) Kevin is not liable for battery because Kevin did not know Ben was throwing the rock

    (D) Kevin is not liable for assault because the rock did not hit Kevin

    (E) Kevin is not liable for battery because the rock, not Kevin, hit Kevin's backpack

69. Which of the following agencies regulates radio, television, and other forms of interstate communications?

    (A) The Bureau of Consumer Protection

    (B) The Federal Communications Commission

    (C) The Federal Trade Commission

    (D) The Interstate Commerce Commission

    (E) The Federal Regulatory Commission

70. David offered to sell his house to Shelly for $250,000. Shelly responded, "I have to think about $250,000, but I could pay $200,000 if you are interested." Shelly's response can best be described as

    (A) a suggestion to negotiate new terms, because the response indicates a desire to continue considering the offer

    (B) a rejection, because the response fails the mirror-image rule

    (C) a counteroffer, because the response makes a new offer

    (D) an acceptance, because modern law no longer requires that an acceptance correspond with all terms of the original offer

    (E) a rejection, because the response fails to indicate a clear desire to keep the offer open

71. Which of the following functions could NOT be performed by the Equal Employment Opportunity Commission?

    (A) Investigating of employees' discrimination claims

    (B) Creating of plans to address discriminatory practices

    (C) Issuing an injunction against employers

    (D) Issuing rules designed to implement antidiscrimination laws

    (E) Bringing suit in federal court

72. A contract created by a form agreement that does not allow one party to negotiate its terms is called

    (A) an investment contract

    (B) an adhesion contract

    (C) a unilateral contract

    (D) an executory contract

    (E) a form contract

73. Nicole entered into a contract with Charles pursuant to which Charles agreed to pay Nicole $500 and Nicole agreed to give Charles two golf lessons. Two days later Nicole told Charles that she would not give Charles his lessons unless he paid her $600. If Charles agrees to pay Nicole $600, a court is likely to find that the agreement is

    (A) unenforceable because it lacks consideration

    (B) unenforceable because it violates the Statute of Frauds

    (C) unenforceable because it is an executory contract

    (D) enforceable because it is supported by consideration

    (E) enforceable because both parties assented to it

74. A foreign government's decision to take a business or asset from a person who is not one of its citizens is called

    (A) a takings

    (B) expropriation

    (C) appropriation

    (D) a tariff

    (E) an export

75. Which of the following statements regarding a buyer's right to reject goods is true?

    (A) A buyer can reject goods under installment contracts only if the nonconformity substantially impairs the value of the contract.

    (B) A buyer can reject goods only if they represent a reasonable percentage of the total contract.

    (C) A buyer must reject all goods or accept all goods.

    (D) A buyer cannot reject goods after delivery.

    (E) A buyer cannot reject goods unless they significantly deviate from the contract terms.

76. Unconscionability is based on a judgment that a

    (A) contract is against public policy

    (B) contract is misleading

    (C) contract is one-sided and unfair

    (D) contract is fraudulent

    (E) contract is illegal

77. All of the following are related to creditors' rights EXCEPT

    (A) a financing statement

    (B) a proxy statement

    (C) a security agreement

    (D) an equity redemption

    (E) a foreclosure

78. A contract for the sale of goods may be modified without consideration if

    (A) it is in writing

    (B) there exists some substitute for consideration

    (C) it is in writing and signed by the party to be bound

    (D) it is not material

    (E) it occurs in good faith

79. Which of the following is a recognized exception for employment discrimination?

    (A) A bona fide occupational qualification

    (B) A restricted job market

    (C) Economic necessity

    (D) An important business rationale

    (E) An important government interest

80. Which of the following statements regarding the Securities Act is true?

    (A) It provides benefits for people in retirement.

    (B) It regulates the offer and sale of securities.

    (C) It protects secured transactions.

    (D) It protects Social Security benefits.

    (E) It regulates fair trade practices.

81. Brian offered to sell his fax machine to Sam for $100. Sam responded by saying, "I can't afford $100, but will you take $50?" When Brian said no to the $50, Sam tried to pay Brian $100 for the fax machine. If Sam sues Brian to enforce the $100 offer, a court will probably hold that

    (A) Brian is liable because Sam never really rejected Brian's offer

    (B) Brian is not liable because Sam's counteroffer terminated Brian's offer

    (C) Brian is liable because he never revoked the offer

    (D) Brian is not liable because the contract is a unilateral one

    (E) Brian is liable because an offeree retains the power to accept an offer

82. Scott, a 10-year-old, stuck his foot out while Eve, another 10-year-old, was running, causing Eve to trip and fall. If Eve sues Scott, which of the following is true?

    (A) Scott cannot be held liable because he is a minor.

    (B) Scott cannot be held liable because the conduct was between two minors.

    (C) Scott can be held liable for an intentional tort only.

    (D) Scott can he held liable for negligence only.

    (E) Scott can be held liable for an intentional tort and negligence.

83. Which of the following statements is true regarding the unemployment compensation program?

    (A) It is administered solely by the federal government.

    (B) It is funded by withholding certain amounts from employees' salaries.

    (C) In exchange for participating in the program, employees must relinquish their rights to sue their employers.

    (D) State law determines the compensation levels.

    (E) Federal law determines employees' eligibility.

84. Alex made an offer to buy Kevin's car. Kevin paid Alex $50 so that Kevin could have 45 days to consider Alex's offer. If Alex dies before the 45 days have passed, what is the status of the offer?

   (A) It has terminated because of Alex's death.

   (B) It has terminated due to lapse of time.

   (C) It is irrevocable until 45 days have lapsed.

   (D) It is revocable by Alex's estate.

   (E) It is irrevocable.

85. Reggie promised to pay Kelly $1,000 for singing at his birthday party. When Kelly arrived at the party to sing, Reggie told Kelly that he had changed his mind and refused to allow Kelly to perform. If Kelly sues Reggie for payment, which of the following is Reggie's best defense?

   (A) The contract is unilateral.

   (B) The contract is bilateral.

   (C) Kelly had only partially performed the contract.

   (D) Reggie had canceled the party.

   (E) Kelly's performance had not yet begun.

86. A lawsuit by shareholders alleging that the directors and officers breached their fiduciary duty is known as

   (A) malpractice

   (B) derivative suit

   (C) demurrer

   (D) *stare decisis*

   (E) suit in equity

87. A communication may NOT be deemed an offer when

    I.   the terms of the communication are not certain

    II.  the intended beneficiaries cannot be determined

    III. the communication requires further negotiation

    (A) I only

    (B) II only

    (C) III only

    (D) I and III only

    (E) I, II, and III

88. Most-favored nation treatment means

    (A) countries should treat all products within their borders equally

    (B) countries should not discriminate among trading partners

    (C) countries should provide special treatment for their own products

    (D) countries should provide special treatment to nations that are less developed

    (E) countries should provide special treatment to nations that are their trading partners

89. Which of the following is an ethical theory that focuses on consequences?

    (A) Categorical imperative

    (B) Natural rights

    (C) Utilitarianism

    (D) Libertarianism

    (E) Deontology

90. On Monday Gloria and Alcynthia entered into a contract pursuant to which Gloria agreed to build a boat for Alcynthia. Alcynthia agreed to pay Gloria $50,000. On Tuesday Alcynthia breached the contract, telling Gloria that she would not pay her for the boat. On Wednesday Denise informed Gloria that she would be willing to pay Gloria $50,000 if Gloria agreed to build her the same boat she had agreed to build for Alcynthia. Gloria refused Denise's offer. If Gloria brings suit against Alcynthia, a court is likely to hold that

    (A) Gloria cannot recover damages against Alcynthia because Gloria had not yet performed under the contract

    (B) Gloria cannot recover damages against Alcynthia because Gloria refused to accept Denise's offer

    (C) Gloria can recover all of her damages against Alcynthia because Alcynthia breached the contract

    (D) Gloria can recover damages against Alcynthia because Denise was not a party to the contract and Denise's offer has no affect on the contract between Gloria and Alcynthia

    (E) Gloria can recover damages against Alcynthia because their contract was a unilateral contract

91. Which of the following decisions could NOT be heard by the Supreme Court exercising original jurisdiction?

    (A) Cases between two or more states

    (B) Cases between the federal government and a state

    (C) Cases involving officials of foreign countries

    (D) Cases between citizens of two or more states

    (E) Cases between the state and citizens of another state

92. All of the following are related to environmental law EXCEPT

    (A) hazardous waste sites

    (B) quality control standards

    (C) misappropriation

    (D) National Priorities List

    (E) Toxic Substance Control Act

93. To which of the following cases will a court apply the rule of *in pari delicto*?

    (A) A battery

    (B) An illegal contract

    (C) Unfair trade

    (D) An ambiguous contract

    (E) A secured transaction

94. Which of the following statements regarding only collective bargaining is true?

    (A) Employees can engage in collective bargaining only if a state statute permits it.

    (B) Employees who engage in collective bargaining cannot engage in strikes.

    (C) Federal law requires employers to bargain directly with employee representatives.

    (D) Federal law allows employers to restrict employee access to labor organizations.

    (E) Collective bargaining was viewed as a fundamental right by the founders.

95. The rule designed to ensure that all products within a given country are treated equally is known as

    (A) equal protection

    (B) equal treatment

    (C) antidiscrimination treatment

    (D) national treatment

    (E) universal treatment

96. On his way from a baseball game, Bruce was walking down the street with his bat and gloves. While he was walking, he noticed a woman getting ready to hit a man with a crowbar. Bruce immediately moved to protect the man by hitting the woman with his baseball bat. If the woman brings suit against Bruce, a court is likely to hold that

    (A) Bruce is not liable so long as he used the amount of force that the man could have used

    (B) Bruce is not liable so long as he reasonably believed the man's life was threatened

    (C) Bruce is not liable unless there is a Good Samaritan statute in the jurisdiction when the suit is brought

    (D) Bruce is liable for battery

    (E) Bruce is liable for assault

97. Which of the following is a distinction that can be made between a grand jury and a petit jury?

    (A) A petit jury hears evidence, and a grand jury does not.

    (B) A petit jury makes decisions regarding criminal cases, and a grand jury only makes decisions involving civil cases.

    (C) The Constitution requires that all cases be decided by a petit jury, and a grand jury is optional.

    (D) There is no distinction between a grand jury and a petit jury.

    (E) A petit jury determines guilt or innocence, and a grand jury determines the sufficiency of the evidence to bring a criminal case.

98. Debbie was in a parking lot when a stranger threw a ball at her. The ball did not hit her. If Debbie did not think the ball would hurt her, which of the following statements is true?

(A) The stranger cannot have any liability because Debbie did not suffer any harm.

(B) The stranger cannot have any liability because Debbie did not fear the ball.

(C) The stranger can be held liable only if the stranger intended to harm Debbie.

(D) The stranger can be held liable if the stranger intended the ball to hit Debbie.

(E) The stranger can be held liable even if the ball slipped from her hands.

99. What action does NOT terminate an offer?

(A) A counteroffer

(B) Mental incompetence

(C) Lapse of time

(D) Changed circumstances

(E) Revocation

100. A defect that results from insufficient warnings can be defined as a

(A) manufacturing defect

(B) product defect

(C) design defect

(D) supplier defect

(E) merchant defect

# CLEP INTRODUCTORY BUSINESS LAW PRACTICE TEST 2

## === Answer Key ===

| | | | |
|---|---|---|---|
| 1. (E) | 26. (C) | 51. (D) | 76. (C) |
| 2. (A) | 27. (B) | 52. (A) | 77. (B) |
| 3. (C) | 28. (B) | 53. (E) | 78. (E) |
| 4. (C) | 29. (E) | 54. (E) | 79. (A) |
| 5. (A) | 30. (C) | 55. (A) | 80. (B) |
| 6. (B) | 31. (C) | 56. (B) | 81. (B) |
| 7. (E) | 32. (C) | 57. (C) | 82. (E) |
| 8. (E) | 33. (A) | 58. (D) | 83. (D) |
| 9. (B) | 34. (E) | 59. (B) | 84. (C) |
| 10. (D) | 35. (B) | 60. (C) | 85. (E) |
| 11. (D) | 36. (E) | 61. (B) | 86. (B) |
| 12. (C) | 37. (B) | 62. (B) | 87. (E) |
| 13. (A) | 38. (A) | 63. (D) | 88. (B) |
| 14. (B) | 39. (D) | 64. (B) | 89. (C) |
| 15. (B) | 40. (A) | 65. (A) | 90. (B) |
| 16. (C) | 41. (B) | 66. (D) | 91. (D) |
| 17. (D) | 42. (C) | 67. (E) | 92. (C) |
| 18. (E) | 43. (D) | 68. (A) | 93. (B) |
| 19. (D) | 44. (E) | 69. (B) | 94. (C) |
| 20. (B) | 45. (B) | 70. (A) | 95. (D) |
| 21. (C) | 46. (E) | 71. (C) | 96. (A) |
| 22. (A) | 47. (C) | 72. (B) | 97. (E) |
| 23. (D) | 48. (C) | 73. (A) | 98. (D) |
| 24. (A) | 49. (A) | 74. (B) | 99. (D) |
| 25. (B) | 50. (B) | 75. (A) | 100. (C) |

# DETAILED EXPLANATIONS OF ANSWERS

## PRACTICE TEST 2

1.   **(E)**   Product liability actions can be brought as tort or contract claims. They can also be brought as warranty claims. (E) includes all those possibilities.

2.   **(A)**   Promissory estoppel is based on a theory of unjust enrichment. (B) is not correct because reliance damages are designed to refund a party. (C) is incorrect because restitution is designed to return a party to her original position. (D) is incorrect because liquidated damages are set damages designed to give the parties some certainty regarding their damage remedy. (E) is incorrect because capacity is not a damage remedy.

3.   **(C)**   A judgment n.o.v. can be made after the jury has entered a verdict. In fact, it is referred to as a judgment notwithstanding the verdict. A directed verdict (A) comes at the end of the plaintiff's presentation of her case. Summary judgment (B) motions are made prior to a full trial. A demurrer (D) is made before the defendant files a response. Venue (E) is a motion that must be made at the first available opportunity or it will be lost.

4.   **(C)**   The Uniform Commercial Code governs the sale of goods. The Parol Evidence Rule (A) concerns when certain evidence will be admitted to help define the meaning of a written agreement. The Statute of Frauds (B) is a rule that governs which contracts must be in writing. The Restatement of Contracts (D) relates to common-law contracts. A Law of Promissory Estoppel (E) does not exist.

5.   **(A)**   The contract between Alice and May is subject to the condition that the pool is open in the summer. As a result, if the condition does not arise, neither party will have an obligation to perform. (B) is incorrect

247

because one party cannot change the contract by creating a different condition. Although a condition may be excused based on substantial performance, a person's preparation for performance (C) is not enough. Thus, the fact that Alice purchased swimwear would not excuse the condition and require May to perform. The lack of a condition (D) occurring means that neither party has to perform and does not create a breach. (E) is incorrect because there has been no performance. The failure of the condition to occur means that there was never an obligation to perform.

6.    **(B)**    The Americans with Disabilities Act requires employers to make reasonable accommodations for employees with disabilities. None of the other acts requires employers to make accommodations for employees covered by the act.

7.    **(E)**    When a third party reasonably believes that an agent has the authority to act, then apparent authority is created and binds the principal. Notice terminates apparent authority. (A) and (B) are incorrect because the agent does not need to expressly consent or ratify the agent's actions. Those represent alternative ways for authority to be created. However, since apparent authority exists, these other forms are not necessary. (C) and (D) are incorrect as well because they merely represent rephrasing of the notion that the principal must take some affirmative action to be held liable; instead, the principal will be liable based on the third party's reasonable impression.

8.    **(E)**    Courts differ on how they treat acceptances that contain different terms. The three formulations represent the three different approaches to the treatment of additional terms. Because the other responses do not include all three approaches, they are incorrect.

9.    **(B)**    A contract will be taken out of the Statute of Frauds when there has been performance, an admission, or promissory estoppel. However, while part performance is sufficient for other forms of contracts, there must be full performance on contracts that are not capable of being performed within a year. All of the other responses represent exceptions to the Statute of Fraud and are incorrect.

10.  **(D)**    The Supreme Court generally gives deference to appeals court decisions. However, the Court does not provide that deference with respect to interpretations of law. Thus the Court reviews such interpretations without regard to the lower court's determination. The Court does not give deference

to all decisions (A), nor does it give deference to interpretations of the law (B). In addition, the Court does not give greater scrutiny for errors. Thus (C) and (E) are incorrect.

11. **(D)** Randy has engaged in short-swing profits because he has made a profit by buying and purchasing shares within a six-month period. A private placement (A) is an offering to sophisticated investors. A public offering (B) is an offering to people who are not sophisticated. Investment profits (C) is not a securities law term. Insider trading (E) is trading on the basis of material nonpublic information.

12. **(C)** Gary most likely has committed an assault because it does not require physical touching, just that a person has reasonable apprehension that touching would arise. That standard should apply to Frank. Battery (A) requires some actual contact. Defamation (B) refers to using language to harm a person's reputation. Negligence (D) requires some physical harm. (E) is also incorrect because it requires some extremely outrageous conduct, and the conduct at issue likely does not qualify.

13. **(A)** Since Meredith never exchanged a promise with Donald, his action of taking care of her bushes appears to be a gift. As such, she cannot be held liable. (B) is incorrect because while Meredith will not be held liable, the lack of a written agreement does not matter. Although justifiable reliance may cause the court to hold a party liable, a court will not find that reliance is justified when a person confers a gift outside an emergency situation. Thus (C) and (D) are incorrect. (E) is incorrect because the fact that Donald may have suffered a detriment is not enough; an exchange of promises must be proven as well.

14. **(B)** The Equal Employment Opportunity Commission oversees the implementation of employment discrimination laws and outlines procedures for filing a claim against an employer. (A) and (E) are incorrect because neither agency exists. The National Labor Relations Board (C) regulates collective bargaining arrangements. The Federal Trade Commission (D) regulates unfair trade practices.

15. **(B)** Section 5 of the Securities Act requires registration of securities unless there is a proper exemption. However, liability for failing to register is imposed under Section 12(a)(1). Thus (B) is correct and (E) is incorrect. Section 11 relates to misstatements in a registration statement, while 12(a)(2) relates to misstatements in a prospectus. Thus, (A) and (C) are

incorrect. Section 4 exempts certain private placements from registration, so (D) is incorrect.

16. **(C)** When one party transfers a right to another, it is referred to as an assignment. A third-party beneficiary contract (A) does not involve transferring any rights. A delegation (B) refers to transferring a duty. A unilateral contract (D) refers to a contract in which a person's act of performance is also acceptance. A bilateral contract (E) refers to one in which two promises are exchanged.

17. **(D)** Of the listed items, only an agreement to extinguish a debt qualifies as consideration because it involves a legal detriment of giving up a right that a person is not obligated to give up. All the other items either do not involve a bargain or do not involve refraining to do something that a person is not otherwise obligated to do. Thus none of the other responses is appropriate.

18. **(E)** The Comprehensive Environmental Response, Compensation, and Liability Act regulates the cleanup of abandoned hazardous wastes. The National Environmental Policy Act (A) establishes the nation's policy with regard to the environment. The Environmental Protection Agency (B) oversees pollution control efforts. The Clean Water Act (C) focuses on ensuring that the nation's water supply remains free from harmful pollutants. The Resource Conservation and Recovery Act (D) regulates disposal for active waste sites.

19. **(D)** Chapter 13 enables debtors to create a plan to repay their debts. Chapter 5 (A) and Chapter 15 (E) do not reflect bankruptcy proceedings. Chapter 7 (B) refers to liquidations, and Chapter 11 (C) refers to reorganizations.

20. **(B)** A company registered under the Securities Exchange Act is referred to as a reporting company. A private company (A) is not registered. An investment company (C) invests in other companies. Neither (D) nor (E) is a company regulated by the federal securities laws.

21. **(C)** Substantial performance refers to a situation in which a party has substantially performed but has committed a minor breach. If there has been a significant breach (A), then substantial performance has not occurred. A substantial performance also means that there has not been a material breach (B). Because substantial performance does reflect some

breach, (D) is incorrect. Similarly (E) is also incorrect because a person always has an obligation to fully perform the contract.

22. **(A)** Common law is a system of judge-made laws. (B), (C), and (D) refer to the civil or code law system. (E) is incorrect because the common law system does not refer to laws but rather to court decisions.

23. **(D)** Corporate social responsibility refers to the notion that corporations should focus on all corporate stakeholders. Shareholder primacy (A) is a theory that supports a corporate focus primarily on shareholders. Fiduciary responsibility (B) refers to the duty corporate officers and directors as well as other agents owe to perform their duties in the best interests of their respective entities. Corporate charitable giving (C) is a component of social responsibility because it represents, a corporation's efforts to give to charitable causes. However, it is just one aspect of social responsibility. (E) is also incorrect because it is a concept that is embodied in social responsibility but does not refer to the theory itself.

24. **(A)** In this case Tanya has entered into a contract, and then a change occurred that frustrated her purpose for entering into the contract. Because of the accident, she no longer has a reason for her contract. A unilateral mistake (B) refers to a situation in which a person enters into a contract based on a mistake. Unconscionability (C) refers to contracts that are outrageous. Duress (D) refers to contracts that are entered into because of some inappropriate threat. Promissory estoppel (E) refers to a court enforcing a contract despite lack of consideration.

25. **(B)** Judicial review is the process of reviewing decisions to ensure that they are constitutional. Neither judicial examination (A) nor constitutional examination (C) are concepts recognized in constitutional law. Federalism (D) refers to a system of shared power between states and the federal government. Precedent (E) refers to prior case law.

26. **(C)** The First Amendment protects the freedom of speech. However, not all speech merits protection. When speech creates a danger to the public, the government may regulate the speech because it is not protected under the First Amendment. That is the case with speech such as Andy's, which may cause panic and potential harm to a large number of people. Courts assess that kind of speech under the clear and present danger test. (A) is incorrect because Andy's speech will not be subject to strict scrutiny, and if it were, then it makes it easier for Andy to avoid liability because it requires the government to have

a compelling reason to restrict speech. (B) is not the best response because time, place, and manner restrictions refer to restrictions that are content neutral. Both (D) and (E) are not correct because Andy's ability to exercise his freedom of speech and his freedom of association are not absolute, so his rights do not give him the freedom to endanger the lives of others.

27. **(B)** The Due Process clause protects a defendant's rights to a fair trial. The Takings Clause (A) refers to governmental takings. The Equal Protection Clause (C) reflects a provision that prohibits discrimination. The Supremacy Clause (D) makes federal laws and treaties the supreme law of the land. The Proper Procedure Clause (E) does not exist.

28. **(B)** Under the mailbox rule, an acceptance is the only communication that is effective on dispatch. An offer (A) must be communicated to the offeree. Under the mailbox rule, all other communications are effective when they are received. Thus (C), (D), and (E) are incorrect.

29. **(E)** When there are misstatements in a registration statement, a director may avoid liability by raising a diligence defense. In that defense the director must demonstrate that she had a reasonable basis to believe that the statement was true. An issuer is strictly liable, so (A) is not correct. Experts are only liable for misstatement in portions that they certified, thus (B) is not correct. Defendants can raise different diligence defenses, so (C) is not correct. Directors only have an obligation to investigate information that is not within an expert portion of the registration, so (D) is incorrect.

30. **(C)** This question focuses on assignments and delegations. (C) is not true because an assignment does not require the prior consent of the obligor. (A) is true because a personal service cannot be delegated. (B) is true because a party must receive notice so that she can know to whom she owes service after an assignment. (D) is true because the lack of notice relieves Benny of liability. (E) is true because notice of assignment means that the assignment must be held for the assignee.

31. **(C)** Flow-through tax treatment means that there is no tax at the entity level. Instead, people get taxed on their share of the profits. Shareholders do not get taxed on the corporation's profits. They are taxed on their portion of any distributions. Thus (A) is not correct. Because employees also do not get taxed on an entity's profits, (B) is not correct. (D) is incorrect because partners do have some tax liability. (E) is incorrect because employees do not have such tax liability.

32. **(C)** The Parol Evidence Rule covers the admissibility of particular evidence. When an agreement is integrated, oral and written evidence are not admissible to determine the meaning of the agreement. (A) and (B) are not correct because the Parol Evidence Rule does not relate to whether oral agreements can be in writing. (D) is not correct because the Parol Evidence Rule relates to more than just oral evidence. (E) is incorrect because when a contract is partially integrated, oral and written evidence may be admitted.

33. **(A)** This question demonstrates the process of proximate cause. In this case Vicki is likely to be held liable because the injury was a foreseeable result of her driving without reasonable care. This is true even though the pole was an intervening force, because it was foreseeable that the pole would hit someone and cause that person injury. (B) is not correct because in negligence actions a person must show actual or "but for" cause as well as proximate cause; actual cause by itself will not support liability. (C) is incorrect because Kim can be liable for injuries caused by other forces if those forces are foreseeable. (D) is incorrect because every person has an obligation to use reasonable care and hence can be liable if they fail to use reasonable care and harm strangers as a result. (E) is incorrect because there is no need to demonstrate the forseeability of the extent of the harm so long as the injury itself is foreseeable.

34. **(E)** A plaintiff must establish both personal and subject manner jurisdiction as well as proper venue before bringing a suit in court.

35. **(B)** An investment contract requires a showing of an investment of money in a common enterprise that relies on the efforts of others. None of the other elements represents a component of investment contracts.

36. **(E)** Contracts that are not capable of being performed within one year are covered by the Statute of Frauds. This includes contracts that take more than one year to complete. Because this contract will take five years, it falls within the Statute of Frauds. For contracts that cannot be completed within a year, full performance is necessary to take the contract out of the Statute and make it enforceable. Wendy's partial performance (A) is not enough to take the contract out of the Statute. (B) is not correct because a contract falls within the Statute if the entire contract cannot be performed within a year. It does not matter that Wendy began performing within a year if she cannot also complete that performance by the end of the year. (C) is not true. (D) is not correct because a contract needs to be in writing and

signed by the party to be bound to be enforceable; both parties' signatures are not necessary.

37. **(B)** Remediation consists of reducing the health risks associated with a site. Perfection (C) refers to ensuring that a priority is established for a security interest. Attachment (D) refers to creating a security interest. (A) and (E) are incorrect because they are generic terms for cleaning up hazardous materials.

38. **(A)** The Securities and Exchange Commission ("SEC") is an administrative agency. None of the other terms applies to the SEC.

39. **(D)** The contract Joe entered into with Monica is likely unenforceable based on duress, because Joe made an improper threat to expose embarrassing details and he appeared to leave Monica with no other alternative since she is new to the neighborhood. (A) is incorrect because Monica appears to have a defense to enforcement. (B) is not correct because an improper threat for purposes of duress does not need to be illegal. (C) is not correct because the contract did not have mutual assent; Monica's assent appeared to have resulted from duress. (E) is incorrect because contracts that violate public policy must stem from some policy found in a statute or some other legislative action.

40. **(A)** Interference with business relations requires that there be a valid business relationship or expected relationship, that the defendant knew of the relationship, that the defendant intentionally interfered with the relationship in a manner that caused its breach or termination, and that the plaintiff was damaged as a result of the interference. (B) is not correct because the defendant's motives are not important. (C) is not correct because the plaintiff must have suffered only some damage, not severe loss. The claim does not involve cure (D), nor does it require that the relationship be long-standing (E).

41. **(B)** A limited liability partnership imposes liability on partners for personal actions and those of people being supervised by them. A limited partnership (A) imposes full liability on all the general partners and limited liability on the limited partners. A limited liability company (C) and a corporation (D) enable all owners to have limited liability. All partners have liability in a general partnership (E).

42. **(C)** A security interest requires that some consideration be given to be enforceable. (A) and (B) are not correct because both these actions may establish perfection, but they are not necessary to ensure that the security

interest is enforceable. A debtor, not a creditor, must sign the security agreement, so (D) is not correct. A security interest does not require notice before enforcement, thus (E) is not correct.

43. **(D)** The Supremacy Clause makes federal law, the Constitution, and federal treaties the supreme law of the land. None of the other items falls within the scope of the Supremacy Clause.

44. **(E)** A tie-in is a vertical agreement that is not necessarily illegal. The other agreements are horizontal agreements that are illegal because they are deemed to be restraints on trade.

45. **(B)** A motion for lack of personal jurisdiction must be made at the first opportunity or it will be deemed waived. A motion for summary judgment (A) can be filed at any time. A motion for directed verdict (C) must occur at the end of the plaintiff's case. A motion for lack of subject matter jurisdiction (D) can be made at any time. A judgment n.o.v. (E) can only be made after the verdict.

46. **(E)** Lawrence has created an anticipatory repudiation because he has demonstrated his express intent not to perform when performance comes due. Kelly can treat the contract as terminated because Lawrence's repudiation represents a total breach. (A) is incorrect because Lawrence has repudiated despite having time to perform. (B) is incorrect because his notification is what reveals his repudiation and hence makes him liable. Kelly does not have to demonstrate that she changed her position for Lawrence's repudiation to be effective (C). Lawrence is liable; the amount of time he gave Kelly is irrelevant (D).

47. **(C)** A mutual mistake is when both parties are mistaken about a basic assumption of the contract that has a material impact on performance, and the party seeking to avoid performance could not have assumed the risk of the mistake. (C) is the correct response because issues of control are not an element of mutual mistake.

48. **(C)** An appeals court can perform all the listed functions other than examining or reexamining witnesses because such an examination occurs in the context of a trial and an appeals court does not conduct trials.

49. **(A)** Vicarious liability is a general rule covering situations in which someone is held liable for the tort actions of third parties. In the context

of employment, vicarious liability means that the employer is liable for all the torts of an employee that occurred within the scope of employment. Because the torts must occur within the scope of employment, (B) is not the correct response. (C) is not correct because vicarious liability does not focus on contracts; agency law holds an employer liable for an employee's contracts. Thus (D) is also not correct. In addition, an employer is generally not liable for intentional torts of the employee. (E) is not correct because an employer will be held liable even if the employee does not obey the employer's instructions.

50. **(B)** If an event occurs after contract formation, it is known as a changed circumstance and can serve as the basis for avoiding a contract. In this case Michael's death makes performance literally impossible. Unconscionability (A) relates to a contract that is shocking or outrageous. Although frustration of purpose (C) is one of the doctrines of changed circumstances, it applies when a contract loses its value even though performance can still occur. In this case, performance cannot occur; thus impossibility is the more appropriate doctrine. Mutual mistake (D) refers to a mistake made during formation and thus is not applicable to this setting. Duress (E) occurs when a contract is entered into because of an improper threat, and that has not occurred here.

51. **(D)** Carl's actions constituted an anticipatory repudiation because he indicated his intention not to perform. However, he can retract the repudiation by indicating a willingness to perform. In this case his retraction appears valid. (A) is not correct because Carl's call does not become a counteroffer. (B) is not correct because a breach cannot occur until the repudiation has been finally accepted, and here it has been retracted in time so there is no breach. (C) is not correct because there is no need for the offer to be in writing. (E) is not correct because a contract can be breached by repudiation when it has not been effectively retracted.

52. **(A)** *Res ipsa loquitor* is a doctrine used to establish a breach of a duty when an action normally occurs as a result of negligent conduct.

53. **(E)** When a contract has been substantially performed but has some defect, the ordinary measure of damages is cost of completion. However, when there would be economic waste, the measure of damages becomes diminution in value, which means the difference in value between the defective performance and a proper performance. Here reconstructing the doghouse would produce economic waste because of the significant cost

involved. As a result, the damage award will be diminution in value. (A) is not correct because the subject matter of the contract does not matter. (B) is not correct because substantial performance means that there has been a breach, and liability will be imposed whenever there is a breach. (C) is not correct because it does not relate to a recognized damage remedy. (D) is not correct because it is the normal award for damage but does not take into account economic waste.

54.  **(E)**   This contract is a third-party beneficiary contract because it aims to benefit Lisa. Lisa is an intended beneficiary because the contract recognizes her. In addition, Lisa is a creditor beneficiary because the contract is entered into to satisfy a debt that Roger owes to Lisa. As a result, Lisa can enforce the claim against Chris as well as Roger because he still owes her money. Roger also can enforce the claim against Chris because Chris has an obligation to perform on Lisa's behalf. Chris can raise any defenses against Lisa that he could raise against Roger, thus he can raise the issues of Roger's breach. However, Chris cannot raise a claim that is personal to Roger and Lisa's contract. Thus he cannot raise a claim regarding Lisa not owing Roger any money.

55.  **(A)**   A jury verdict generally has to be unanimous. (B) is incorrect because jury verdicts in a civil trial must be decided based on the preponderance of the evidence. (C) is not correct because a court can overturn the verdict based on improper application of the law. (D) is not correct because juries must receive instruction from the judge. (E) is not correct because a verdict must be reached without reliance on a judge's opinion.

56.  **(B)**   Contracts with mentally incompetent people are voidable by the mentally incompetent person. The general rule is that the parties must be restored to their original positions. Hence, it would appear that Kevin would need to restore the remaining $4,000. However, when a person has reason to know of the incompetence, the contract can be avoided without having to restore the parties to their original positions.

57.  **(C)**   The Fair Labor Standards Act provides minimum wage and overtime for both full- and part-time employees. The Act also prohibits employers from hiring children under a certain age. However, the Act does not regulate labor practices.

58.  **(D)**   Personal jurisdiction relates to a court's ability to exercise jurisdiction over a person, while subject matter jurisdiction involves the ability

to exercise jurisdiction of the subject of the particular case. This scenario involves a question about personal jurisdiction. Because Jan is employed by a company that is headquartered in the state where suit is brought, there is likely enough minimum contacts to justify personal jurisdiction. (A) and (E) are not correct because the facts at issue do not implicate subject matter jurisdiction. (B) is not correct because minimum contacts allow a person to be sued in a state even when the person has never been in it. (C) is incorrect because personal jurisdiction can arise in ways other than through consent and because the issues do not implicate subject matter jurisdiction.

59. **(B)** The Sandy Springs law classifies people on the basis of sex and thus implicates the Fourteenth Amendment. Sex is not a suspect classification but is quasi-suspect and must survive intermediate scrutiny in order to be upheld. Sex is not a suspect classification and thus does not have to meet strict scrutiny (A). A classification based on sex does not get a rational basis review (C). The rule of reason test (D) is a standard of review for trade practices. The time, place, and manner test (E) is a standard of review in First Amendment cases.

60. **(C)** The Necessary and Proper Clause grants Congress the power to make all laws necessary to effectuate its legislative powers. The Supremacy Clause (A) makes certain laws and treaties the supreme law of the land. (B) is not correct because it governs fair processes. (D) is not correct because such a clause does not exist. (E) is not correct because it involves Congress's ability to regulate interstate commerce.

61. **(B)** Novation is the correct term. (A) is incorrect because it transfers a right. Accord and satisfaction (C) is an agreement between the same parties to accept different performance that extinguishes rights. By contrast, Novation occurs when an agreement is taken over by a third party. Rescission (D) relates to terminating a contract, not taking one over. (E) is not correct because it refers to a contract in which both parties continue to have performance obligations.

62. **(B)** Normally, a contract with a minor is voidable by a minor during the period he is minor and a reasonable time after he reaches majority. This is true even if the contracting party believes a person is not a minor. There are exceptions, including a contract for necessities, a contract with a minor who is married, and a contract with a minor who deliberately misrepresented her age. Thus (A), (C), and (E) are not correct responses because

they reflect recognized exceptions. (D) is incorrect because it reflects the idea that a contract must be disaffirmed within a reasonable time.

63. **(D)**   Piercing the corporate veil is a doctrine that disregards the usual protection of limited liability within a corporation and holds directors and officers liable for the debts of the corporation. It is generally only used for fraud or illegality. In all other circumstances, directors cannot be held liable for those debts; thus, (A) and (B) are incorrect. (C) is not correct because it is just a statement of limited liability and does not reflect the piercing doctrine. (E) is not true and also does not reflect the piercing doctrine.

64. **(B)**   When a change occurs after contract formation, it may give rise to the ability to avoid enforcement. In this case the change is a law. Courts view such change as making the contract impossible to perform, even though it is not literally impossible to do so. There is still consideration despite the illegal nature of Gina's agreement, because when she entered into the contract there was a legal detriment. Thus, (A) is incorrect. (C) is incorrect because there remains a mutual obligation, even though one person can no longer perform her obligation without violating the law. (D) is incorrect because the contract is no longer enforceable. (E) is incorrect because Alice's reaffirmation does not make the contract valid.

65. **(A)**   Because government contracts tend to benefit members of society, they generally are deemed to have intended beneficiaries only when they give a private right of enforcement. All the other contracts listed do not have intended beneficiaries.

66. **(D)**   Administrative agencies are given a lot of discretion. To appeal an administrative agency's opinion, all administrative remedies must be exhausted. (A) is not correct because courts can overturn agency rules. (B) is not correct because such agencies are required to have public meetings. (C) is not true because actions involving interpretations of laws outside of an agency's area of expertise are not given deference. (E) is not true because an agency's action can be appealed to the federal courts.

67. **(E)**   A contract may be unenforceable for various reasons. However, it does not become unenforceable just because it is more difficult to perform. All the other responses reflect valid reasons why a contract may be unenforceable.

68. **(A)** A battery occurs when someone touches another person in a harmful or offensive manner. The contact can be made to the person or something connected to the person. In this case the fact that the contact was made to the backpack, does not negate the battery. Assault refers to a situation when a person has reasonable apprehension of a battery. In his case, because Kevin's back was turned, he could not have any reasonable apprehension of contact. Thus, (B) is not correct. Because battery does not require knowledge of the contact, (C) is incorrect. (D) is not correct because assault does not require actual contact. (E) is not correct because battery does not require that the defendant actually make contact, only that the defendant put in motion the contact—in this case throwing the rock.

69. **(B)** The Federal Communications Commission regulates radio, television, and other forms of communication.

70. **(A)** A counteroffer is a rejection followed by a new offer. For a response to be deemed a rejection, it typically must clearly indicate a desire not to accept an offer. When the response is ambiguous and the offeree reveals a willingness to continue considering the offer, courts are more likely to define a person's response as a suggestion for change, rather than a counteroffer or rejection. (B) is incorrect because the response does not appear to be a rejection. (C) is incorrect because the response does not appear to be a clear rejection, and hence it is less likely that there is a counteroffer. In addition, (C) is incorrect because the response does not appear to make a new offer but is a suggestion for discussion of new terms. (D) is incorrect because the response does not appear to manifest acceptance and because the terms seem sufficiently different from the original offer that there could not be acceptance based on the response. (E) is incorrect because a rejection must indicate a clear desire not to accept.

71. **(C)** The Equal Employment Opportunity Commission has broad powers to regulate discrimination in the workplace. However, it cannot issue an injunction; that is something only a court can do. All the other responses are correct reflections of the Commission's authority.

72. **(B)** A form contract is known as an adhesion contract. An investment contract (A) is a security. (C) is incorrect because it refers to a contract where a promise is made for a performance. (D) is incorrect because it refers to a contract that continues to have performance obligations for both parties. (E) is incorrect because it is not the term for a form contract.

73. **(A)**  Because Nicole already has an obligation to give Charles golf lessons, his agreement to pay the additional money would be unenforceable because it lacks consideration under the preexisting duty rule. Because this is not a contract for goods, the UCC, which allows contracts to be modified without consideration, does not apply. (D) is not correct because there is no new consideration on Nicole's part. (E) is not correct because assent does not substitute for consideration. (B) and (C) are not correct because they are not applicable.

74. **(B)**  Expropriation refers to foreign government takings. A takings (A) occurs when a person's own government takes their property. Appropriation (C) is not recognized in this context. Both tariffs (D) and exports (E) relate to trade and thus are not applicable.

75. **(A)**  Under the UCC, the buyer's ability to reject goods in installment contracts is limited. Outside the installment contract, the UCC allows a buyer to reject goods if they do not conform in any respect with the contract terms.

76. **(C)**  Unconscionability is a doctrine that allows for contract avoidance when a contract "shocks the conscience" which means the contract must be extremely one-sided and unfair.

77. **(B)**  A proxy statement is issued in connection with the solicitation of a shareholder's vote and is not related to creditors' rights. All the other documents and terms are related to creditors' rights.

78. **(E)**  Under the UCC, a contract for the sale of goods can be modified without consideration so long as the modification occurs in good faith. Each of the other responses is incorrect.

79. **(A)**  Only a bona fide occupational qualification has been recognized as an exception to employment discrimination. The other responses relate to economic justifications that are not recognized as valid reasons for employment discrimination.

80. **(B)**  The Securities Act regulates the offer and sale of securities. The rest of these statements are inapplicable.

81. **(B)**  A counteroffer is a rejection followed by a new offer. Once an offer has been rejected based on a counteroffer, the rejection terminates the

offeree's ability to accept the offer. (B) is the best answer because Sam's response appears to be a counteroffer, which serves to reject Brian's offer, terminating Sam's ability to accept. (A) is incorrect because Sam's counteroffer was a rejection. (C) is incorrect because Brian does not have to revoke the offer; the offer also can be terminated by Sam's counteroffer. (D) is incorrect because whether the contract is a unilateral one has no impact on Sam's rejection based on the counteroffer. (E) is incorrect because an offeree does not have the power to accept an offer that has been terminated by revocation, rejection, or some other means.

82. **(E)** Although Scott is a minor, he can be held liable in tort and for negligence. With regard to negligence, the reasonable-person standard will be adapted to a standard of care appropriate for Scott's age and skill. The fact that Scott is a minor does not prevent him from having liability. Thus both (A) and (B) are incorrect. (C) and (D) are incorrect because they do not take into account that Scott can be held liable for both negligence and an intentional tort such as battery.

83. **(D)** The unemployment compensation program is a combined federal and state program. Thus (A) is incorrect. Because it is funded by state funds and by employer funds (B) is not correct. Unlike Workers' Compensation, employees do not give up any rights to participate in the program, so (C) is incorrect. State law determines both eligibility and compensation levels making (E) incorrect.

84. **(C)** By paying $50 to keep the offer open for 45 days, Kevin has created an option contract. Although ordinarily an offer terminates upon the offeror's death, that rule does not apply to an option contract. Instead, the offer must remain open until the end of the option period. (A) is incorrect because Kevin has an option contract, which changes the general rule that the offer terminates at the offeror's death. (B) is incorrect because there is an option contract covering a 45-day period, and hence you cannot conclude that Kevin has waited too long to accept, causing the offer to lapse. (D) is incorrect because Alex's estate cannot revoke an option contract. (E) is incorrect because the offer can be revoked once the option period has concluded.

85. **(E)** The contract between Reggie and Kelly is a unilateral contract because acceptance appears to occur on performance. With a unilateral contract, acceptance cannot occur and a contract cannot be formed until performance occurs. If the contract were not unilateral, Reggie could revoke his

offer prior to Kelly's performance because an offeror can revoke a contract before acceptance. However, with a unilateral contract an offer cannot be revoked once performance has begun. Instead, the offeror must give the offeree the chance to complete performance and accept the contract. Therefore, Reggie's best defense is (E) because if Kelly's performance has not occurred, he does not have to allow her to complete her performance, but instead can revoke his offer. (A) is incorrect because while the contract is unilateral, that fact on its own does not determine if Reggie can avoid the contract. (B) is incorrect because the contract is a unilateral one and because if the contract were bilateral, then presumably Kelly's acceptance occurred at the time she agreed to come to the party. If this is true, then Reggie cannot revoke. (C) is incorrect because the facts do not reveal that Kelly began performance. In addition, if this fact were true, it would defeat Reggie's claim. Because this is a unilateral contract, if Kelly had begun performance, Reggie would be obligated to allow her to complete the performance. (D) is incorrect because Reggie's decision to cancel his party has no impact on whether or not an offer or acceptance has occurred.

86. **(B)** A lawsuit by shareholders regarding a breach of fiduciary duty claim is a shareholder derivative suit. The other responses do not relate to shareholder actions and thus are incorrect.

87. **(E)** Each of the three responses can be used to demonstrate that an offer has not been made. The terms of a communication must be certain and definite for the communication to be deemed an offer. In addition, when a communication is made to a broad group so that the intended offerees cannot be determined, the communication is less likely to be construed as an offer. For this reason advertisements are generally not construed as offers. Finally, when a communication requires further negotiation, it is not likely to be deemed an offer but should be considered an invitation to make an offer.

88. **(B)** Most-favored nation treatment is designed to promote fair trade and thus means that countries should not discriminate among trading partners. The notion that nations should treat all products in the borders equally (A) is called national treatment. Both of these treatments are antidiscrimination rules, so (C), (D) and (E) are incorrect.

89. **(C)** Utilitarianism is a consequentialist theory that maintains that the best ethical rule is to do the greatest amount of good for the greatest number

of people. (A), (B), and (E) focus on duty-oriented ethics. Libertarianism (D) focuses on individual liberties.

90. **(B)** Although Alcynthia has breached the contract, Gloria's ability to recover damages will depend on whether she complied with her duty to mitigate damages. That duty requires Gloria make a reasonable effort to reduce the amount of damages created by Alcynthia's breach. In this case, Gloria had the ability to mitigate her damages completely by accepting Denise's offer, but Gloria refused to do so. This refusal will prevent Gloria from recovering any damages from Alcynthia. (A) is not correct because even if Alcynthia has not performed under the contract, a contract had been created. Gloria's lack of performance does not impact her ability to recover damages so long as Alcynthia breached the contract. (C) is incorrect because when a party breaches a contract, the breach does not necessarily entitle the non-breaching party to damages. Instead, damages will be reduced by any losses and costs avoided. Since the losses could have been avoided, Gloria will not recover from Alcynthia. (D) is incorrect because the fact that Denise was not a party to the contract does not impact the duty to mitigate. (E) is incorrect because the contract was not a unilateral contract and also because the type of contract does not impact the duty to mitigate.

91. **(D)** The Supreme Court's jurisdiction over cases involving citizens of different states is diversity jurisdiction. That jurisdiction is shared with state courts. The Supreme Court has original jurisdiction over all the other types of cases listed.

92. **(C)** Misappropriation relates to a theory that expands the number of people who can be liable for insider trading and does not relate to environmental laws. The remaining responses do have some association with environmental regulations.

93. **(B)** *In pari delicto* refers to the notion that a court will leave the parties as it finds them. A court is most likely to apply this principle when a contract is illegal because the court does not want to enforce an illegal bargain. As a result, courts may not award any remedy to parties engaged in an illegal contract. The other doctrines are not applicable.

94. **(C)** Federal law protects employees' ability to bargain collectively. As a result, employers must bargain directly with employee representatives. The other statements are incorrect because federal law not only permits collective bargaining but also permits strikes and requires that employers allow

employees to join labor organizations. (E) is incorrect because collective bargaining was not viewed as a right and historically was restricted.

95. **(D)** National treatment is the rule that aims to prevent discrimination between products within a nation's borders. The other doctrines are not applicable to trade in foreign countries.

96. **(A)** Bruce will be seeking to use the defense-of-others defense to avoid liability for his battery. That defense can be used whenever a person reasonably believes force is necessary. The person who uses force on another's behalf may use the amount of force that the victim could have used. (B) is incorrect because the defense of others is not limited to situations where someone's life is threatened. So long as the person is threatened with injury, defense of others can be used to help them. (C) is incorrect because a Good Samaritan statute may shield a person who comes to the rescue of someone else, but if Bruce is successful with his defense-of-others claim, he will not need the protection of that statute. Also, if Bruce is successful, he will not be liable for battery or assault; thus (D) and (E) are not the best answers.

97. **(E)** A grand jury determines if a criminal case can be brought against a defendant, and a petit jury delivers a verdict. Both juries hear evidence, so (A) is not correct. A grand jury (B) only makes decisions on criminal cases. A grand jury is required by the Constitution, so (C) is incorrect. Because there are differences between a grand jury and a petit jury, (D) is incorrect.

98. **(D)** Battery stems from an intentional contact. If the stranger intended the contact with Debbie, the stranger will be held liable. Battery does not require that a person fear the contact (B) or suffer physical injury (A). From the defendant's perspective, battery does not require intent to harm (C). However, battery requires intentional contact, and thus if the ball slipped (E), there would be no intent.

99. **(D)** Changed circumstances do not terminate an offer. All the other responses terminate an offer.

100. **(C)** An inadequate warning defect is also known as a design defect. Thus (A) is incorrect. (B) is incorrect because *product defect* is a general term whereas *design defect* reflects the more particular type of product defect. (D) and (E) are incorrect because they are not recognized forms of product defect.

# CLEP INTRODUCTORY BUSINESS LAW—TEST 1

1. Ⓐ Ⓑ Ⓒ Ⓓ Ⓔ
2. Ⓐ Ⓑ Ⓒ Ⓓ Ⓔ
3. Ⓐ Ⓑ Ⓒ Ⓓ Ⓔ
4. Ⓐ Ⓑ Ⓒ Ⓓ Ⓔ
5. Ⓐ Ⓑ Ⓒ Ⓓ Ⓔ
6. Ⓐ Ⓑ Ⓒ Ⓓ Ⓔ
7. Ⓐ Ⓑ Ⓒ Ⓓ Ⓔ
8. Ⓐ Ⓑ Ⓒ Ⓓ Ⓔ
9. Ⓐ Ⓑ Ⓒ Ⓓ Ⓔ
10. Ⓐ Ⓑ Ⓒ Ⓓ Ⓔ
11. Ⓐ Ⓑ Ⓒ Ⓓ Ⓔ
12. Ⓐ Ⓑ Ⓒ Ⓓ Ⓔ
13. Ⓐ Ⓑ Ⓒ Ⓓ Ⓔ
14. Ⓐ Ⓑ Ⓒ Ⓓ Ⓔ
15. Ⓐ Ⓑ Ⓒ Ⓓ Ⓔ
16. Ⓐ Ⓑ Ⓒ Ⓓ Ⓔ
17. Ⓐ Ⓑ Ⓒ Ⓓ Ⓔ
18. Ⓐ Ⓑ Ⓒ Ⓓ Ⓔ
19. Ⓐ Ⓑ Ⓒ Ⓓ Ⓔ
20. Ⓐ Ⓑ Ⓒ Ⓓ Ⓔ
21. Ⓐ Ⓑ Ⓒ Ⓓ Ⓔ
22. Ⓐ Ⓑ Ⓒ Ⓓ Ⓔ
23. Ⓐ Ⓑ Ⓒ Ⓓ Ⓔ
24. Ⓐ Ⓑ Ⓒ Ⓓ Ⓔ
25. Ⓐ Ⓑ Ⓒ Ⓓ Ⓔ
26. Ⓐ Ⓑ Ⓒ Ⓓ Ⓔ
27. Ⓐ Ⓑ Ⓒ Ⓓ Ⓔ
28. Ⓐ Ⓑ Ⓒ Ⓓ Ⓔ
29. Ⓐ Ⓑ Ⓒ Ⓓ Ⓔ
30. Ⓐ Ⓑ Ⓒ Ⓓ Ⓔ
31. Ⓐ Ⓑ Ⓒ Ⓓ Ⓔ
32. Ⓐ Ⓑ Ⓒ Ⓓ Ⓔ
33. Ⓐ Ⓑ Ⓒ Ⓓ Ⓔ
34. Ⓐ Ⓑ Ⓒ Ⓓ Ⓔ

35. Ⓐ Ⓑ Ⓒ Ⓓ Ⓔ
36. Ⓐ Ⓑ Ⓒ Ⓓ Ⓔ
37. Ⓐ Ⓑ Ⓒ Ⓓ Ⓔ
38. Ⓐ Ⓑ Ⓒ Ⓓ Ⓔ
39. Ⓐ Ⓑ Ⓒ Ⓓ Ⓔ
40. Ⓐ Ⓑ Ⓒ Ⓓ Ⓔ
41. Ⓐ Ⓑ Ⓒ Ⓓ Ⓔ
42. Ⓐ Ⓑ Ⓒ Ⓓ Ⓔ
43. Ⓐ Ⓑ Ⓒ Ⓓ Ⓔ
44. Ⓐ Ⓑ Ⓒ Ⓓ Ⓔ
45. Ⓐ Ⓑ Ⓒ Ⓓ Ⓔ
46. Ⓐ Ⓑ Ⓒ Ⓓ Ⓔ
47. Ⓐ Ⓑ Ⓒ Ⓓ Ⓔ
48. Ⓐ Ⓑ Ⓒ Ⓓ Ⓔ
49. Ⓐ Ⓑ Ⓒ Ⓓ Ⓔ
50. Ⓐ Ⓑ Ⓒ Ⓓ Ⓔ
51. Ⓐ Ⓑ Ⓒ Ⓓ Ⓔ
52. Ⓐ Ⓑ Ⓒ Ⓓ Ⓔ
53. Ⓐ Ⓑ Ⓒ Ⓓ Ⓔ
54. Ⓐ Ⓑ Ⓒ Ⓓ Ⓔ
55. Ⓐ Ⓑ Ⓒ Ⓓ Ⓔ
56. Ⓐ Ⓑ Ⓒ Ⓓ Ⓔ
57. Ⓐ Ⓑ Ⓒ Ⓓ Ⓔ
58. Ⓐ Ⓑ Ⓒ Ⓓ Ⓔ
59. Ⓐ Ⓑ Ⓒ Ⓓ Ⓔ
60. Ⓐ Ⓑ Ⓒ Ⓓ Ⓔ
61. Ⓐ Ⓑ Ⓒ Ⓓ Ⓔ
62. Ⓐ Ⓑ Ⓒ Ⓓ Ⓔ
63. Ⓐ Ⓑ Ⓒ Ⓓ Ⓔ
64. Ⓐ Ⓑ Ⓒ Ⓓ Ⓔ
65. Ⓐ Ⓑ Ⓒ Ⓓ Ⓔ
66. Ⓐ Ⓑ Ⓒ Ⓓ Ⓔ
67. Ⓐ Ⓑ Ⓒ Ⓓ Ⓔ
68. Ⓐ Ⓑ Ⓒ Ⓓ Ⓔ

69. Ⓐ Ⓑ Ⓒ Ⓓ Ⓔ
70. Ⓐ Ⓑ Ⓒ Ⓓ Ⓔ
71. Ⓐ Ⓑ Ⓒ Ⓓ Ⓔ
72. Ⓐ Ⓑ Ⓒ Ⓓ Ⓔ
73. Ⓐ Ⓑ Ⓒ Ⓓ Ⓔ
74. Ⓐ Ⓑ Ⓒ Ⓓ Ⓔ
75. Ⓐ Ⓑ Ⓒ Ⓓ Ⓔ
76. Ⓐ Ⓑ Ⓒ Ⓓ Ⓔ
77. Ⓐ Ⓑ Ⓒ Ⓓ Ⓔ
78. Ⓐ Ⓑ Ⓒ Ⓓ Ⓔ
79. Ⓐ Ⓑ Ⓒ Ⓓ Ⓔ
80. Ⓐ Ⓑ Ⓒ Ⓓ Ⓔ
81. Ⓐ Ⓑ Ⓒ Ⓓ Ⓔ
82. Ⓐ Ⓑ Ⓒ Ⓓ Ⓔ
83. Ⓐ Ⓑ Ⓒ Ⓓ Ⓔ
84. Ⓐ Ⓑ Ⓒ Ⓓ Ⓔ
85. Ⓐ Ⓑ Ⓒ Ⓓ Ⓔ
86. Ⓐ Ⓑ Ⓒ Ⓓ Ⓔ
87. Ⓐ Ⓑ Ⓒ Ⓓ Ⓔ
88. Ⓐ Ⓑ Ⓒ Ⓓ Ⓔ
89. Ⓐ Ⓑ Ⓒ Ⓓ Ⓔ
90. Ⓐ Ⓑ Ⓒ Ⓓ Ⓔ
91. Ⓐ Ⓑ Ⓒ Ⓓ Ⓔ
92. Ⓐ Ⓑ Ⓒ Ⓓ Ⓔ
93. Ⓐ Ⓑ Ⓒ Ⓓ Ⓔ
94. Ⓐ Ⓑ Ⓒ Ⓓ Ⓔ
95. Ⓐ Ⓑ Ⓒ Ⓓ Ⓔ
96. Ⓐ Ⓑ Ⓒ Ⓓ Ⓔ
97. Ⓐ Ⓑ Ⓒ Ⓓ Ⓔ
98. Ⓐ Ⓑ Ⓒ Ⓓ Ⓔ
99. Ⓐ Ⓑ Ⓒ Ⓓ Ⓔ
100. Ⓐ Ⓑ Ⓒ Ⓓ Ⓔ

# CLEP INTRODUCTORY BUSINESS LAW—TEST 2

1. Ⓐ Ⓑ Ⓒ Ⓓ Ⓔ
2. Ⓐ Ⓑ Ⓒ Ⓓ Ⓔ
3. Ⓐ Ⓑ Ⓒ Ⓓ Ⓔ
4. Ⓐ Ⓑ Ⓒ Ⓓ Ⓔ
5. Ⓐ Ⓑ Ⓒ Ⓓ Ⓔ
6. Ⓐ Ⓑ Ⓒ Ⓓ Ⓔ
7. Ⓐ Ⓑ Ⓒ Ⓓ Ⓔ
8. Ⓐ Ⓑ Ⓒ Ⓓ Ⓔ
9. Ⓐ Ⓑ Ⓒ Ⓓ Ⓔ
10. Ⓐ Ⓑ Ⓒ Ⓓ Ⓔ
11. Ⓐ Ⓑ Ⓒ Ⓓ Ⓔ
12. Ⓐ Ⓑ Ⓒ Ⓓ Ⓔ
13. Ⓐ Ⓑ Ⓒ Ⓓ Ⓔ
14. Ⓐ Ⓑ Ⓒ Ⓓ Ⓔ
15. Ⓐ Ⓑ Ⓒ Ⓓ Ⓔ
16. Ⓐ Ⓑ Ⓒ Ⓓ Ⓔ
17 Ⓐ Ⓑ Ⓒ Ⓓ Ⓔ
18. Ⓐ Ⓑ Ⓒ Ⓓ Ⓔ
19. Ⓐ Ⓑ Ⓒ Ⓓ Ⓔ
20. Ⓐ Ⓑ Ⓒ Ⓓ Ⓔ
21. Ⓐ Ⓑ Ⓒ Ⓓ Ⓔ
22. Ⓐ Ⓑ Ⓒ Ⓓ Ⓔ
23. Ⓐ Ⓑ Ⓒ Ⓓ Ⓔ
24. Ⓐ Ⓑ Ⓒ Ⓓ Ⓔ
25. Ⓐ Ⓑ Ⓒ Ⓓ Ⓔ
26. Ⓐ Ⓑ Ⓒ Ⓓ Ⓔ
27. Ⓐ Ⓑ Ⓒ Ⓓ Ⓔ
28. Ⓐ Ⓑ Ⓒ Ⓓ Ⓔ
29. Ⓐ Ⓑ Ⓒ Ⓓ Ⓔ
30. Ⓐ Ⓑ Ⓒ Ⓓ Ⓔ
31. Ⓐ Ⓑ Ⓒ Ⓓ Ⓔ
32. Ⓐ Ⓑ Ⓒ Ⓓ Ⓔ
33. Ⓐ Ⓑ Ⓒ Ⓓ Ⓔ
34. Ⓐ Ⓑ Ⓒ Ⓓ Ⓔ

35. Ⓐ Ⓑ Ⓒ Ⓓ Ⓔ
36. Ⓐ Ⓑ Ⓒ Ⓓ Ⓔ
37. Ⓐ Ⓑ Ⓒ Ⓓ Ⓔ
38. Ⓐ Ⓑ Ⓒ Ⓓ Ⓔ
39. Ⓐ Ⓑ Ⓒ Ⓓ Ⓔ
40. Ⓐ Ⓑ Ⓒ Ⓓ Ⓔ
41. Ⓐ Ⓑ Ⓒ Ⓓ Ⓔ
42. Ⓐ Ⓑ Ⓒ Ⓓ Ⓔ
43. Ⓐ Ⓑ Ⓒ Ⓓ Ⓔ
44. Ⓐ Ⓑ Ⓒ Ⓓ Ⓔ
45. Ⓐ Ⓑ Ⓒ Ⓓ Ⓔ
46. Ⓐ Ⓑ Ⓒ Ⓓ Ⓔ
47. Ⓐ Ⓑ Ⓒ Ⓓ Ⓔ
48. Ⓐ Ⓑ Ⓒ Ⓓ Ⓔ
49. Ⓐ Ⓑ Ⓒ Ⓓ Ⓔ
50. Ⓐ Ⓑ Ⓒ Ⓓ Ⓔ
51. Ⓐ Ⓑ Ⓒ Ⓓ Ⓔ
52. Ⓐ Ⓑ Ⓒ Ⓓ Ⓔ
53. Ⓐ Ⓑ Ⓒ Ⓓ Ⓔ
54. Ⓐ Ⓑ Ⓒ Ⓓ Ⓔ
55. Ⓐ Ⓑ Ⓒ Ⓓ Ⓔ
56. Ⓐ Ⓑ Ⓒ Ⓓ Ⓔ
57. Ⓐ Ⓑ Ⓒ Ⓓ Ⓔ
58. Ⓐ Ⓑ Ⓒ Ⓓ Ⓔ
59. Ⓐ Ⓑ Ⓒ Ⓓ Ⓔ
60. Ⓐ Ⓑ Ⓒ Ⓓ Ⓔ
61. Ⓐ Ⓑ Ⓒ Ⓓ Ⓔ
62. Ⓐ Ⓑ Ⓒ Ⓓ Ⓔ
63. Ⓐ Ⓑ Ⓒ Ⓓ Ⓔ
64. Ⓐ Ⓑ Ⓒ Ⓓ Ⓔ
65. Ⓐ Ⓑ Ⓒ Ⓓ Ⓔ
66. Ⓐ Ⓑ Ⓒ Ⓓ Ⓔ
67. Ⓐ Ⓑ Ⓒ Ⓓ Ⓔ
68. Ⓐ Ⓑ Ⓒ Ⓓ Ⓔ

69. Ⓐ Ⓑ Ⓒ Ⓓ Ⓔ
70. Ⓐ Ⓑ Ⓒ Ⓓ Ⓔ
71. Ⓐ Ⓑ Ⓒ Ⓓ Ⓔ
72. Ⓐ Ⓑ Ⓒ Ⓓ Ⓔ
73. Ⓐ Ⓑ Ⓒ Ⓓ Ⓔ
74. Ⓐ Ⓑ Ⓒ Ⓓ Ⓔ
75. Ⓐ Ⓑ Ⓒ Ⓓ Ⓔ
76. Ⓐ Ⓑ Ⓒ Ⓓ Ⓔ
77. Ⓐ Ⓑ Ⓒ Ⓓ Ⓔ
78. Ⓐ Ⓑ Ⓒ Ⓓ Ⓔ
79. Ⓐ Ⓑ Ⓒ Ⓓ Ⓔ
80. Ⓐ Ⓑ Ⓒ Ⓓ Ⓔ
81. Ⓐ Ⓑ Ⓒ Ⓓ Ⓔ
82. Ⓐ Ⓑ Ⓒ Ⓓ Ⓔ
83. Ⓐ Ⓑ Ⓒ Ⓓ Ⓔ
84. Ⓐ Ⓑ Ⓒ Ⓓ Ⓔ
85. Ⓐ Ⓑ Ⓒ Ⓓ Ⓔ
86. Ⓐ Ⓑ Ⓒ Ⓓ Ⓔ
87. Ⓐ Ⓑ Ⓒ Ⓓ Ⓔ
88. Ⓐ Ⓑ Ⓒ Ⓓ Ⓔ
89. Ⓐ Ⓑ Ⓒ Ⓓ Ⓔ
90. Ⓐ Ⓑ Ⓒ Ⓓ Ⓔ
91. Ⓐ Ⓑ Ⓒ Ⓓ Ⓔ
92. Ⓐ Ⓑ Ⓒ Ⓓ Ⓔ
93. Ⓐ Ⓑ Ⓒ Ⓓ Ⓔ
94. Ⓐ Ⓑ Ⓒ Ⓓ Ⓔ
95. Ⓐ Ⓑ Ⓒ Ⓓ Ⓔ
96. Ⓐ Ⓑ Ⓒ Ⓓ Ⓔ
97. Ⓐ Ⓑ Ⓒ Ⓓ Ⓔ
98. Ⓐ Ⓑ Ⓒ Ⓓ Ⓔ
99. Ⓐ Ⓑ Ⓒ Ⓓ Ⓔ
100. Ⓐ Ⓑ Ⓒ Ⓓ Ⓔ

# Index

**D**

## E

# INSTALLING REA's TEST*ware*®

## SYSTEM REQUIREMENTS

Pentium 75 MHz (300 MHz recommended) or a higher or compatible processor; Microsoft Windows 98 or later; 64 MB Available RAM; Internet Explorer 5.5 or higher

## INSTALLATION

1. Insert the CLEP Introductory Business Law TEST*ware*® CD-ROM into the CD-ROM drive.
2. If the installation doesn't begin automatically, from the Start Menu choose the RUN command. When the RUN dialog box appears, type d:\setup (where *d* is the letter of your CD-ROM drive) at the prompt and click OK.
3. The installation process will begin. A dialog box proposing the directory "Program Files\REA\CLEPBusLaw" will appear. If the name and location are suitable, click OK. If you wish to specify a different name or location, type it in and click OK.
4. Start the CLEP Introductory Business Law TEST*ware*® application by double-clicking on the icon.

REA's CLEP Introductory Business Law TEST*ware*® is **EASY** to **LEARN AND USE**. To achieve maximum benefits, we recommend that you take a few minutes to go through the on-screen tutorial on your computer.

## SSD ACCOMMODATIONS FOR STUDENTS WITH DISABILITIES

Many students qualify for extra time to take the CLEP Introductory Business Law exam, and our TEST*ware*® can be adapted to accommodate your time extension. This allows you to practice under the same extended-time accommodations that you will receive on the actual test day. To customize your TEST*ware*® to suit the most common extensions, visit our website at *www.rea.com/ssd*.

## TECHNICAL SUPPORT

REA's TEST*ware*® is backed by customer and technical support. For questions about **installation or operation of your software**, contact us at:

**Research & Education Association**
**Phone: (732) 819-8880 (9 a.m. to 5 p.m. ET, Monday–Friday)**
**Fax: (732) 819-8808**
**Website: www.rea.com**
**E-mail: info@rea.com**

**Note to Windows XP Users:** In order for the TEST*ware*® to function properly, please install and run the application under the same computer administrator-level user account. Installing the TEST*ware*® as one user and running it as another could cause file-access path conflicts.

# REA's Test Preps
## The Best in Test Preparation

- REA "Test Preps" are **far more** comprehensive than any other test preparation series
- Each book contains up to **eight** full-length practice tests based on the most recent exams
- **Every** type of question likely to be given on the exams is included
- Answers are accompanied by **full** and **detailed** explanations

*REA publishes over 70 Test Preparation volumes in several series. They include:*

**Advanced Placement Exams (APs)**
Art History
Biology
Calculus AB & BC
Chemistry
Economics
English Language & Composition
English Literature & Composition
European History
French Language
Government & Politics
Latin
Physics B & C
Psychology
Spanish Language
Statistics
United States History
World History

**College-Level Examination Program (CLEP)**
Analyzing and Interpreting Literature
College Algebra
Freshman College Composition
General Examinations
General Examinations Review
History of the United States I
History of the United States II
Introduction to Educational Psychology
Human Growth and Development
Introductory Psychology
Introductory Sociology
Principles of Management
Principles of Marketing
Spanish
Western Civilization I
Western Civilization II

**SAT Subject Tests**
Biology E/M
Chemistry
French
German
Literature
Mathematics Level 1, 2
Physics
Spanish
United States History

**Graduate Record Exams (GREs)**
Biology
Chemistry
Computer Science
General
Literature in English
Mathematics
Physics
Psychology

**ACT** - ACT Assessment

**ASVAB** - Armed Services Vocational Aptitude Battery

**CBEST** - California Basic Educational Skills Test

**CDL** - Commercial Driver License Exam

**CLAST** - College Level Academic Skills Test

**COOP & HSPT** - Catholic High School Admission Tests

**ELM** - California State University Entry Level Mathematics Exam

**FE (EIT)** - Fundamentals of Engineering Exams - For Both AM & PM Exams

**FTCE** - Florida Teacher Certification Examinations

**GED** - (U.S. Edition)

**GMAT** - Graduate Management Admission Test

**LSAT** - Law School Admission Test

**MAT** - Miller Analogies Test

**MCAT** - Medical College Admission Test

**MTEL** - Massachusetts Tests for Educator Licensure

**NJ HSPA** - New Jersey High School Proficiency Assessment

**NYSTCE** - New York State Teacher Certification Examinations

**PRAXIS PLT** - Principles of Learning & Teaching Tests

**PRAXIS PPST** - Pre-Professional Skills Tests

**PSAT/NMSQT**

**SAT**

**TExES** - Texas Examinations of Educator Standards

**THEA** - Texas Higher Education Assessment

**TOEFL** - Test of English as a Foreign Language

**TOEIC** - Test of English for International Communication

**USMLE Steps 1,2,3** - U.S. Medical Licensing Exams

---

### Research & Education Association
61 Ethel Road W., Piscataway, NJ 08854
Phone: (732) 819-8880     **website: www.rea.com**

**Please send me more information about your Test Prep books.**

Name _____

Address _____

City _____ State _____ Zip _____